Hoover Institution Publications 134

Herbert Hoover and Famine Relief to Soviet Russia: 1921-1923

Herbert Hoover and Famine Relief to Soviet Russia: 1921-1923

Benjamin M. Weissman

Rutgers University
Newark, New Jersey

Hoover Institution Press
Stanford University
Stanford, California

The Hoover Institution on War, Revolution and Peace, founded at Stanford University in 1919 by the late President Herbert Hoover, is a center for advanced study and research on public and international affairs in the twentieth century. The views expressed in its publications are entirely those of the authors and do not necessarily reflect the views of the staff, officers, or Board of Overseers of the Hoover Institution.

Permission to use quotations and citations from the published and unpublished works of Herbert Hoover granted by the Herbert Hoover Foundation, Inc.

Material from "Herbert Hoover's 'Treaty' with Soviet Russia: August 20, 1921," by Benjamin Weissman, published in *Slavic Review,* Volume 28, Number 2, June 1969 included courtesy of *Slavic Review.*

Hoover Institution Publications 134
International Standard Book Number 0-8179-1341-6
Library of Congress Card Number 73-75888
© 1974 by the Board of Trustees of the
   Leland Stanford Junior University
All rights reserved
Printed in the United States of America

To Rae
and Evelyn, Anne, and Joe

Contents

Acknowledgments

The author is grateful to all the friends and strangers who helped in the preparation of this book. Professors Stanley Page (College of the City of New York) and Michael Luther (Hunter College) provided early advice and encouragement. Professor Alexander Dallin of Columbia University read and criticized the study with infinite care and insight. Through the kind assistance of Harold H. Fisher, ARA historian and professor emeritus of Stanford University, the author was able to make contact with participants in the relief mission. These ARA veterans—Cyril J. C. Quinn, Herschel Carey Walker, Henry Wolfe, and Perrin Galpin—furnished invaluable firsthand descriptions of the mission and its setting. Librarians at the Herbert Hoover Archives of the Hoover Institution on War, Revolution and Peace and at the Slavonic Room of the New York Public Library were endlessly patient and helpful. Barbara Pronin edited the manuscript with a masterful if merciless hand.

No foundation, institution, or agency sponsored this study, although Rutgers University did provide a semester's respite from teaching assignments. The author is solely responsible for the biases, interpretations, and conclusions that follow.

List of Abbreviations

ACRFR	American Committee for Russian Famine Relief
ARA	American Relief Administration
Cheka	Soviet internal security police
CRB	Commission for Relief in Belgium
FSR	Friends of Soviet Russia
GPU	Soviet secret police
Gubispolkom	Provincial Soviet Executive Committee
Ispolkom	Town Soviet Executive Committee
JDC	American Jewish Joint Distribution Committee
Kompomoshch	Commission for Famine Relief
Mezhrabpom	International Workers' Committee for Aid to the Starving in Russia
NEP	New Economic Policy
Pomgol	Central Commission for Aid to the Starving
Posledgol	Central Commission for the Struggle against the Consequences of the Famine
RAKPD	Russian-American Committees for Help to Children
USGC	United States Grain Corporation
VTsIK	All-Russian Central Executive Committee of the Soviet Government

Introduction

In 1921, one of the worst famines in history threatened the lives of millions of Russians as well as the continuance of Soviet rule. On 13 July of that year, the writer Maxim Gorky appealed to the world for help. On 20 August the American Relief Administration (ARA), a private organization directed by Herbert Hoover, then secretary of commerce, concluded an agreement with the Soviet government to provide famine relief in the stricken area. For the next twenty-two months, a small group of Americans representing the ARA fed the starving throughout most of Russia. The total cost of the mission was relatively small; the money provided by the American government would not support a minor war today for more than a week. Yet, the mission was in many ways the most intimate engagement between the two countries to date.

Soviet commentators have accorded the American relief mission a prominent, though not usually an honored, place in the history of Soviet-American relations. American interest in the mission has been slight. The most extensive treatment by an American scholar is a detailed account written in 1927 by the ARA's official historian.[1] Soviet critics unanimously condemn the relief operation as an anti-Soviet intervention entirely devoid of humanitarian inspiration or effect. Contrary opinion sees it as a purely charitable, nonpolitical enterprise. George F. Kennan writes:

> The best that may be said in retrospect is that, despite all the friction and difficulty, both sides got, basically, what they most wanted. The ARA did not become a source of conspiracy; the Soviet Government was not overthrown. Several million children, who would otherwise have died, were kept alive.[2]

The purpose of this book is to examine the relief mission objectively in the light of several basic assumptions, to test these assumptions against the information uncovered, and to come to some balanced judgement on the conflicting assessments of the mission.

The Special Problem

Otherwise sophisticated scholars have not hesitated to judge the event solely on the basis of their impressions of Hoover's personality, his attitude toward communism, or—strangely, but typically—his record as president during the Great Depression. A senior professor of political science told the author flatly that Hoover "could not possibly have helped starving Russians. He didn't even care about starving Americans." This, of course, is an extreme instance of blind bias. But preliminary reading and informal conversations have convinced the author that nobody, including the author himself, is unbiased about Hoover. A veteran of the depression, the author freely acknowledges that he undertook this study bearing a fairly strong antipathy toward Hoover and his political philosophy. An objective evaluation involved at least temporary suppression of this prejudice. The reader will have to judge whether the effort has been successful.

The Basic Theory

Hoover's influence on the relief mission was very great; but there were literally millions of other actors on the scene, including Lenin and all the leading Bolsheviks of the period. History provided the setting and prologue. Parochial and national interests, personal and ideological compulsions provided the plot.

Kennan's statement that "both sides got basically what they most wanted" leaves much to be explored. Initial agreement between the Soviet Union and the United States on the desirability of a goal has never meant the end of political contention but only its transfer to another level. And neither the urgency nor the nobility of the common purpose automatically guarantees the success of the undertaking. Thus, even if the leaders on both sides shared a deep commitment to rescuing the starving Russians in 1921, they would still have had to contend with their own ideological compulsions, the conflicting demands of their various roles, and the bitter antagonism between the two countries. This, at any rate, is the basic idea behind the present study. Since there is not yet universal agreement on some of the terms used above, a brief elaboration is in order.

Antagonism and Ideology

The contrast between American and Soviet political institutions does not, in itself, account for the antagonism that has existed between the two countries since the Bolshevik seizure of power in 1917. The United States has managed to coexist comfortably, and even make alliances, with national regimes that range from moderately authoritarian to outright dictatorial. Hostility between the United States and the Soviet Union is rooted in ideological animosity. It would be difficult to find two leaders who symbolized this kind of enmity better than Herbert Hoover and V. I. Lenin. On 28 March 1919 Hoover wrote to President Woodrow Wilson: "We cannot even remotely recognize this murderous [Soviet] tyranny without stimulating actionist radicalism in every country in Europe and without transgressing on every national idea of our own."[3] Lenin's fulminations against "capitalist enslavement" have been widely quoted and are well known.

Definitions of "ideology" have varied considerably since Marx first used the term as a synonym for the "false consciousness" of the ruling class. Oddly enough, Western scholarship has preserved the pejorative meaning of the word and used it against the Communists; avowed Marxists have removed its sting. This convenient revision of Marx's concept enables Soviet commentators to draw invidious comparisons between communist and capitalist ideologies without elaborate footnoting.

There seems to be merit in combining both approaches and borrowing selectively from several others.[4] "Ideology" will be used in this study to signify a strongly held set of beliefs based on one or another principle that is proclaimed as immutable and universal. Historical examples of principles exalted in this manner include the exclusive authority of a particular divinity, the omnipotence of science, the inevitably benign operation of "free capitalism," and the negation of all evil by the revolutionary proletariat.

To some degree, ideology determines the believer's values, perceptions of reality, and behavior. In its extreme effect, it distorts interpretation of the real world by oversimplifying the complex or by rejecting dissonant facts. This rehabilitation of Marx's notion of "false consciousness" is only partial; our definition does not see ideology as a peculiar attribute of the capitalist class or any other.[5] There is, as Marxists might agree, a dialectical dynamic in ideology. It seems to originate and develop in opposition to an earlier ideology. The counter ideology generates its own messianic passion as its adherents proceed from rejection of the repugnant doctrine to constant, almost reflexive hostility toward its institutions, leaders, and goals.

Pending the predicted "end of ideology," it is worthwhile to examine the influence of this powerful ingredient in interpreting any encounter between two countries that have symbolized opposing ideologies since the Bolshevik Revolution. There is, of course, a danger in elevating this factor, or any other, to the level of absolute determinism. Such an approach would be, according to our definition, ideological.

The Leaders and Their Roles

Perhaps the most complicated problem of this study concerns the motives of its principal figures. The roles that each was expected to fulfill were diverse and not necessarily congruent on any given decision or action. Hoover was not only the world's most celebrated famine-fighter but also secretary of commerce, champion of Republican liberalism, and a leading opponent of recognition of Soviet Russia. Lenin was the head of the Soviet government, leader of the Bolshevik party, and the living symbol of world revolution. Although these two leaders were not merely "clerks" of their various constituencies, it can be assumed that the hopes and fears of the different groups that looked to them for leadership affected their decisions to some degree.[6] A satisfactory unraveling of this tangled motivational skein may not be entirely possible. It must nevertheless be attempted.

The Natural and Human Environments

The physical environment is usually treated as an objective factor that imposes definite limitations on even the most talented and effective leaders. But great innovators have often succeeded in transcending limitations that were accepted as such by their contemporaries. Furthermore, it is often difficult to distinguish between the objective and human elements of a given biophysical event. A famine, for instance, has certain natural physical characteristics and consequences. The cause, extent, and even the existence of a famine, however, may be interpreted quite differently by various observers and become subjects of fierce political controversy. The distinction between the physical and human features of this "natural" event then becomes blurred.

The same is true of the institutional environment. According to David Easton, "No less than the obvious limitations of the physical environment, the formalized institutionalized human environment serves as a constraint on decision and action, independent of human motivation."[7] But in considering the actions of such strong, confident leaders as Hoover and Lenin, one must take into account the powerful impulse to alter, eliminate, or ignore inhibiting institutions. In many, perhaps most, instances, the leaders will fail in such an attempt. It is the long series of exceptional cases, however, that makes up the body of human history.

This book is about a moment in history when the lives of millions of people seemed to depend on the ability of men to transcend political animosity in a common interest. Today, more than a half-century since the famine of 1921, the stakes involved in such a test are much higher. Although the present study deals with a unique set of events and with special people, it is hoped that it may cast light on the problems that arise when leaders of antagonistic countries decide to collaborate on a great humanitarian undertaking.

The Politics of Famine Relief

By the early summer of 1921 the peasants of the Volga region knew that they faced a famine year. They prayed for a miracle. All one could do was pray. Even if the rains finally came, it would be too late to plant and harvest a crop. As far back as the oldest peasant could remember, a prolonged drought in the spring meant famine and slow death for millions.

Many believed that God was punishing them for sins committed earlier in the year. But even the most devout knew that the widespread starvation that followed the loss of the crop was in some measure the fault of human authority. Men in power far from the fertile plains of the Volga made decisions that left the peasant with little or no reserve grain to sustain life if the rains failed. In 1891, for instance, when the wheat died in the fields during another drought, the peasants were already nearly destitute. Liberation from serfdom thirty years earlier had not lifted them from poverty. Primitive techniques of agriculture still prevailed throughout Russia. The expense of maintaining the huge tsarist bureaucracy was exacted mainly from the peasants in the form of direct taxes and a series of indirect taxes on vodka, sugar, tobacco, and matches. Added to this burden were the redemption payments—annual installments owed the government for land settled on the peasants in the emancipation edict. Any surplus, whether in cash or in crops, that may have been realized in a good harvest was thus absorbed. The loss of one season's crops confronted the peasant with starvation. In the Volga area, where drought was a constant threat, the peasant eked out his life under a suspended sentence of death.[1]

At first, the government of Alexander III refused to acknowledge the existence of the 1891 famine. The starving peasants found a voice, however, in an appeal to the world for help written by Count Leo Tolstoy. The government responded to the worldwide publicity about the disaster by permitting the organization of private relief activity in the stricken area.[2]

The abdication of the government from direct responsibility for relief of the starving was a political blunder. Famine relief became a training school for reform and revolution. The *zemstva* (local self-government councils), whose powers had been severely curtailed by a series of special decrees, took on new life in the fight against the famine. Their revival kept active in public life a group that would later press for reform of the autocracy.[3] Famine relief also reactivated certain revolutionary groups that had been paralyzed by official repression after the assassination of Alexander II in 1881. This new revolutionary movement was inspired and strengthened by direct contact with the impoverished peasants.[4]

One group of revolutionists—the Marxist "Emancipation of Labor"—seemed strangely insensitive to the plight of the peasants as well as to the political potentialities of famine relief. Georgi Plekhanov, founder and leader of this group, asserted that the proper role for a revolutionary socialist was not to engage in famine relief but to organize the destruction of the system that breeds famines.[5] Among those who agreed with this view was a young Marxist lawyer, Vladimir Ulyanov, who was living in Samara when famine struck the area in 1891. Ulyanov scorned the philanthropic efforts of the local intelligentsia as typically philistine diversions from the primary task of building the revolution.[6]

When famine struck again in 1921, the passage of thirty years had transformed Ulyanov into V. I. Lenin and had elevated him to supreme authority in Russia. Perhaps better than anyone else, Lenin realized the threat that a famine posed to the existence of the Bolshevik regime. As early as March, 1921, he had warned the Tenth Congress of the Russian Communist party:

> If there is a crop failure, it will be impossible to appropriate any surplus because there will be no surplus. Food would have to be taken out of the mouths of the peasants. If there is a harvest, then everybody will hunger a little, and the government will be saved; otherwise, since we cannot take anything from people who do not have the means of satisfying their own hunger, the government will perish.[7]

Again, as in 1891, the peasant was helpless against the onslaught of famine, partly because of government policy. Throughout the years of civil war and foreign intervention against the Bolshevik regime, the government had systematically appropriated grain from the peasants by means of special "collection" squads. Several months before the outbreak of the famine, Lenin frankly admitted the harshness of this policy: "The peculiarity of 'war communism' was that we actually took from the peasant his entire surplus, and, sometimes we took not only the surplus but part of his necessary supply in order to meet the expenses of the army and to support the workers."[8]

At Lenin's insistence, the system of forced requisitions was finally replaced by a moderate tax in kind. The change was part of the New Economic Policy (NEP)—a retreat from the rigidities of "war communism." To stimulate the revival of economic activity, especially in agriculture, the regime had decided to permit a limited amount of private enterprise and free trade in farm produce. But for the peasants of the Volga, the change had come too late. There had been no time to pile up reserve stocks. When drought struck, the stage was set for a reenactment of the age-old tragedy of the eastern plains.

THE FAMINE OF 1921

In the spring of 1921, reports of a devastating drought began to circulate in Moscow. Months had passed without rain in the Volga region.[9] On 26 June *Pravda* carried the grim announcement that a famine worse than that of 1891 was raging in the Volga area. Several days later, *Pravda* reported that the people in the stricken area were "in mass flight."[10] The prospects for immediate relief were dim. One Soviet economist estimated that the government would be able to muster no more than 20 percent of the food needed to supply the people in two of the starving provinces, Samara and Saratov.[11]

Toward the end of July, the full dimensions of the disaster became apparent. In a series of radio messages intercepted by the American commissioner at Constantinople, the Party leadership in Moscow alerted activists throughout the country to the dangers presented by the famine. The peasants in the Samara region were eating grass, leaves, bark, and clay.[12] The Central Committee of the Communist party urged its members in the area to try to stop panic and migration, "since the flight of the peasants from the affected area will cause the situation to be worse for years to come" and "will ruin entirely our economic life." On 23 July the Central Committee admitted that the situation was desperate: "The Soviet government is unable to help."[13]

The regime withheld official announcement of the famine to the outside world for more than a month after the first reports in *Pravda*. Finally, on 2 August the government released a formal communiqué on the famine as a "Note from the Government of the RSFSR [Russian Socialist Federated Soviet Republic] to the Heads of All Governments." The message, signed by Georgi Chicherin, commissar of foreign affairs, acknowledged the existence of "unusual conditions" in ten Russian provinces inhabited by about eighteen million people. The stricken areas were in immediate need of forty-one million poods [one pood equals about thirty-six pounds] of grain in order to provide half-rations to the rural population. "The starving regions," according to the note, "have no grain stocks with which to relieve the famine, and shipments from other provinces can be only extremely limited." Chicherin admitted that there was some movement of "terror-stricken people" from the drought areas but declared that the "migration has not assumed a character that threatens social order and security in the slightest." He concluded with a cautious appeal for help: "The Soviet government welcomes the help of all providing it does not involve political considerations. We thank all foreign organizations and groups that offered their assistance."[14]

In one part of the communiqué, Chicherin expressed the hope that the official announcement would "correct a total misunderstanding about the situation in the starving provinces." He evidently had in mind rumors about an imminent collapse of the economy, and possibly of the Soviet authority itself, at least in the famine areas. These rumors were being fed by confusion within Soviet ranks about the famine situation. While members of the Soviet Legation in Warsaw were telling foreign correspondents that conditions in the drought areas were desperate, *Izvestia* was publishing encouraging reports from the same region.[15] A month later, Soviet officials in Moscow still disagreed about the stand to be taken on the famine. According to the *Times* (London), one official would attempt to minimize the extent of the suffering, while another would "exaggerate the already sufficient terrible facts."[16]

The British press was the most fruitful source of "terrible facts" about the famine. In 1921, the foreign capitalist press was still barred from Soviet Russia. Because of the presence of a British trade mission in Moscow at the time, however, the London newspapers were able to relay to the world all the horror stories current in the Russian capital. According to one report, people in Moscow were fainting in the streets from hunger.[17] The number of those actually starving was estimated at thirty-five million by the head of the British trade mission.[18]

During the fall and winter of 1921, various relief commissions conducted extensive surveys of the famine regions. The most detailed investigation was carried out by the official Soviet relief agency, the Central Commission for Aid to the Starving (abbreviated in Russian as *Pomgol*). According to a *Pomgol* report issued in 1922, seventeen provinces, with an estimated population of over twenty-five million people, were directly affected by the famine in the fall of 1921.[19] The number of those who were actually starving ranged from 55 percent of the population in Perm to 90 percent in Samara.[20] In five provinces of the Ukrainian Republic, 12 percent of the entire population of ten million faced death by starvation in December 1921. This figure rose to 48 percent by April 1922.[21] Nevertheless, by August 1922, over 1,100 carloads of food were shipped from the Ukraine to the eastern provinces of Russia; the contribution of the famine-stricken provinces was 74 carloads.[22]

The first of a series of special representatives sent to Russia by Herbert Hoover gave a much more optimistic report. James P. Goodrich, former governor of Indiana, was commissioned by Hoover in September 1921 to make an independent survey of conditions in Russia with the consent and assistance of the Soviet government. On 1 November 1921, Goodrich reported that European Russia could easily supply the needs of the starving region. He acknowledged that conditions in Kazan, Simbirsk, and Saratov were very bad, but he called some of the accounts in the American press exaggerated and recommended withholding assistance until the Soviet government exhausted all its available resources of food and gold.[23]

An entirely different picture was presented by two top-ranking specialists from Hoover's organization—the American Relief Administration (ARA). After an exhaustive firsthand investigation of conditions in Russia and the Ukraine, they estimated that the drought had reduced the total crop in Russia by about seven million tons; a net deficit of some three million tons within the country was certain. They concluded that outside help was absolutely necessary if disaster was to be averted.[24]

The most pessimistic report of all was issued by Fridtjof Nansen, a Norwegian who was at that time head of the International Committee for Russian Relief. Nansen estimated that nineteen million people in Russia were facing death from starvation in 1921 and that ten to twelve million would certainly die if substantial outside help were not obtained.[25]

In 1922, the League of Nations issued a comprehensive report on the famine. According to this report, agriculture throughout Russia had declined to a dangerous level by the time the drought struck. Years of war, counterrevolutionary struggle, blockade, and boycott had aggravated a shortage of farm equipment and railway cars. The division of farm acreage into small holdings after the Revolution had led to a regression to primitive methods of cultivation. The shortage of manufactured goods brought on by the hasty nationalization of industry had virtually destroyed the market for farm products and thus reduced the peasant's incentive to increase cultivation and sowing.[26]

The final blow was the requisition policy pursued by the Bolshevik government during the Civil War. The area under cultivation shrank to 70 percent of the average sown during the five years immediately preceding World War I. The reduction in the Volga region was even greater.[27] According to the League report, the effect of the drought under these circumstances was to bring on the worst famine to strike Europe in modern times. The number of deaths directly attributable to hunger and disease in the famine areas was estimated at one to three million.

The actual extent of the famine will probably never be known. Most contemporary observers, however, agreed that between ten and thirty million people faced starvation and that the government had neither the resources nor the organizational capability to cope with the disaster.

To the Bolshevik regime, the famine posed one of the most crucial challenges since the seizure of power in 1917. The tight discipline of the Civil War years had already become dangerously attenuated. The government frankly admitted widespread disaffection.

Parallel with the dissatisfaction of the peasant there is increased discontent on the part of the workers, who were starving when there was actually bread in the villages. As a result, there is a decline in manufactured goods; factories are standing idle; there is poor work; we can see failure of our economic plans and a deterioration in the international situation.

Even within the Party, the vanguard of the working class, a decline in morale in the face of these great problems is noticeable here and there. . . .[28]

Lenin's prophecy that the government would fall if there were a crop failure was not unrealistic. The abortive 1921 uprising of the garrison in the devoutly revolutionary city of Kronstadt had served warning that Bolshevik rule was not yet secure. But as long as the government still commanded the loyalty of the Red Army, the *Cheka* (internal security forces), and Party activists throughout the country, there was little danger that the starving peasants in the famine areas could mount a successful revolt against the regime. The real menace to stable rule was the serious disruption of the natural and social environments.

Hunger-crazed peasants were beginning to leave their homes by the thousands, frequently abandoning their children to certain death.[29] Vidkun Quisling, at that time a member of Nansen's staff, reported that he had spoken with peasants who had eaten their own children, sisters, or brothers.[30] An ARA supervisor declared that cannibalism was widespread in his area.[31]

During a famine, however, cannibalism is less destructive than the consumption of horses and cats. The slaughter of horses reduces the possibility of effective plowing for a new crop. The disappearance of cats causes a sharp increase in the rodent population and thus in the incidence of rat-borne diseases.

Famine reaches disaster level when the starving muster their last energies to flee to other areas. This eliminates the last hope of a new crop. The refugees rapidly drain the resources of nonfamine areas; hoarding increases; food supplies disappear. Famine and pestilence sweep across new areas, reducing even further the number of plowers and sowers upon whom ultimate rescue depends. As the process continues, the possibility of reversing it diminishes. Family ties, social loyalties, and finally the authority of government fall away. A regime that manages somehow to maintain its rule becomes indeed "lord of the flies."[32]

Lenin and the Crisis

To Lenin, the famine was "a disaster that threatened to nullify the whole of [the Bolsheviks'] organizational and revolutionary work."[33] The acute suffering of the masses, which Lenin had always seen as the necessary cost of building a new social order, had aroused, in his words, "the opposition of not only a significant part of the peasantry, but of the workers."[34] For the first time since 1917, there seemed no group in society to which the Bolsheviks could turn for support. Clinging to power in the face of this new catastrophe, they seemed to be standing alone.

Not surprisingly, Lenin's attitudes and decisions strongly influenced the final outcome. The serious dissension among the Bolsheviks that surfaced at the Tenth Party Congress in March 1921 emphasized once again that only Lenin had enough authority to impose unity on the various factions. Against determined opposition to some of his policies, he nevertheless won majority support for his economic program as well as for his proposal to stifle organized factions within the Party. Major decisions on foreign policy, economic management, operations of government, and internal Party affairs would continue to be dominated by Lenin.

As the crisis deepened, however, Lenin's health began to deteriorate. "I am so tired," he wrote to Maxim Gorky on 9 August, "I can't do the least little thing."[35] He assigned some of his functions to subordinates, but he would not surrender them entirely. In foreign affairs especially, he insisted on retaining final authority. Even on day-to-day matters, he continued to issue instructions down to the wording of letters, communiqués, and directives.[36] The fate of each agreement negotiated by Commissar of Foreign Trade Leonid Krasin depended ultimately on Lenin's judgments concerning the intentions of the participants and the long-range effects on the Russian economy.[37] It was inevitable that any negotiations with foreign countries about famine relief would fall under Lenin's close critical scrutiny.[38]

Lenin's attitude toward human suffering had not changed substantially since the famine of 1891, when he had scorned the relief efforts of the intelligentsia as an evasion of revolutionary duty. In his view, the proletariat could not shrink from sacrificing the welfare of the peasants, and even the workers, in the interest of the Revolution.[39] In 1921, however, there was no conflict between Lenin's political goals and ordinary humanitarianism. To spark relief campaigns in Russia and throughout the world, he issued personal appeals for donations. On 2 August 1921 he directed a plea to the peasants of the Ukraine: "The well-protected Ukraine gathered an excellent harvest this year. Workers and peasants of the starving Volga region, who are presently suffering a catastrophe worse than the horrible disaster of 1891, expect help from the Ukrainian farmers."[40]

The amount of assistance available from the "well-protected Ukraine" was far from sufficient, however. Several provinces were badly in need of help themselves; the harvest in this area ranged from poor to practically nothing.[41] It is not surprising that Lenin was ignorant of conditions in this region; the nominally independent government of the Ukrainian Republic seemed unaware that the famine had spread into its own territory. In the meantime, thousands of refugees from the Volga region poured into Ukrainian provinces that were themselves suffering an acute shortage of food.[42] The famine was gaining momentum, and the need for outside help was desperate.

Lenin did not expect assistance from the United States or any other capitalist government. In the middle of July, several days after Gorky issued his appeal to the world, Lenin told Willi Münzenberg, a member of the Executive Committee of the Communist International, that there was little hope of any substantial assistance from the capitalist powers; Russia would have to rally the international proletariat in a gigantic relief campaign.[43]

During the same week, Lenin refused an unusual opportunity to make a conciliatory gesture toward the United States. On 14 July the Norwegian relief expert, Fridtjof Nansen, advised Gorky that the Americans alone were in a position to extend significant aid to Russia but that no help could be expected unless several Americans who were being held in prison on various charges were released.[44] Nansen was right on both counts. On the following day, Joseph I. France, U.S. senator from Maryland, urged Lenin to reconsider the case of one of the prisoners, Mrs. Marguerite Harrison.

The fact that the senator was an energetic advocate of recognition of Soviet Russia did not move Lenin to take his request seriously. He wrote to Chicherin:

I have just finished a conference with Senator France. . . . He told me how he came out *for* Soviet Russia at large public meetings together with Comrade Martens [an unofficial Soviet representative in the United States]. He is what they call a "liberal," *for* an alliance of the United States plus Russia, plus Germany, in order to save the world from Japan, England, and so on, and so on.[45]

The letter went on to relate that Mrs. Harrison was the sister-in-law of the governor of Maryland and that the senator's reelection from that state might be jeopardized by her continued incarceration. Lenin passed the senator's request on to Chicherin and to the *Cheka* without recommendation.

Chicherin refused to entertain the senator's request, advising Lenin that "France was admitted under the condition that he start no discussion about imprisoned persons, and, since he violated this stipulation, there is no need to meet him halfway." About the substance of Senator France's request, Chicherin was equally adamant.

> Until America becomes reconciled with us and guarantees favorable relations, there is danger of American support of some kind of insurrection like Kronstadt, and to allow an American spy to go to America is dangerous. Since his electoral interests are of no value to us whatsoever, the sacrifice is excessive.[46]

A public offer of assistance by Herbert Hoover, at that time U.S. secretary of commerce and head of the largest relief organization in the world, did not alter Lenin's plan to mobilize the workers of the world in the fight against the famine. His appeal to the international proletariat, published on 2 August 1921, sternly indicted the imperialists, landowners, and capitalists of all countries, whom he held responsible for the famine. "Help is needed," Lenin declared. "The Soviet republic of workers and peasants expects that help from laboring people, from the industrial workers, and from small farmers." He expressed confidence that the oppressed people of the world would instinctively realize the necessity of helping the Soviet state, "which had been obliged to be the first to assume the joyous but difficult task of overthrowing capitalism." He warned the workers that the capitalists were at that very moment planning intervention and counterrevolution. The appeal ended with a declaration of faith that the international proletariat would react to these conspiracies by coming to the rescue of the Soviet state "with still greater energy."[47]

Western workers and farmers, however, were in no position to provide the tremendous resources needed to alleviate the famine. Unemployment was high; prices and wages were falling; the most enthusiastic campaign could be expected to yield only minimal results. The only country that emerged from war with a large stockpile of food and a tremendous capacity for agricultural production was the United States. The world's most prosperous nation, however, was also the most adamantly anti-Communist. In 1921, when the major European powers were already scrambling for a privileged place in the Russian market, the United States clung to its policy of total isolation from the Soviet regime. Unless this obstacle were somehow overcome, the prospects for U.S. assistance were grim.

Lenin and the United States

Unlike his more doctrinaire colleagues, Lenin was willing to collaborate with the capitalist powers. He believed that it was absolutely essential to the success of the New Economic Policy that foreign capital and technology be enlisted in the immense task of economic reconstruction. Even before the initiation of the NEP, America seems to have occupied a special place in Soviet plans. When foreign factories were confiscated in 1918–19, the Soviet government exempted such American firms as Singer Sewing Machine, International Harvester, and Westinghouse Air Brake.[48] In 1920, Lenin himself actively promoted a long-term concession for Americans in Kamchatka, brushing aside objections that such a policy would prolong the existence of capitalist states by helping them to overcome economic crises.

> Our existence and the hastening of our deliverance from a critical situation and from hunger are powerful revolutionary forces that are more important than the pennies in the scale of the world economy that they will obtain from us.... If the capitalists could prevent crises in their countries, capitalism would be eternal. They are unquestionably blind pawns in the overall mechanism—the imperialist war proved that.[49]

As it turned out, the United States did not become a partner in the development of Kamchatka. It is clear, however, that Lenin would not be deterred by ideological considerations from entering into an advantageous relationship with the most powerful of the capitalist countries. A more serious obstacle was his fear of a new intervention. The approval with which the American press greeted the Kronstadt uprising evoked a clear expression of this fear in an interview with an American correspondent.

> In America it is believed that the Bolsheviks are a small group of ill-intentioned people who are ruling tyrannically over a large number of educated people who could form an excellent government upon the abolition of the Soviet regime. This opinion is entirely false. Nobody is in a position to replace the Bolsheviks with the exception of the generals and the bureaucrats, who long ago demonstrated their bankruptcy. If the significance of the Kronstadt uprising is exaggerated abroad, and if support is rendered to it, it is because the world has divided into two camps—the capitalist countries and communist Russia.[50]

Lenin's apprehension that Americans might be tempted to aid the Kronstadt rebels was not fantastic. On 13 March, two days before the interview with Lenin was published in the United States, the American Legation at Helsingfors (now Helsinki), Finland, suggested such a course to the Secretary of State.

> Kronstadt has sufficient supplies for two weeks only. . . . Fortress will be reduced unless provisioned from the outside. British Government is not inclined to render assistance. Finnish Government is in a position to do so but cannot risk compromising its neutrality. However, if food supplies were delivered to Simon, American Methodist relief representative at Viborg, transportation could be surreptitiously arranged.[51]

Neither the United States nor any other foreign power came to the assistance of the insurrectionists. But for Lenin, a renewal of foreign intervention during this time of great danger to the Bolshevik regime remained a real possibility: he was bound to be wary of capitalists bearing gifts.

The "Bourgeois" Famine Relief Committee

The appeal that elicited Hoover's offer of help was not officially sponsored by the Soviet government. From the evidence now available, it seems doubtful that even the idea of such an appeal originated among the Bolsheviks. In any case, it was not Lenin who appealed to bourgeois humanitarianism but Maxim Gorky in his capacity as member of a public famine committee composed mainly of the most prominent anti-Bolsheviks in the country.

Gorky himself was not remarkably sympathetic toward the Russian peasants. In a book published during the famine, he described them as "the half-savage, stupid, and heavy people of the Russian villages and countryside" and even expressed a hope that "they would die out,"[52] presumably not, however, in a horrible famine. According to Ekaterina Kuskova, an anti-Communist intellectual and long-time acquaintance of Gorky, the "eagle of Russian literature" reacted coldly to news about the famine: "We had to stimulate him, since he seemed so cold and calm, to move the Kremlin—to which he was close—to search for a solution."[53] The suggestion that Gorky approach Lenin directly apparently came from S. N. Prokopovich, a noted economist and former minister in the Provisional Government. The plan was to obtain official approval for the formation of a public committee to help the starving.[54] Kuskova relates that Gorky agreed without great enthusiasm to transmit the proposal to Lenin.

Recruiting diverse elements in society in the difficult task of economic reconstruction was at that time considered vital to the success of the New Economic Policy. Specialists of all kinds, including the former owners of private businesses, were encouraged to reassume their former roles. Thus, Lenin saw no reason why the "remnants" of the former regime, including two former ministers in the Provisional Government, should not be allowed to contribute to the campaign against the famine. On 28 June, he wrote to Ivan Teodorovich: "Received draft 'Committee for Famine Relief' from Gorky. Get it from Rykov in a quarter of an hour when he has finished reading it. Tomorrow we will make our decision at the Politburo. It seems to me personally that we can go along with Gorky's project."[55]

The Politburo gave its approval. Lev Kamenev was appointed to negotiate with Kuskova. The two met in the Kremlin and quickly came to an agreement. On 3 July, the creation of the All-Russian Famine Relief Committee was announced in *Izvestia*.[56]

Not all Bolsheviks agreed with the plan to sanction the return to public life of such well-known anti-Bolsheviks as Kuskova, Prokopovich, and Dr. S. N. Kishkin. On 12 July, Lenin sent one of the objectors, Commissar for Public Health N. A. Semashko, a playful little note revealing a cynical, almost careless attitude toward the whole project.

> Don't be willful, dear fellow! . . . Don't be jealous of Kuskova. There is a directive pending in the Politburo to-day: Render Kuskova completely harmless. You will be in the "Communist cell." Be on the alert; watch those people carefully.
>
> From Kuskova we will get her name, her signature, and a couple of carloads from people like her and from those who sympahize with her. NOTH-ING more.
>
> There should be no difficulty in accomplishing this.[57]

Apparently, at least at the outset, Lenin had neither great expectations nor fears in regard to the "bourgeois" committee. All he hoped for were "a couple of carloads" of food, and "Gorky's project" seemed a harmless way to obtain this. Quite possibly, Gorky obtained Lenin's approval before issuing the appeal that opened the way to the American relief mission. In any case, the government and the members of the committee saw Gorky's appeal as only one step in the campaign to rally non-Bolshevik support for the fight against the famine. A week after the appeal was issued, the committee held a preliminary session to iron out differences prior to formal promulgation. Among those present were Kamenev, Teodorovich, Krasin, (commissar of foreign trade), and A.V. Lunacharsky (commissar for education), all representing the government. The public members included Kishkin, Prokopovich, Kuskova, Gorky, and Alexandra Tolstoya, daughter of Leo Tolstoy. "The government," commented *Pravda,* "looks with full sympathy at this initiative and is ready to give it full support."[58]

On the following day, the government authorized the establishment of the All-Russian Famine Relief Committee consisting of sixty-one members. The "Communist cell" was increased to ten members, including Semashko, as Lenin had promised. The presence of prominent Bolsheviks on the committee and the election of Kamenev as chairman of its presidium led to considerable confusion since Kamenev was also the head of the official famine relief commission appointed by the All-Russian Central Executive Committee of the Soviet Government *(VTsIK).*

The authorizing decree granted the public committee the right to obtain food in Russia and abroad and to distribute it directly to the starving. It was empowered to collect money, publish its own newspaper, initiate public works to relieve unemployment in the famine area, and to take "any steps necessary" to ensure the success of its undertakings. It was recognized as a legal body with all attendant privileges and was granted immunity from supervision by the watchdog agency of the government, the Commissariat of Workers' and Peasants' Control.[59]

At the first meeting of the committee, the "bourgeois" members elected a non-Communist majority to the presidium. More startling was the publicity given to the opinions advanced by two members who had served as ministers in the deposed Provisional Government. "In a country like this," declared Kishkin, "where the government mechanism is weak, and outlying districts are scarcely connected in any way with the center, where law and order hardly exist, the kind of organization must be formed that can learn at a moment all the peculiarities of the situation." Prokopovich commented that only the public committee and not the government was capable of getting help from abroad. *Izvestia* published their remarks on the following day.[60]

The Unanticipated Consequences

While Hoover's response to Gorky was en route to Russia, rumors that the Soviet regime was disintegrating were speeding across the cables to the United States. An American observer informed Secretary of State Charles Evans Hughes on 25 July that "the crisis presents an opportunity which, if rightly used, may lead to the liquidation of the Bolshevist regime and the beginning of restoration." He saw the All-Russian Famine Relief Committee as

> . . . not only an agency through which we can hope to extend assistance and relief to the people of Russia without strengthening the Bolshevist regime, but, what is more important perhaps, a group actively functioning in Russia, which, if it is properly and adequately supported by the generous cooperation of this and other nations, can develop into the representative government of Russia. . . .[61]

Other opponents of the Soviet regime were equally sanguine. On

24 July, the *New York Tribune* proclaimed on its front page, "Bolsheviki in Panic, Call on Opposition to Save Russia." The head of a Russian émigré organization in Paris begged the American ambassador to ask his government to send relief to Russia "without waiting for the fall of the Bolshevik regime," which he described as "weakened and in full disintegration."[62] The little welfare project that Lenin had expected to control through the "Communist cell" was rapidly becoming the focus of counterrevolutionary hopes around the world. While the Bolshevik regime pondered this development, interested observers everywhere turned their attention to a man who seemed to embody both the hopes and fears of Lenin and his associates—Herbert Hoover.

—2—

The Roles of Herbert Hoover

On 13 July 1921 Gorky launched the All-Russian Famine Relief Committee's campaign for outside assistance by issuing an appeal to the world in his own name. There is no evidence that he expected a reply from Herbert Hoover or that his appeal would mark a turning point in the grim course of the famine. Gorky was only a minor actor in the strange drama in which he became involved; when Hoover entered the scene, Gorky faded into the background. Hoover insisted on negotiating directly with the leaders of the Soviet government, knowing that the obstacles on the road to a successful relief mission could be cleared away only by a confrontation at the top.

Ironically, one of the most formidable obstacles was deep-rooted suspicion of Hoover's own motives. A liberal magazine of the period declared it self-evident that Hoover would attempt to exploit famine relief in Soviet Russia for his own political ends.

> Everything that is known of Mr. Hoover, his sentiments and opinions, his experience, training, commercial and political association, and finally his position as an executive officer in the United States Government, conveys ample assurance that he would use his position in Russia for political purposes; indeed that he could hardly help doing so if he tried.[1]

But the editorialist omitted the one role that had made Hoover's name a byword throughout Europe and America—his spectacular performance as a famine fighter. It was Hoover's success in rescuing the population of Belgium from starvation during World War I and in feeding millions of Europeans during the Armistics period that had made him one of the best-known Americans of the time. Only the politically aware in Europe and America (a small minority) knew or cared that Hoover was also a retired capitalist of considerable wealth, the U.S. secretary of commerce, and a dedicated, unrelenting anti-Communist. Hoover's critics were confident that he would use the famine to make one last attempt on behalf of world capitalism to overthrow the Soviet regime. Hoover's admirers—undoubtedly including the overwhelming majority of the public at the time—were equally certain that the "savior of Belgium" would devote himself single-mindedly to rescuing the starving millions in Soviet Russia.

The controversy concerning Hoover's motives persists, if only within a small circle of scholars. His more impassioned critics refuse to credit him with any but counterrevolutionary intentions in offering relief to Soviet Russia.[2] His admirers—and several nonadmirers as well, including George F. Kennan—insist that he wanted nothing more than to feed the hungry.[3] Another scholar, however, claims that the relief effort was "simply" an expression of Hoover's animosity toward the Bolshevik regime "in a form more devious than frank counterrevolution."[4]

The current argument about Hoover's intentions is only a minor footnote to the actual event. In 1921, however, the suspicions and fears excited by Hoover's dramatic offer of help strongly affected the course of the mission itself. From the outset, the success of the program depended heavily on the opinions of Lenin and his associates about Hoover's motives. Was Hoover (American capitalism) forced to come to the aid of Soviet Russia because of the economic crisis brought on by overproduction of food and other war supplies? Or was relief only a disguise for a new intervention against the first socialist state? The first possibility promised some sort of rapprochement between the United States and Soviet Russia, at least for purposes of trade; the second posed a threat to the Soviet regime that rivaled the one presented by the famine itself.

To the Soviet leadership, all that mattered was which section of the American bourgeoisie Hoover represented; his personal eccentricities, philanthropic or otherwise, were insignificant. As Trotsky put it: "Of course, help to the starving is spontaneous philanthropy, but there are few real philanthropists—even among American Quakers. Philanthropy is tied to business, to enterprises, to interests—if not to-day, then to-morrow." Trotsky compared relief workers to the advance guard of missionaries that precedes soldiers and merchants; the goal of relief missionaries in 1921 was obviously to open the Russian market to the bourgeosie and thus to relieve "the great and unprecedented trade-industrial crisis all over the world, especially in America and England."[5]

Hoover insisted that he had always separated his philanthropic work from his other activities. In response to a charge by the editor of the *Nation* that he had used food as a weapon against bolshevism in Hungary in 1919, he wrote, "You have slid to second base by running away from your original [point] . . . and now you mix America's private charities with her official organizations and national policies—which I have never done, or allowed to be done."[6]

Nevertheless, Hoover's career offered dramatic proof that a rigid separation between politics and famine relief was not always possible or even desirable. By 1921, he was widely recognized as expert in both fields. In creating the principles and refining the techniques used in rescuing the starving Belgians during the First World War, Hoover transformed famine relief into a resource rivaling propaganda, diplomacy, and military force as an instrument of policy. He succeeded in harnessing politics and famine relief for the most effective promotion of each. As sole manager of this new resource, he entered the political arena with a worldwide constituency. His rise to national political leadership was almost irresistible, as was his emergence as champion of American individualism and American interests. But the complicated interplay among his various roles aroused controversies that haunted his rescue missions, especially the one to Soviet Russia.

THE ENGINEER—FAMINE FIGHTER

Hoover's description of himself as a former mining engineer was extremely modest. Even in its broadest sense, the word "engineer" does not encompass the range of activities that enabled Hoover to retire from business at the age of forty. As a partner in the British management firm of Bewick, Moreing, and Company from 1902 to 1908, he set up or reorganized mining companies in sixteen countries. His functions included technological direction, capitalization of new enterprises, and administrative management. According to a traditional company arrangement, individual partners were permitted to invest in their own mining ventures, which they then turned over for management by Bewick, Moreing on a fixed-fee and profit-sharing basis. In 1905, Hoover invested his own funds in an abandoned mine in Burma and transformed it into one of the richest sources of lead, zinc, and silver in the world.[7]

By 1908, Hoover had established a reputation in the worldwide mining industry as an innovative technologist, a brilliant administrator, and a highly successful financial organizer. He left Bewick, Moreing and set up an informal management concern in association with a group of younger engineers. The new organization was not a "firm" in any legal sense. It was not registered as a partnership or as a corporation. Its offices in New York, London, San Francisco, and later in St. Petersburg were identifiable as branches of an international enterprise by the same simple legend on the door: *Herbert C. Hoover*.[8]

One of the criticisms leveled against Hoover both during and after the Soviet relief mission concerned his business activities in tsarist Russia in association with the British promoter Leslie Urquhart. One U.S. senator charged that Hoover's offer of relief to Russia was directly connected with Urquhart's efforts to obtain a concession in the Urals area from the Soviet government.[9] Hoover acknowledged that he had served as "engineering director of certain metallurgical concerns in Russia" but denied that he still maintained any connection with the corporation that had been set up to coordinate mining activities in the area. He claimed that he had disposed of his "small interest" in all Russian properties and resigned from all companies connected with such interests around 1915. "Therefore," he wrote to the senator, "I have not for many years had any direct or indirect personal interest in Russia."[10]

According to a later account by Hoover himself, his prewar association with the Russo-Asiatic Corporation and its chairman, Leslie Urquhart, was extensive and extremely lucrative. Urquhart had requested Hoover's assistance in organizing and operating a diversified exploitation of some million-and-a-half acres that belonged to Baron Mellor Zakomelsky, a distant relative of the tsar. The property, known as the Kyshtim estate, was rich in agricultural, lumber, copper, iron, and chemical resources. Hoover reorganized the finances of the property and instituted a system of management that combined technological renovation, wage incentives, and close supervision. The project prospered; profits soared; stockholders and managers realized a net return of approximately $2 million a year.

In 1912, representatives of the tsarist government requested similar development by the Urquhart-Hoover group of the Cabinet Mines, an extensive property in Siberia owned by the royal family. This enterprise, according to Hoover, was enormously successful; he obtained an interest in the Irtysh mines near Omsk, which he described as the richest single source of ore ever developed.[11]

In 1921, Urquhart was engaged in negotiations with the Soviet government for a long-term lease of the Kyshtim estate and several other Russo-Asiatic holdings that had been confiscated shortly after the Bolshevik Revolution. Hoover was thus accused of trying to recoup through relief what Russo-Asiatic had lost through revolution. But the actual record casts no doubt on Hoover's claim that he had severed all connections with the firm in 1915. In 1921, in fact, he was pessimistic about the prospects for foreign concessions in Soviet Russia. His former associate, Urquhart, had suggested to Hoover the formation of an international consortium for the purpose of obtaining long-term leases in Russia.[12] Hoover replied, "I question whether the time is ripe either inside or outside Russia as a further swing to the right is vital before confidence can be created abroad upon which such vitally constructive plans as yours can be erected."[13]

In somewhat different terms, Hoover tried to discourage American concession hunters also. In 1922, he told a meeting of the International Chamber of Commerce that he would not entertain pleas for assistance by those seeking concessions because "we cannot approve of anybody exploiting the Russian people."[14] A year later, he denounced "foreign concession hunters who would endeavor to establish even tenuous title to the heritage of the Russian peoples—their natural resources—which could be subsequently used as the groundwork for pressure of their governments in the exploitation of the Russian people."[15]

Hoover's indignation about his own former profession was, understandably, not convincing to his critics, who continued to suspect him of hoping to stake out an exclusive claim in the mineral-rich hills of eastern Russia for himself and his old associates.[16] This suspicion was reinforced by Hoover's reticence about his personal affairs and by the profound faith of the American public in the corruptibility of politicians. But close examination of Hoover's past by his opponents failed to yield any evidence to support a charge of venality. Indeed, Hoover seemed to have lost all interest in moneymaking some years earlier, when he suddenly found a much more rewarding outlet for his unique talents and skills.

Wartime Genesis—The Relief of Belgium

When World War I broke out, Hoover was doing business as usual at the London headquarters of his international mining concern. At the request of a former associate, he agreed to serve as chairman of a committee for the repatriation of Americans who were stranded in Europe at the outbreak of hostilities. By the end of September 1914 the committee had completed its work. Hoover was himself preparing to return to the United States when his assistant on the repatriation committee, Edgar Rickard, came to him with an unusual plea. Would Hoover help to clear a shipment of grain through the British blockade of the continent? The supplies were badly needed in Belgium; its nine million inhabitants were completely cut off from their major source of food when the country was occupied by the German Army in August 1914.

The British government maintained that it was the responsibility of the occupying authorities to provide food for the population. For their part, the Germans attributed the plight of the Belgians to the British blockade and proceeded to deplete the food supply even further by requisitioning grain for the occupying troops. A hastily organized relief group, the *Comité Central de Secours et d'Alimentation,* tried to stave off disaster in Brussels by arranging to ship 2,500 tons of grain through the blockade. The British, however, were reluctant to accept a written guarantee by the German authorities that none of the relief supplies would be requisitioned.[17] Hoover agreed to try to break the deadlock.

Following a conference with Hoover on 6 October, the U.S. ambassador to Great Britain, Walter Hines Page, requested permission from the secretary of state to accept consignment of the stalled shipment to the American minister at Brussels in accordance with the conditions set down by the British government.[18] Within two weeks, the German governor-general of occupied Belgium agreed to exempt the relief supplies from military requisition, the U.S. State Department accepted consignment of the goods, and the British government released the shipment.[19] For the time being, Brussels was spared.

In the meantime, requests for similar assistance were pouring into the offices of the *Comité Central* from other cities in Belgium and were promptly forwarded to Hoover. At the request of Ambassador Page, Hoover agreed to direct a neutral committee to provide food for the entire country. On 22 October 1914 he announced the formation of the American Committee for the Relief of Belgium under the sponsorship of the American envoys to London, Brussels, The Hague, Berlin, and Paris. The word "American" was dropped from the name when the Spanish ambassador to Great Britain and the Netherlands minister at Le Havre were added to the executive committee. The working complement of the new Commission for Relief in Belgium (CRB), however, remained exclusively American.[20]

Persuading the British to suffer a permanent breach in their blockade of the continent was not easy. The purpose of the blockade was not to stabilize the enemy's rear area but to disrupt it. Furthermore, it was by no means certain that the Germans would really allow the Belgian population to starve if the British refused to permit relief shipments. Aside from the moral issue, there was the practical difficulty of maintaining an occupation army in the midst of a doomed population. Finally, the British had to reckon with the real possibility that the German Army might seize relief shipments for its own use.

Although the Minister of War, Lord Kitchener, and the First Lord of the Admiralty, Winston Churchill, obviously resented advice about the conduct of the war from an American businessman, Hoover pressed his argument with confidence and authority.[21] He warned David Lloyd George, chancellor of the exchequer, that the Germans would not deprive their own people in order to feed the Belgians. It was up to the British, he declared, who had gone to war "for the sole purpose of maintaining the Belgian people and their national integrity," not to abandon their defeated ally. The cost to Britain's war effort, according to Hoover, would be quite small; loosening the blockade to feed the Belgians might extend the war by a few days. But Hoover did not depend on persuading the British with military or moral arguments alone. His strategy was to intensify the competition between England and Germany for the sympathy and support of the neutral countries, particularly the United States. He warned Lloyd George:

> In the matter of public sentiment in the neutral world, I can only speak for my own country . . . . I cannot too strongly emphasize the fact that should this relief work fail to receive the sympathy and support of the English people, it would have a most serious bearing on the whole attitude of public sentiment in the United States.[22]

This was substantially the same argument that Hoover had used some ten days earlier in a discussion with the German Foreign Minister, Gottlieb von Jagow, in Berlin. He told von Jagow that the United States would remain neutral if the Germans were able to gain the sympathy of at least half of the American public. He said that he was "absolutely satisfied that in order to win American opinion Germany must mend her methods toward Belgium."[23]

Hoover succeeded in convincing each side that the relief of Belgium was advantageous to its cause. The Allies accepted Germany's written guarantee that only the Belgian population would receive the benefits of the relief effort and that the distribution of all food, including the harvest in the occupied area, would be under the control of the CRB. The personnel of the relief mission were granted freedom of action in their work.[24]

In spite of numerous disputes between the British and Germans about alleged violations of the agreement, Hoover was able to maintain the arrangement for the relief of Belgium throughout the war. Shortly after the entry of the United States into the war, American personnel operating in occupied territory were replaced by representatives of the Spanish and Netherlands governments. The CRB continued to provide the money, shipping, and general administration for the relief effort.[25]

Hoover's Private Relief Organization

The organization that Hoover created for the relief of Belgium was entirely unique. With little exaggeration, an official of the British Foreign Office described the CRB as a "piratical state organized for benevolence." Hoover "seized" ships for transportation of supplies at cost price or less; commandeered the services of business friends, Rhodes scholars, and army officers, and extracted from the diminished treasuries of Great Britain and France subsidies that ultimately amounted to over $300 million. The CRB fleet sailed under its own flag, protected by privileges and immunites denied by the belligerent powers to all other ships. CRB credentials served as passports for travel in regions where most official passports were invalid.

The organization's staff took its order only from "the Chief" (as Hoover was commonly referred to in internal communications) or from his appointed representative. Hoover negotiated a series of "treaties" with the warring powers and usually succeeded in enforcing compliance through prudent use of a threat to cancel the mission.[26] According to Hoover, Senator Henry Cabot Lodge threatened an investigation of Hoover's negotiations with England and France to determine whether these acts were in criminal violation of a federal law that forbade usurpation of diplomatic power by a private citizen. Hoover replied that his negotiations and agreements were undertaken with the full approval of several American ambassadors. Lodge did not pursue the matter.[27] Hoover continued to make "treaties" with foreign governments until the end of the relief mission to Soviet Russia.

One of his closest associates characterized the governing principles of Hoover's relief organization as "the same as those successful in American engineering enterprises and particularly those controlled in foreign countries by Mr. Hoover."[28] For Hoover, the major objective of a relief operation was volume. Josephus Daniels, secretary of the navy during the First World War, wrote that Hoover described his work in Belgian relief "as coldly as if he were giving statistics of production. From his words and manners, he seemed to regard human beings as so many numbers."[29]

In order to achieve maximum "production," Hoover carried over into his relief work the operating principles that he had found most effective in his mining enterprises—namely, heavy outside financing, strict accounting, tight economical administration, and above all, undisputed one-man authority. Hoover was convinced that "famine fighting is a gigantic economic and governmental operation handled by experts and not 'welfare' work of benevolently handing out food hit or miss to bread lines. . . . Some individual with great powers must direct and coordinate all this. Such an operation would be hopeless in the hands of international commissions or committees."[30]

The CRB and its successors were living illustrations of this theory of leadership. They had no identity apart from the Chief; his exclusive authority to initiate, expand, diminish, or terminate relief missions, and even the organization itself, was unquestioned. No contract or constitution limited his power to set up policies and establish procedures. The accomplishments of the group were credited directly to Hoover. Criticism of any aspect of a mission by outsiders was regarded as a personal attack on Hoover.

The aura of authority that attached to this calm, unsentimental, almost impersonal leader was not transferable; thus, no conflicts about succession to the Chief disturbed the unity of his executive staff. The hard core of Hoover's top-ranking assistants remained with him throughout his relief operations. Trusted subordinates were granted wide latitude in the implementation of Hoover policies. CRB representatives in the field negotiated agreements with German military commanders without prior consent from the London head-quarters. Information and advice from below were always welcomed, indeed demanded, by Hoover as indispensable to efficient control.

Criticism of central policy to outsiders meant dismissal but it was rarely necessary to invoke this sanction. The awe that Hoover inspired in his subordinates by his confident working of miracles during the relief of Belgium, and by his later successes, pervaded the organization. Compliance with the wishes of the Chief became anticipatory.[31]

Hoover's private relief organization was managed by fewer than sixty full-time staff members throughout the mission to Belgium. His top-ranking assistants received no pay; the rest of the staff drew subsistence allowances. But, as the balance sheet of this tiny "firm" reveals, the relief of Belgium assumed the proportions of a major industry. From the wartime governments of the United States, Great Britain, and France, Hoover obtained subsidies that totaled over $700 million. International appeals to private institutions and individuals yielded another $50 million. Another source of income was the surplus realized on the sale of food. Belgians who could afford to pay were obliged to buy rations from normal retail channels, which were in turn supplied by the CRB at prices slightly above cost. Whenever food was in danger of spoilage owing to a shortage of shipping or other facilities, the CRB sold grain and meat to nonoccupied countries at market prices. Because of the low overhead of the operation and the high prices that prevailed during the war, the relief mission was able to realize over $135 million in profit from its commercial activities. This surplus was used to increase the number and size of relief rations. In its four-and-one-half years of operation, the CRB disbursed a grand total of over $880 million—a sum that exceeded the annual budget of the United States government for any of the prewar years since the Civil War.[32]

The spectacular relief of Belgium brought Hoover to the attention of an immense, sympathetic audience. His personal correspondence with heads of state, philanthropic organizations, governors, business leaders, educators, and editors multiplied with the expansion of the mission. By the time the United States entered the war, millions of Europeans and Americans and most of their leaders saw Hoover as "the savior of Belgium." The door was open to a political career at the highest level.

"FOOD REGULATOR OF THE WORLD"

When Hoover returned to the United States in May 1917, President Woodrow Wilson offered him the chairmanship of a board that would be responsible for control of the nation's wartime food supply. To Hoover, such a dilution of one-man authority represented an unnecessary sacrifice of efficiency. He told the president that commissions had been ineffective in Europe because of their "inevitable frictions, indecisions, and delays," adding that "the whole genius of American business, and even governmental administrations, prescribed a single responsible executive with boards only in advisory, legislative, or judicial functions." The president agreed to replace the proposed board with a powerful food administrator—Hoover himself—but not without misgivings.[33]

As it turned out, the "food dictator" relied heavily on voluntary cooperation rather than on arbitrary regulations in controlling the food supply. The federal monopoly of key commodities and flexible control of profit margins were convenient instruments of control that made rationing and price control unnecessary. "We knew," Hoover later commented, "that, although Americans can be led to make great sacrifices, they do not like to be driven."[34]

To assist him, Hoover enlisted the services of "old Belgian hands," such as Edgar Rickard and Vernon Kellogg, and a new group of talented young "Hoover men," including Lewis L. Strauss and Robert A. Taft. With the Chief confidently at the helm, the tight organization of food administrators provided food for the U.S. armed forces and the civilian population, supplemented the provisioning of the Allies, and maintained the relief of Belgium throughout the rest of the war. When the war ended, Wilson asked Hoover to serve as an adviser to the American delegation at the Peace Conference in Paris and to take over direction of American relief to Europe.[35]

The struggle for control of food relief began at once. On 24 October 1918 Hoover advised the president that some Allied leaders were pressing plans for international control of food distribution. "My own instinct," wrote Hoover, "is entirely against any such agreements. . . . If we maintain our independence we can confer favors instead of complying with agreements and we can use our resources to make economic exchanges which will maintain justice all around."[36] He instructed his representative to register American opposition to the Allied plan.[37] He could not approve, he declared in a memorandum on 14 November 1918, leaving the important matter of food relief to "the second-class minds and jealousies of the present inter-Allied bodies." What was urgently needed was a commander-in-chief of food operations with powers similar to those granted to Marshal Foch during the war: "This man should be an American—the disinterested nation; the nation having to furnish the bulk of the supplies; the nation that could increase its supplies by call from its own citizens."[38]

The Allied leaders naturally objected to being denied a visible role in the relief of postwar Europe, but resistance to Hoover's plan was futile. Impatient with the protracted negotiations, Hoover ordered his organization to start shipments to southern Europe, where the food shortage was acute. The president had given his approval only the day before.[39] The Allies surrendered. On 23 December the French and Italian foreign ministers agreed to American management of European relief. On 3 January the American Commission to Negotiate Peace announced the appointment of Herbert Hoover as director general of an inter-Allied council for the relief of Europe. By that time, approximately 150,00 tons of American food had already been dispatched.[40]

Hoover's victory was complete. General John J. Pershing called him "food regulator of the world." Unencumbered by any outside control, he launched the most massive relief program in history. During the nine months following the Armistice, he organized the delivery of nearly $1 billion worth of goods to twenty-two countries.[41] In all, over four million tons of relief supplies were delivered to Europe. The heads of government throughout Europe, including those who had vigorously opposed Hoover's drive for solitary control, expressed their deep appreciation.[42]

In the course of the struggle over the control of food relief, Hoover had moved toward the development of an exclusively American relief organization. At Hoover's prompting, Wilson asked Congress for an appropriation of $100 million for the relief of "such populations in

Europe, outside of Germany, as may be determined by me from time to time as necessary."[43] On 25 January 1919 Hoover urged Wilson to establish an independent American relief organization to manage the funds voted by Congress the day before. A month later, Wilson issued an executive order (drawn up by Hoover) stipulating that all functions connected with the disbursement of the appropriated funds "shall be conducted under the direction of Herbert Hoover who is hereby appointed Director General of the American Relief Administration with full power to determine which of the populations named in said Act the supplies shall be furnished and in what quantities."[44]

The new agency grew rapidly into an international relief network with its own communications system. Its staff of 4,000 volunteers was made up of experienced "old Hoover hands," Rhodes scholars, and army officers who were relieved of military duties for the period of their service to the ARA. In addition to supervising relief in thirty-two countries, the ARA, according to Hoover, frequently acted as a source of information and as an instrument of political action for the Allied Council and President Wilson.[45] During the turbulent Armistice period, this meant deep involvement in the new conflict that preoccupied the Allied leaders—the struggle against bolshevism.

THE AMERICAN ANTI-COMMUNIST

One of Hoover's arguments against Allied control of food was that Great Britain and France would attempt to use relief for "political and economic objectives." "The sole object of relief," he declared, "should be humanity. It should have no political objective or other aim than the maintenance of life and order."[46] But Hoover was also convinced that there was no possibility of securing "life and order" in areas controlled or threatened by bolshevism. In advocating the use of food as an antidote to communism, Hoover saw no compromise of the canons of philanthropy. On 22 November 1918 he wrote in a memorandum on the reconstruction of Europe:

> From a political point of view, the urgent necessity of setting up supplies need not be placed on a higher plane than—
> First: To stem the tide of Bolshevism, for no stability of Government can be maintained in starving populations and stability can be

established by placing food supplies in the hands of some government
recognized as of stable qualities.[47]

The only alternative to using relief in this manner, according to the
memorandum, was military resistance at considerable "expense and
loss of life."

Relief and Diplomacy: the Hoover-Nansen Proposal

The idea of substituting food for guns in the war against communism appealed to President Wilson. Early in 1919, the president
wrote to the chairman of the House Appropriations Committee:
"Bolshevism is steadily advancing westward, is poisoning Germany.
It cannot be stopped by force, but it can be stopped by food."[48]

He was also attracted, however, to a negotiated settlement of the
Civil War in Russia and adjacent territories. His proposal to arrange
a meeting between representatives of the contending forces on the
island of Prinkipo was ratified at a meeting with the Allied leaders on
21 January 1919. When this scheme collapsed due to French opposition, Wilson's personal representative, Colonel Edward M. House,
worked out a plan to send a State Department emissary, William C.
Bullitt, on a secret mission to Soviet Russia with a specific proposal
for a truce and a conference of the belligerent parties. Bullitt left
Paris on 22 February and returned at the end of March with a Soviet
commitment to accept an Allied proposal substantially along the
lines suggested, provided that such an offer were made by 10 April.
According to Bullitt's later testimony before the Senate Foreign
Relations Committee, the American delegation at Paris agreed that
the Soviet proposal provided a suitable basis for a truce.[49]

At this point, Hoover presented an alternative plan to Wilson. In a
memorandum written on 28 March, Hoover suggested offering food
relief to Soviet Russia in return for a unilateral cessation of "all militant action across definite boundaries" on the part of the Bolsheviks.
In support of his plan, he offered an analysis of communism
remarkably like the approach adopted by liberal social scientists of a
later generation. After noting that the Bolsheviks were scoring vic-
tories only in areas formerly governed by "reactionary tyranny," he
declared that "where the gulf between the middle classes and the
lower classes is large, and where the lower classes have been kept in
ignorance and distress, this [communist] propaganda will be fatal

and do violence to normal democratic development."[50]

Since these conditions did not exist in the United States, there was no danger that America would succumb to communist subversion. Hoover was not sure whether the Bolsheviks would try to impose their system on others by force, but "if this spirit is inherent in their doctrine," he recommended that the United States "disregard all other questions and be prepared to fight." Pending conclusive evidence on this matter, he did not favor military intervention. "The American people cannot say that we are going to insist that any given population work out its internal social problems according to our particular conceptions of democracy."

Although Hoover's arguments resembled those advanced by advocates of some sort of rapprochement with Soviet Russia, to Hoover, such a compromise was out of the question. He recommended that Wilson refuse to recognize Soviet Russia and use his prestige to expose the "utter foolishness" of bolshevism and at the same time to denounce the "reactionaries" for their opposition to social reform. As an immediate, more concrete measure to halt the spread of bolshevism, he offered his relief program. He proposed the establishment of an organization similar to the Commission for Relief in Belgium under the leadership of "some neutral of international reputation for probity and ability."[51]

Hoover's plan obviously ruled out approval of the Bullitt agreement, which provided for the ending of hostilities by all contending groups and the immediate removal of all foreign troops from Russia. Hoover's proposal called for a cessation of military activities by the Bolsheviks only. The Bullitt agreement stipulated that the Allied blockade against Soviet Russia was to be lifted and that all existing governments in Russia were to extend to each other, and receive from the Allied and associated governments, all the privileges necessary to insure the resumption of travel and trade. The Hoover plan did not call for a change from the existing policy of assistance to the counterrevolutionary forces and strict isolation of Soviet Russia except for the proposed relief assistance.

While Bullitt waited on the president for approval of the agreement with the Soviet leaders, Hoover acted on his own plan. By 3 April, he had persuaded Fridtjof Nansen to head the neutral relief commission and to petition the president for approval and for financial support of the relief mission. The letter, which had been drafted in advance by Hoover and his associates,[52] mentioned no political or military conditions. The relief effort was to be "devoted solely to the humanitarian purpose of saving life" and "would raise no question of political recognition or negotiations between the Allies with the existing authorities in Russia."[53] The letter was released immediately to the press. According to Bullitt, Colonel House informed him that he favored the relief plan as "an easier way to peace" and asked him to prepare a reply to Nansen's petition. Bullitt was evidently unaware that Hoover had drafted a reply that contained several of the conditions that he had outlined in his 28 March memorandum to the president.

On 4 April Bullitt submitted a draft of a reply that was in essence a summary of the conditions already approved by the Soviet government. The addition of an offer of relief served to relate the Bullitt draft to Nansen's letter. According to Bullitt, Colonel House reacted favorably to the draft but insisted on submitting it for final review to two experts on international law. One of the experts was Gordon Auchincloss, House's secretary and official contact with Hoover.[54]

The "revision" that was returned to Bullitt later that day was an entirely different proposal, probably the one that Hoover claims to have drawn up at the same time that he framed the Nansen letter. The key provisions of this version were "a cessation of hostilities by Russian troops" and control of the Russian transportation system by the new relief commission. Bullitt was then permitted to amend the proposal by including a ban on military action by troops of all nationalities and on the transfer of all military supplies and troops to or within the entire region. The draft was then returned for final revision.[55]

According to Lewis Strauss, who was Hoover's secretary at the time, "This reply, which was the heart of the matter, had the most careful editing and was once more rewritten by Mr. Hoover."[56] The heads of state of the victorious powers, constituted as the Council of Four, signed the proposal on 9 April 1919. After some delay, apparently owing to obstructive tactics on the part of the French authorities, the reply to Nansen was sent to the Soviet government.[57] In the meantime, the deadline for Allied approval of the Bullitt agreement had passed.

When the reply to Nansen's letter was published, it was greeted with a barrage of criticism. A liberal magazine saw it as a plan to feed counterrevolutionaries and starve Bolsheviks.[58] The French Foreign

Minister, Stephen Pichon, publicly denounced the proposal to which Premier Georges Clemenceau had put his name. The émigré Russian Political Conference, led by Prince Lvov, the first premier of the Provisional Government, called the plan a prop under a Red government that was about to collapse. A massive Soviet retreat in March and April under the pressure of General Kolchak's White armies lent weight to this argument.[59]

The attacks on the Allied relief proposal were wasted. On 14 May the Soviet Commissar of Foreign Affairs, Georgi Chicherin, notified Nansen by radio that the conditions set forth for granting food relief were unacceptable. He commended Nansen for his humanitarian offer but condemned the Allied powers for having "fundamentally disfigured" his original proposal. He stated that the cessation of hostilities was strictly a political matter, and that while the Soviet government was always ready to consider peace negotiations, it was not willing "to make any concessions referring to the fundamental problems of our existence under the guise of a presumably humanitarian work." Chicherin concluded by inviting Nansen to meet with Soviet delegates to work out a suitable relief plan.[60]

The Allied powers were not disposed to seeing only the philanthropic aspects of their plan implemented. After meeting with Hoover, the representatives of Great Britain and Italy instructed him to notify Nansen that they deemed it "extremely inadvisable" to arrange any meeting with Soviet representatives at the moment. Nansen resigned himself to the evident fact that the issue was dead along with his hope of reconciling Soviet Russia with the rest of the world through food relief.[61]

Chicherin's reply indicated that Soviet leaders took the tacit rejection of the Bullitt agreement as proof that the United States, like the Allied powers, was not interested in negotiating a peace that left the Bolshevik regime in power. The relief proposal, with its suspect military-political conditions, appeared as a cynical misuse of philanthropy. Hoover's later comment that "the effort died at no cost but words" underestimates the price of his failure to displace conventional diplomacy with food relief.[62]

The Soviet leaders had given notice that they would not submit to a limitation of their own authority by an outside group merely to relieve hunger; Lenin's concept of humanitarianism did not stretch that far. The Civil War in Russia, with its frightful toll of death and suffering, continued.

In the meantime, Hoover continued to administer food relief as a positive antidote to what he regarded as the twin diseases of central Europe—hunger and bolshevism. When the Allied-supported government of Austria appeared in danger of being overthrown toward the end of April 1919, Hoover saw his function as "a race against both death and Communism." To counter a reported uprising in Vienna scheduled for 1 May, he authorized the city government to post the following proclamation on the city walls:

> Any disturbance of public order will render food shipments impossible and bring Vienna face to face with absolute famine.

> HERBERT HOOVER

In his description of the incident, Hoover states tersely, "May 1 came and went quietly."[63]

The threat to withhold food seemed to deter revolution. Could it also be used to stimulate an anti-Communist uprising? Hoover saw the opportunity to test the hypothesis two months later in Soviet Hungary. On 26 July the Allied Council of Four issued a declaration, written by Hoover, warning the Hungarian people that food relief would not be forthcoming unless a government that was more representative and reponsible than the Communist regime of Bela Kun came into power. On 1 August the Kun government was overthrown by a combination of army and trade union leaders. Although Hoover later expressed doubt that the Red regime fell because of the threat to stop food shipments, he did not deny that such had indeed been the purpose of the announcement.[64]

The New ARA and Counterrevolution

Although Hoover had achieved considerable autonomy in the distribution of food in Europe, the Allied authorities were not inclined to give him free rein in relief matters concerning Soviet Russia. Hoover chafed under their restraints, convinced that he understood the intricacies of relief politics better than the Old World politicians did. He especially resented the interference of the French representatives, as in the Nansen affair.[65] As the peace conference drew to a close, Hoover was faced with the problem of how to maintain an exclusively American relief organization in Europe after the United States delegation left Paris. When the term of the congressional appropriation was coming to an end, Hoover took steps to insure continuity for the ARA and to enhance his own control over its activities.

Of the original $100 million appropriated by Congress, approximately 88 percent had been disbursed as loans to various governments for the purchase of relief supplies. The remaining 12 percent had been donated to private organizations set up in each country served by the ARA.[66] One of the groups so endowed was the Children's Relief Bureau, which had begun operations in April 1919 with a grant of $7.5 million from the ARA, $4.8 million from various European governments, and $300,000 from private sources.[67] On 17 July 1919 Hoover informed the ARA New York office that he intended to announce the succession of this private organization to the functions of the official government agency; he had obtained approval for this from the president a month earlier. The new agency was to be named the American Relief Administration European Children's Fund. "We are holding on to the first three words partly because we wish to secure the political effect of continued American interest in European welfare," Hoover wrote, "as the whole withdrawal of the Relief Administration will create the most serious apprehension, and secondly it is desirable to maintain the established prestige."[68]

The last three words in the title soon fell into disuse, and the ARA emerged in its final form as Hoover's private relief agency, a unique creation deliberately designed to live in the best areas of both the private and the official worlds. As a private philanthropy, the new ARA was immune from the "frictions, indecisions, and delays" imposed by formal, official procedures. Yet it was able to inherit the name, the prestige, and a substantial amount of the power of the government agency it superseded. Indirectly endowed with a congressional appropriation, the new ARA could and did undertake humanitarian tasks that were far beyond the capabilities of other welfare organizations. And to millions of Europeans, the ARA continued to symbolize America—the generous, successful giant who dispensed food to entire populations at the stroke of Herbert Hoover's pen.

The political implications of the reorganization of the ARA were momentous. As the head of a private organization, Hoover was not subject to the restraints that governed the actions of a politically accountable official. The director general of a U.S. government relief agency could not, according to Hoover, accede to the request of the Allied Supreme Council that he provision the anti-Soviet White armies in Russia because Congress had never intended such use of the appropriation.[69] The Chief of the private ARA, however, felt free to conclude an agreement between his own organization and the political arm of the White forces—the so-called "Provisional Government of Russia." According to the terms of this "treaty," the ARA would deliver to the counterrevolutionary Northwestern Army Corps, and to the detachment operating in the vicinity of Riga, food for both military and civilian personnel. The distribution was placed in the hands of the "Provisional Government" or its designated representatives, "subject to the general direction and approval of the American Relief Administration, and in accord with the dictates of humanity."[70]

In creating the new ARA, Hoover had found a way to avoid involving the United States officially in the anti-Bolshevik military intervention and yet supply the White armies with food during a critical phase of the Civil War. His warning against American participation in military intervention apparently did not rule out material assistance to Russian anti-Soviet forces in the field by an American relief organization, or, for that matter, by the United States government itself. On 30 August 1919 he advised the secretary of state from Paris:

> It appears to our staff that General Yudenich could at an early date take Petrograd in which event their supplies would last but a few days. My own view is that it is wholly illogical to support Kolchak and not to support Yudenich with arms and supplies and that no greater relief of human misery could be undertaken than the occupation of Petrograd.[71]

To Hoover, the White Guard generals represented the last hope of establishing "constitutional government and fundamental personal liberties" in Russia.[72] He strove to keep this hope alive by supplying the anti-Bolshevik armies with gasoline, food, and clothing needed to sustain the offensive against Petrograd during the summer and fall of 1919.[73] In appreciation of this support, the commander of the Northwest Russian Army wrote the following testimonial addressed to "Mr. Hoover, Food-Dictator of Europe":

The North-Western Russian Army, which is fighting against the Bolshevists in the direction of Petrograd for the restoration of the lawful order of things in Russia, is now existing practically upon American flour and bacon.

A regular food supply of the starving population and the Army is at least as important as rifles and ammunition in our fight for the liberation of our great country from the red terror.

We Russians will never cease to thank the great Nation of the United States of America for its help and assistance.

At this time, when we are only beginning our drive for Petrograd, which, I am sure, will be crowned with full success, I am asking the American Relief Administration representative in Russia to convey to you this message of gratitude and appreciation from all soldiers, officers, and myself to the American people as well as our conviction that its generous assistance will also continue further on to accompany us in our struggle with the bitterest enemy of mankind, law and order—Bolshevism.[74]

The State Department joined in the effort to supply General Yudenich's army during the last days of its unsuccessful offensive against Petrograd. The ARA managed to turn over to the embattled White armies the food that had been gathered from other areas and assembled in Finland, but by the time the State Department cargo arrived at the ARA warehouse, the anti-Bolshevik forces were in full retreat from Petrograd, pausing only to loot the ARA storehouses in their path.[75]

The Abortive Relief Mission of 1920

Hoover's antipathy toward the Bolshevik regime did not deter him from trying to reach an agreement with Soviet authorities about feeding children in Bolshevik-controlled territory. The first occasion for direct negotiations between the ARA and the Soviet government arose in the summer of 1920 during the war between Poland and Russia. The ARA had been feeding over a million children in Poland proper as well as in the territory occupied by the Polish Army in Soviet Russia.

In July, the tide of battle turned. ARA relief stations throughout Poland seemed in imminent danger of being overrun by Soviet forces. The ARA London office advised New York headquarters on 22 July that some arrangement must be concluded with Bolshevik authorities if the feeding program in Poland was to continue.[76] Even before the message was received, however, Hoover had instructed field workers to continue operations in Soviet-held territory, "if our men think it at all safe." "After the preliminary mess of invasion," he wrote, "they may be able to set up again in Bolshevik-occupied Poland under some kind of arrangement."[77]

To provide the victims of this new war with food, Hoover was willing to accept reasonable risks, both in regard to his men in the field and to the official American policy of maintaining a strict diplomatic quarantine of Soviet Russia—a policy in which he concurred wholeheartedly. The State Department, however, would support no activity that involved recognizing Soviet authority in any area for any reason. The ARA had therefore to negotiate with the Bolsheviks as a private welfare organization with no official backing.[78]

On 24 July, Walter Lyman Brown, director of the ARA in Europe, opened negotiations in a cable to Chicherin, transmitted by George Lansbury, editor of the *London Daily Herald*. Brown stated that the ARA had been feeding more than a million children in Europe for fifteen months and wished to continue, "irrespective of the Government in control." He asked whether the Soviet government would agree and whether it was prepared to guarantee the safety of ARA stores and equipment.[79]

In his reply of 4 August, Chicherin noted the prominence of former U.S. Army officers on the ARA staff but indicated that this would not impede continued operations if the Americans agreed to certain conditions, including control of all ARA activities by the official Soviet relief organization and limitation of all feeding operations to nonmilitary zones.[80]

Anticipating Hoover's approval, Brown notified Chicherin that he was sending an ARA representative to Minsk with the Polish armistice delegation to discuss terms. The former army officers on the ARA staff had been demobilized for a year, he explained, and had "always been under the strictest instructions to preserve neutrality both in action and spirit, their work being benevolent relief and nothing else."[81]

Without waiting for an answer, Brown authorized the departure of his emissary, Maurice Pate, together with an ARA medical officer, Dr. Herschel C. Walker, who was familiar with the Minsk area. On 14 August, Pate and Walker crossed the Soviet lines with the Polish delegation.[82] On the same day, the Polish Army counterattacked successfully, thereby removing the imminent danger to Warsaw and to most of the ARA stations in Poland.

In Minsk, Pate and Walker were immediately placed under confinement. The local Soviet authorities declared that they had no knowledge of a message announcing the arrival of ARA men. While the Polish delegation delayed its own negotiations, presumably to gain advantage from the advances of the army, Walker and Pate awaited permission to proceed to Moscow. Allowed the liberty of the city under the surveillance of guards, they later reported that the ARA relief kitchens were in operation and that the Bolsheviks had confiscated none of the supplies. Finally, an official escort arrived at Minsk to accompany the ARA delegation to the capital.[83] On 28 August Chicherin notified Brown that the representatives, who had arrived "without our authorization" were on their way to Moscow to proceed with negotiations.[84]

After several conferences with Pate and Walker, Soviet officials from the People's Commissariat of Foreign Affairs agreed to a substantial modification of Chicherin's original terms. They proposed the establishment of a Russian-American committee consisting of delegates from five or six Soviet organizations and several Americans to control accounts, warehouses, and distribution.[85]

The sessions were long and difficult as Soviet officials suspected the Americans' motives. When the conferences were concluded, however, the ARA delegates were convinced that they had laid the groundwork for a suitable agreement. After a meeting with Pate and Walker in London, Brown informed Hoover, "It is possible to carry on child-feeding in Russia under a general scheme of Russian-American Committee control."[86] By this time, however, the advance of the Polish Army had removed the threat to the ARA stations in Poland. The Soviet-Polish Armistice of October 1920 secured the border between the two countries pending the conclusion of a peace treaty. Hoover's interest in concluding a relief agreement with the Soviet regime was apparently limited to the areas in Poland that had fallen under occupation by the Red Army. Negotiations were not resumed.

In some ways, the encounter between the ARA and the Soviet government was a preview of the one that would take place some nine months later. In 1920, the ARA tried to obtain the control over its own operations that it had enjoyed in countries under more permissive governments. The Soviet representatives saw this kind of autonomy as a threat to their own sovereignty and to security as well. The conflict was not resolved by an agreement on "joint supervision" as ARA negotiators were not convinced that the conference had agreed on a mutual interpretation of that term.

The ARA delegates were surprised at the bitterness and suspicion that met their proposals for the relief of children. To the Soviet representatives, there were no disinterested actors or neutral activities in the struggle between capitalism and communism.[87] What they already knew about the ARA, both as an official government agency and as a private relief organization, only reinforced this conviction. Yet, Hoover was prepared to feed the starving in Soviet territory, even if it meant some compromise of both national policy and of his own position as a dedicated anti-Communist. It was, after all, Hoover himself who had developed the theory that relief to the hungry serves to stabilize the existing regime in a given area. Was the unrelenting enemy of bolshevism yielding to the philanthropic relief administrator? The Bolsheviks were mystified and skeptical.

Several months later Hoover again attempted to reach into Soviet territory with relief supplies. On 26 January 1921 he offered the Friends Service Committee, a Quaker group engaged in relief activity in Russia, $100,000 worth of ARA food on the condition that American citizens who were being held by the Soviet government on various charges be released.[88] The head of the Quaker relief agency, Wilbur Thomas, was reluctant to intercede on behalf of American prisoners because he believed that some of them were guilty of the crimes charged. He agreed, however, to relay Hoover's proposal to the Soviet authorities. Hoover then asked the Quakers to arrange at least for food and medical attention for two prisoners with whose cases he was familiar.[89] On 10 March the Friends Service Committee in Moscow notified Hoover that they had received permission to deliver two packages to the two American prisoners. On 14 March the Quakers sent word that the Soviet government was willing to release all the Americans, including spies, if the United States officially negotiated the transaction. Concerning Hoover's proposal, the Quakers declared, "We do not regard it to be the mission of a Children's Relief Organization to demand or negotiate the release of political prisoners."[90]

Hoover was incensed at the Friends Service Committee's decision to maintain professional neutrality while Americans languished in

Soviet prisons, but he nevertheless released the credits for the ARA food to the Quakers in Russia. When he became convinced that the Quakers would not accept the responsibility for feeding the American prisoners, he cut off all further aid.[91]

The negotiations with the Friends and the grant of food were transacted without publicity or prior consultation with the State Department. When the secretary of state learned that the ARA had shipped food to Russia, he requested that Hoover furnish him with full information about the circumstances surrounding the grant. On 13 August Hoover sent the secretary correspondence with the Friends Service Committee as proof that his intentions were to insure the adequate feeding of the American prisoners.[92] Evidently Hoover believed that, as the head of a private relief agency, he was not obliged to obtain advance clearance from the State Department in such matters. But when he decided to answer Gorky's appeal for help to Soviet Russia in July 1921, he was no longer able to act as a free agent. The client was now the Soviet government itself, and Hoover was now a high-ranking official of the American government.

THE CABINET MEMBER

The appointment of Hoover as secretary of commerce in 1921 placed him in a position of unique influence in the administration of Warren G. Harding. The president himself had insisted on Hoover over the vigorous objection of the Old Guard leaders of the Republican party.[93] Hoover's ability and international prestige counted less with the "stand-pat" champions of business privilege than his association with Democrats under the Wilson administration and his reputation as a liberal. He entered the cabinet free of obligations to the party establishment. Indeed, he was able to exact a price for lending his presence to an administration which, with the exception of the Secretary of State, Charles Evans Hughes, was singularly lacking in talent. Hoover accepted the post in Commerce only with the understanding that he would have some voice in policy outside his own department.[94] Once in office, he made common cause on many issues with the secretary of state. The alliance between the State and Commerce departments was cemented not only by the mutual admiration of their secretaries but by their close agreement on policy toward Soviet Russia.[95]

Shortly after taking office, Hoover issued an official statement on this subject.

> The question of trade with Russia is far more a political question than an economic one as long as Russia is in control of the Bolsheviki. Under their economic system, no matter how they moderate it in name, there can be no real return to production in Russia, and therefore Russia will have no considerable commodities to export and consequently, no great ability to obtain imports.

According to the statement, this was not strictly a Russian problem: "Europe cannot recover its economic stability until Russia returns to production."[96]

The Washington correspondent of the *New York Times* interpreted Hoover's pronouncement as an expression of "the opinion that has been held by experts in the American Government for many months."

> It is for this reason that the Bolshevik regime, it is held, must be overthrown, so that the Russian people may have the opportunity to install an economic and political system along liberal, democratic lines, that would bring Russia back into the ranks of the great producing nations of the world.[97]

Hoover's stand on trade with Soviet Russia stimulated a declaration of firm support by a group of leading figures who shared his deep animosity toward the Bolshevik regime. Among the signers were the presidents of the United States Steel Corporation, the National City Bank, the Baltimore and Ohio Railway Company, and the Carnegie Institute; the former president of Harvard University; the entire executive board of the International Longshoremen's Association; and the American Legion Committee on Anti-American Activities.[98]

On 26 March the secretary of state issued a policy statement that was described in the press as an echo of Hoover's views. Hoover welcomed Hughes' statement as a sign that the entire administration agreed with his views on the renewal of trade with Russia. Senator Henry Cabot Lodge and most of the other members of the Senate Foreign Relations Committee added their voices to the chorus of approval.[99]

For the most part, public opinion was in tune with official policy toward the Bolshevik government. In 1919 and 1920 fear of communism was effectively transmitted to millions of Americans through a well-publicized drive by Attorney General Mitchell Palmer against radicals of all descriptions. Although the "Red scare" had largely subsided by the end of 1920, a substantial residue of animosity toward radicals, revolutionists, and Russia remained. By 1921, anti-communism had become a permanent feature of the American political landscape.[100]

Ironically, the wall of hostility between Soviet Russia and the United States, which Hoover had helped to erect and maintain, would have to be breached by Hoover himself in order to clear the way for a relief mission. Where could he find justification for a move that was certain to be widely interpreted as a new departure in American policy? He could appeal to the humanitarian instincts of the American public by citing the desperate need of starving Russian children. He could also present his own immaculate anti-Communist credentials as assurance that American food would not be used to strengthen Bolshevik rule. Finally, as secretary of commerce, he could try to persuade American leaders that a relief mission to Russia held the promise of great economic benefit to the United States.

American farmers were staggering under the burden of a tremendous crop surplus; in one year the price of farm products had declined by almost 50 percent.[101] This fact alone was a powerful argument in favor of a great food relief project. As Julius Barnes, vice-chairman of the ARA, stated the case when the mission was already under way:

> Six weeks ago this was the world situation: On the American farm a great surplus of grain production, selling in the market, under the pressure of its own supplies, at less than the cost of production, and far out of balance with the prices of those things that the farmer had to buy. Across the seas, in Russia, a famine, partly economic and partly climatic, threatening the total extinction of 30,000,000 of human beings, whose lives could be preserved by the unsalable surplus burdening the American farm. I conceive that it would have been a grave disaster had individualistic America found no way to bridge the gap between the two countries.[102]

Industrial production was another area in which American resources seemed to match Soviet needs. The U.S. manufacturing facilities developed during the war were capable of producing goods in quantities that could not be absorbed in either the domestic or the foreign market at the time. During the 1921 recession, unemployment climbed to over 5 million from the previous year's level of 1.5 million.[103] In Russia, the decline in the production of manufactured goods was a critical element in the breakdown of the exchange of goods between the cities and the farm areas that had not been affected by drought.

Unlike Russia, however, the United States did not face economic catastrophe. And in spite of pressure from some quarters to follow England's lead in opening trade relations with the Soviet regime, Hoover was not likely to reverse his policy toward Russian trade while communism was in command in that country. Although Lenin's New Economic Policy was widely celebrated in Europe as the abandonment of communist economic principles, Hoover was not convinced that any real guarantee of property rights was possible under Bolshevik rule. The meagre hope of reducing unemployment by providing American businessmen with special access to the Soviet market was, thus, not a serious consideration as far as Hoover was concerned.

In the early spring of 1921, however, a new hope presented itself. From various sources, Hoover heard that the Bolsheviks were losing their grip on the reins of power. On 3 June the ARA New York headquarters alerted its London office to mobilize all its resources for possible emergency action in Russia.

> The information available here from Russia would indicate that there is some chance for a decided change in the Russian situation, and you are aware from our earliest cables and from discussions with Taylor that the Chief wants to be in position to meet any emergency which might arise from such a much-to-be-desired change in Russian conditions.

According to the letter, the ARA was withholding all commitments to other governments in order to build up as large a reserve of food as possible. The message concluded by spelling out the nature of the anticipated change and the possible role of relief.

> If the Soviet Government should be overthrown we are all anxious to show American good will at the earliest possible moment and from

our experience there is nothing which can express this better than the feeding operation such as the A.R.A. is capable of undertaking.[104]

For the moment, all of Hoover's roles seemed in harmony. If the Bolsheviks fell from power, the successor government would be braced against a cruel famine and American influence would be firmly established. If the reports of an imminent Soviet collapse proved incorrect, a great number of lives would still be saved, and the reduction of the farm surplus in the United States would be a welcome by-product of the new mission. Six weeks later, Gorky issued his appeal for help.

Confrontation at Riga

THE APPEAL AND THE RESPONSE

Gorky's appeal "To All Honest People" opened with a horrifying description of suffering in the country that had given the world such geniuses as Tolstoy, Dostoyevsky, Mendeleyev, Pavlov, and Mussorgsky. The message rang with recrimination against those who "so passionately preached fratricidal hatred, thereby withering the enlightening force of ideas developed by mankind through the most arduous labor. . . ." The bitter appeal ended with a request that all "honest European and American people" donate bread and medicine to his suffering countrymen.[1]

Hoover and his ARA staff promptly drafted a reply. Since it was not clear whether the celebrated writer was acting as a spokesman for the Soviet government, Hoover asked for official clearance from the secretary of state.

> You will recollect my conversation of about six weeks ago in which I raised the desirability of extending relief to children and medical relief in Bolshevik Russia. Since that time the food situation has become more difficult, typhus is wider spread. You may also have noticed the appeals being sent out by prominent Russians including Maxim Gorky for help and the curious statements of the Bolshevik government giving the appeals the color of being unauthorized but that the world is wicked in refusing them. Despite this foolishness, I feel very deeply that we should go to the assistance of the children and also provide some medical relief generally.
>
> I would like to suggest, therefore, to you as head of the American Relief Administration [that] I send an offer to Gorky by cable of which I enclose a draft.

I believe it is a humane obligation upon us to go in if they comply with the requirements set out; if they do not accede we are released from responsibility.[2]

Hughes consented and suggested revisions in the text of Hoover's reply to Gorky. The very next day, Hoover's assistant, Christian A. Herter, notified the State Department that the revised message had been sent to Gorky that afternoon.[3] The State Department found the final version satisfactory.[4]

In his cable to Gorky, Hoover wrote that he had read "with great feeling" the writer's "appeal to Americans. "To the whole American people," he declared, "the absolute *sine qua non* of any assistance must be the immediate release of the Americans now held prisoners in Russia, and adequate provision for administration." The message went on to outline the conditions under which he would render assistance as chairman of the ARA—"a purely voluntary association and an entirely unofficial organization." His first requirement was that "the Moscow Soviet authorities" state officially that the ARA's assistance was needed. Hoover wanted it clearly understood that he was offering aid not as the U.S. secretary of commerce but as a relief worker to needy clients. The other conditions that Hoover posed were, in his words, "identically the same as those that have been established in every one of the twenty-three countries where operations have been conducted one time or another in care of upwards of eight million children."

The American relief workers were to be granted "full liberty to come and go and move about Russia," and they were to be allowed to set up local committees "free from government interference." The Soviet government was to pay for the transportation, storage, and handling of ARA supplies, and to continue issuing regular rations to children receiving American relief. For its part, the ARA would feed as many children and invalids as its resources permitted, "without regard to race, creed, or social status." The final stipulation was that ARA representatives and assistants would abstain entirely from any kind of political activity.[5]

Hoover's decision to negotiate directly with the Soviet government instead of with the public famine committee undoubtedly disappointed optimistic anti-Bolsheviks who saw the committee as the imminent successor to the existing regime. The Bolsheviks, on the other hand, must have drawn comfort from Hoover's implicit

The Russian Embassy was considering the formation of committees in this country to work in cooperation with similar committees in all countries of the world, to collect funds or foodstuffs to be turned over for distribution to the Famine Committee. Mr. R. inquired as to our opinion of such a course to which I replied in an entirely non-committal way. He added that the Embassy had at its disposal quite considerable sums, the exact figure unnamed, which it was considering turning over in some way and asked whether the American Relief Administration would consider accepting these funds, or whether such an acceptance would involve political consideration.

In general, Mr. R. felt that sooner or later some very large international body, which he hoped would be headed by Americans, would have to take over economic control of Russia and that undoubtedly that body, or pending its formation, the American Relief Administration, could use to best advantage the existing Famine Relief Committee for the organization of local committees, etc. etc.[12]

As Hoover was to learn within the next several days, rumors about a new intervention against the Soviet regime were already spreading in Europe. The American high commissioner at Constantinople reported to the State Department:

> I am convinced that any combination of the Allies for relieving famine in Russia will contain considerations of a political nature having for their object the demolition of the present Bolshevik regime. . . . To avoid inevitable political complications which will certainly result, I strongly recommend that our Government and institutions should act independently of any foreign control.[13]

From Paris came word to the State Department that the French and British governments were actually formulating plans for relief assistance involving "cooperation with the pan-Russian Committee already set up in Russia."[14]

Apparently rumors about a possible "bread intervention" involving the public famine committee had already reached the Kremlin. On 4 August the Soviet press carried an interview with Kamenev in which he frankly appraised the possibility that the "bourgeois" members of the committee might try to use their positions to overthrow the government. He insisted, however, that the government would still permit them to volunteer their services in the fight against the famine. "The whole movement really favors the

Soviet power," he declared, "and there is no fear of a 'bread intervention's' succeeding any more than the 'military one.'"[15]

Kamenev intended this statement to serve both as a display of confidence and as a warning. By itself, the committee represented no great menace to the regime. The *Cheka* (internal security police) had proved itself capable of suppressing more determined and experienced oppositionists than this gathering of deposed ministers and Moscow intellectuals. But the possible entry upon the scene by capitalist relief missionaries with huge food resources cast a different light on the committee's potential role. Armed insurrection might prove unnecessary if the two groups joined forces and assumed control over allocation of the means of survival. This, of course, was precisely what Ryabushinsky had in mind.

The Bolsheviks, however, had already taken steps to undercut the public committee's authority by assigning most of its functions to *Pomgol.* To proceed further at this point was to risk antagonizing Hoover on the eve of the Riga conference. Ironically, this unusual display of tolerance by the Bolsheviks only convinced their optimistic opponents abroad that the regime had finally lost control of events in Russia. The counterrevolutionary scenario lacked only a strong, confident leader to take command, and the emissary from the Russian Embassy hoped that Hoover would assume this role.

But Hoover would not compromise the relief mission, the ARA, the Harding administration, or himself by allying his organization with any foreign relief committee, especially one that symbolized opposition to the Soviet regime. On 6 August he again notified Brown that he was to make no compact with any body other than the Soviet government itself.[16] In a confidential cable to Brown sent on the day after Ryabushinsky's visit, he laid down the rule of conduct to be followed by ARA representatives in Russia if an agreement was reached in Riga.

> I wish to impress on each one of them the supreme importance of their keeping entirely aloof not only from action but even from discussion of political and social questions. Our people are not Bolsheviks but our mission is solely to save lives and any participation even in discussion will only lead to suspicion of our objects. In selection of local committees and Russian staff we wish to be absolutely neutral and neutrality implies appointment from every group in Russia and a complete insistence that children of all parentage have equal treatment.[17]

Once this injunction reached the lower levels of the ARA, Hoover could be confident of compliance. As all "old Hoover hands" well knew, the penalty for infraction of any orders from the Chief was instant dismissal. The Soviet leaders, however, did not know that Hoover had forbidden any ventures by his subordinates into the business of counterrevolution. Suspicion about his motives would cloud every session of the critical meeting at Riga.

THE NEGOTIATIONS AT RIGA

The Preliminaries

The ARA team of negotiators converged upon the Latvian capital from their posts in Europe. The contingent was composed of Walter Lyman Brown, director of the ARA for Europe with headquarters in London, and his assistants, Cyril J. C. Quinn, ARA director in Poland; Philip H. Carroll, director for Germany; and J. C. Miller, director for the Baltic area.[18] The Soviet government sent Maxim Litvinov, then deputy chairman of the People's Commissariat for Foreign Affairs. A staunch Leninist since the early days of the Bolshevik faction in the Russian Social Democratic party, Litvinov was experienced in dealing with foreign powers. In November 1919 he had shown great skill in arranging the exchange of prisoners with other governments and in negotiating peace treaties with neighboring states.[19] Lenin followed the talks at Riga closely. "As soon as any kind of news arrives from Litvinov about his negotiations with Brown," he instructed Chicherin, "please phone me the most important results."[20]

Hoover's preliminary instructions set the tone of the conference. On 1 August the ARA New York headquarters notified Brown that Hoover saw no reason to modify any of the conditions set down in his reply to Gorky. The message went on, however, to amend the original proposal. Brown was instructed to retreat from Hoover's promise to "furnish the necessary supplement of food, clothing, and medical supplies to a million children in Russia as soon as organization could be effected" and to make no commitment about the number of children to be fed. He was to propose starting relief operations in Petrograd and then extending them to Moscow and

Vologda.[21] Several days later, Hoover asked Brown to obtain assurance that all Americans in Russia who wanted to leave the country would be allowed to do so.[22] The original *sine qua non* was thus broadened to include Americans who were not in prison.

Two days later, Hoover told Brown to inquire about the possibility of establishing ARA warehouses throughout the country,[23] a standard practice in all countries served by the organization. It was also established custom for ARA installations to display prominently the names of the benefactor nation, the relief organization, and its chief, along with his picture.[24] If the Bolsheviks imagined that the ARA's presence in Russia would be inconspicuous, they were in for a surprise. Hoover would not modify standard ARA policy to protect the prestige of the Soviet regime; he considered full publicity a major resource in any relief operation.

Brown caught the Chief's confident mood. On 8 August he inquired about requiring the Soviet government to furnish a deposit of $1 million in gold as insurance against losses in the event that "the masses" seized ARA supplies.[25] Hoover agreed that such a deposit would reassure American contributors, but he cautioned Brown not to make this an absolute condition.[26]

The day before the first meeting with Litvinov, Hoover asked Brown to point out that it would benefit the Soviet government to allow the American press to enter Russia, since "otherwise famine conditions will be misrepresented."[27] On 30 July an ARA director at Prague had reported former Premier Alexander Kerensky's prediction that Hoover's offer of aid to Russia meant the end of "the blockade of ideas which have been denied the Russian people for five years."[28] In actuality, the last communication links between Russia and the West were cut in August 1918 when the German Embassy was withdrawn. Some contacts had been reestablished with the end of the intervention in 1920, but as far as the United States was concerned, the "blockade of ideas" (in both directions) was still in effect.

The Negotiators Meet

The preliminary session went well. Mrs. Marguerite Harrison (the sister-in-law of Maryland's governor) and six other American prisoners had been released and were out of Russia. Furthermore, all provincial administrations had been ordered to release all American citizens, to issue them passports, and to expedite the departure of those who wanted to leave the country. Litvinov stated that although his government had no direct authority over the Ukraine, it would request similar action by the Ukrainian Republic as well.

To Brown's request for a show of official credentials, Litvinov responded by presenting formal documents signed by Kamenev in the name of *Pomgol* and by citing his own position as deputy commissar for foreign affairs. One minor difficulty arose in connection with Hoover's demand that the Soviet government state formally that it needed ARA relief assistance. Litvinov saw no reason for his government to submit to such humiliation. He referred to Chicherin's circular letter of 2 August to all governments announcing the existence of famine conditions. This, he maintained, was sufficient acknowledgment of need.[29] Hoover was satisfied. "Start negotiations," he instructed Brown.[30]

When the negotiators met the next day, Litvinov immediately took issue with some of Hoover's conditions. He objected particularly to the American's insistence on the right to select the areas in which ARA relief would be given and to organize local relief committees independently.[31] Receiving word of the disagreement, Lenin concluded that Hoover's demands were somehow connected with the deliberations of the Allied Supreme Council, then meeting in Paris to consider possible action on the famine. "In conjunction with the Supreme Council, the Americans apparently want to cancel the project that they have undertaken," he warned Litvinov in a radiogram on 11 August. "Be careful. Try to gauge their intentions. Do not let them get insolent with you."[32]

This curt warning only hints at Lenin's fury. In a letter to Molotov the same day, he demanded immediate public exposure of the "baseness" of Hoover and America. "Hoover must be punished," he wrote, "He must be slapped publicly before the whole world. This is *very difficult* to do, but it *must* be done."

I request polling the Politburo immediately by phone. Show this note to *everyone* and collect the votes. Take as a model the German and Norwegian governments. Reject any other approach for reasons that are clear to everybody, and tell it to the world in a loud voice. The secret interventionists must be named (get Unshlikht to help). Reinforce *Kompomoshch* [Commission for Famine Relief] (if it is not strong enough, borrow from the Army for two months).

Collective effort is especially important in the next few days, since political responsibility is most vital in this difficult matter.

P.S. Delicate maneuvers are needed. A series of exceptionally strict measures. Hoover and Brown are insolent liars.

Set down very strict conditions: for the slightest interference in internal matters—expulsion and arrest.[33]

Lenin's colleagues had to respond in some measure to his directives, but since he had not actually ordered breaking off the talks at Riga, a reinterpretation of the "exceptionally strict measures" was in order. The public denunciation of the Americans was commuted to a firm warning contained in an interview with Litvinov that appeared in a Riga newspaper on the following day.

We will never accept any political conditions concerning Russia or any Russian citizen. We will never agree to any conditions that may have the slightest effect of discrediting our government. We will never let any foreign administration or government use the terrible conditions in the Volga District to force the Workers' and Peasants' Government to accept conditions which are against our honor.[34]

There was no mention of Hoover or the "baseness of America." The talks continued.

At this time Hoover was preparing a presidential directive designed to place control of all American relief in Russia in his own hands. On 11 August he wrote to Harding, "Please find enclosed draft of letter addressed to myself which I think would be very helpful in concentrating American effort on Russian relief."[35] The next day Hoover had in hand a letter from the president notifying him that the directive was on its way to him.

Harding's proclamation gave official approval to Hoover's initiative in offering assistance to Russia and directed that all efforts toward relief of the famine "should be carried through by one organization." The State Department was instructed to issue passports to Russia for relief work "only to persons who may be in the service of the American Relief Administration." All contributions to Russian relief were to be channeled through the ARA or organizations committed to cooperation with Hoover's agency.[36]

The secretary of state, too, was glad to see control of American relief placed in Hoover's hands. Under Hoover's supervision, the relief effort would presumably not be used to weaken the official nonrecognition policy. At the same time, the State Department might be able, through the ARA, to perform certain consular functions in Russia that were not possible under the existing estrangement. As a first step in this direction, Hughes relayed to Hoover a request from the secretary of labor. Could Hoover force the Soviet government to accept, as a condition of receiving American assistance, about seventy-five Russian citizens who had been arrested during the Palmer raids? The Soviet authorities had consistently refused to repatriate Russians who did not have passports that had been approved by their own official agencies.[37]

Hoover was as eager as Hughes to deport the Russian radicals, but did not want to jeopardize the negotiations at Riga by presenting a new demand. Accordingly he notified Hughes, "I feel that this is a question which does not properly come within the range of the conditions on which the A.R.A., a private charitable organization, can insist as a *sine qua non* for its relief work."[38] But he saw no harm in asking Brown to find out whether the Soviet government was interested in giving safe harbor to Russian nationals incarcerated in the United States.[39] Litvinov refused even to consider the request. He told Brown that such matters could be taken up only with official representatives of the United States and not with a private relief organization.[40]

As Hoover moved toward control of all American relief to Russia, a group of potential rivals appeared on the scene. The ARA-Soviet talks had attracted to Riga representatives of twelve European nations and several international relief organizations. The International Red Cross and its affiliates were on hand to challenge any ARA attempt to secure a monopoly in a field in which they, too, claimed some expertise and interest.[41] The chairman of an ad hoc joint committee of international relief societies invited Hoover to attend a conference on Russian relief scheduled to be held in Geneva on 15 August. Hoover agreed to send a representative and then enumerated the difficulties that would face an international relief project in Russia.

He argued that the famine was too extensive to be contained by such a group, that the requirements exceeded the resources of all the private charities in the world put together. Even if funds were available, the effective relief of Russia involved "the rehabilitation of transportation, of agriculture, and of industry, necessitating measures again beyond the reach of charity." Finally, he stated that even if the international charities managed somehow to cope with the current crisis, the famine would recur every year until there was a radical change in the economic system of Russia. Hoover proposed that before the international societies attempted any definite action, they first determine exactly how many famine victims each society would undertake to feed and then assign specific areas of responsibility under strict management by a single authority. "Without this data," Hoover declared, "the conference can be of no practical result."[42]

When the conference met at Geneva, the societies offered Nansen and Hoover joint chairmanship of the newly formed International Committee for Russian Relief. Nansen accepted the appointment; Hoover declined, explaining that his position in the American cabinet prevented him from serving on an international committee with such close official connections.[43] Hughes agreed that American interests would best be served if the ARA worked independently of any foreign groups.[44]

In the meantime, Soviet authorities took action to restrict the activities of its own rivals in the area of famine relief. On 13 August the government proposed to the public famine relief committee that it suspend its plans for sending delegates abroad and "confine all its activities to combatting the famine locally." But the members of the committee's presidium were unwilling to become local fund raisers for the regime. The non-Bolshevik majority voted to proceed with its original plans.[45] Ordinarily it would have been easy to disband such a group and possibly arrest its leading members, but the formation of the committee had won the approval of political leaders throughout the "bourgeois" world. On 11 August the British House of Lords heard Lord Emmott, head of the committee of inquiry on the Russian famine, express confidence in the members of the public famine relief committee, including the "moderate Bolshevik" group.[46] In addition, for all the Bolsheviks knew, it may have been Gorky's membership in the "bourgeois" group that had persuaded Hoover to reply to his appeal. Overt repression at this time might endanger the negotiations with the ARA. In any case, the committee was allowed to continue for the moment.

Crisis at Riga

The first two days of negotiation reflected an ever widening gulf of disagreement. Neither Brown nor Litvinov had the authority to retreat from the positions set up for them by their superiors. Brown, in fact, drafted a set of new conditions and on 13 August asked Hoover for permission to incorporate them in a proposal that he intended to present to Litvinov. Brown wanted concrete assurances from the Soviet government that no food would be given to the Red army or navy, to government employees, adults, or to any other groups not specifically designated by the ARA. According to his proposal, the basis for supplemental feeding by the Americans would be the Soviet military ration. Finally, the ARA would be given the unlimited right to set up such organizations as it thought necessary and the power to control or improve sanitary conditions and water supplies wherever there was danger of epidemic disease.[47] Hoover was displeased. "Fear your conditions exceed my original [proposal]," he warned Brown. "Can you not take text of my original telegram [to] Gorky and draw explanatory statements as to working details paragraph by paragraph?"[48]

Lenin, for his part, offered Litvinov several practical suggestions. First, he outlined a counterproposal that would insure Soviet control of ARA activities. The Soviet government would deposit gold in New York in an amount equal to 120 percent of the cost of feeding a million children and sick adults for one month. In exchange, the Americans would have to refrain from "meddling in political or administrative affairs." Local assistance would be supervised by joint committees composed of Russians and Americans. In regard to Hoover's stipulation that ARA food serve as a supplement and not a substitute for the regular Soviet ration, Lenin advised informing the Americans that the Soviet government had never provided any kind of rations in the rural communities.[49]

Litvinov presented Lenin's proposals as a compromise but indicated that he personally preferred a guarantee of reimbursement for losses to a cash deposit. He did not mention Lenin's suggestion for joint committees, insisting rather that the formation of any new committees at all would be a needless duplication of existing machinery.[50]

The differences between two sides were too great to be resolved by trivial compromises. The Americans were insisting on complete freedom of the country for ARA representatives, absolute immunity from search or arrest, and removal of American personnel only on presentation of proof of wrongdoing to the satisfaction of the ARA supervisor in the area. The Bolsheviks wanted ARA work confined to the villages and cities of the Volga region, reserving to themselves relief operations in such big cities as Moscow and Petrograd. Litvinov claimed that acquiescence to the ARA's demands would leave the Soviet government at the mercy of the American organization. Soviet authorities would have no control over the actions of ARA workers, whether they violated Soviet law or not. The government would not even retain the right of expulsion for serious crimes. This, according to Litvinov, far exceeded the immunity usually granted to high-ranking foreign diplomats.

On 15 August Brown notifed Hoover that he was "sitting tight."[51] Later that day, however, he began to have misgivings about the course of the negotiations. It was evident that no agreement would be reached unless one or the other side made substantial concessions. Clearly, traditional ARA principles could not be applied rigidly to Soviet Russia. If the Chief really wanted to go into Russia, some adjustments were necessary. Thus, Brown again cabled Washington pointing out that the ARA had never before attempted to provide relief in a country under a "communistic government whose duty it is to feed all the people"; neither had it ever encountered severe famine conditions over a wide area. These conditions raised special problems that could not be resolved if the ARA insisted on complete autonomy. Brown asked for guidance.

> There may, furthermore, be reasons of policy why, in order to have A.R.A. in Russia, you would be willing to make concessions. Very radical changes in Soviet Government anticipated by best informed American opinion here. Urgent advice requested. We would be assisted in general by all policy indications you can give us in line with the above.[52]

Hoover had meanwhile dispatched to Riga a reply to Brown's earlier cable. He stood firm on all demands. The ARA would not yield freedom of movement or the right to appoint its own local committees, nor would it surrender the right to discipline American relief workers. "Under present lack of judicial procedure no American can be subject to search," he wrote. "If we think Soviets have good cause, we will remove officials." Soviet insistence on a specific statement about how many lives the ARA would undertake to save was, in Hoover's opinion, "preposterous."[53] Brown's uncertainties were resolved: "Acknowledge your Washington 17 which received with acclamation and will be used this afternoon in manner apparently intended." He proceeded to apply what he regarded as Hoover's last word on the subjects in contention.[54] The negotiations were deadlocked.

On 17 August news of the stalemate in Riga was featured on the front page of the *New York Times* together with an accurate description of the differences between the parties. Litvinov was reported to be conferring with representatives of the International Red Cross.[55] In the United States, only Hoover seemed optimistic.[56] What the press did not know was that Hoover had already sent Brown new instructions that represented a substantial shift in position. In his message, Hoover maintained that the Soviet government's attempt to limit the options of the ARA violated accepted principles of relief administration. However, since he wanted "simply to save the lives of children," he was willing to make certain concessions.

> Although we have in 23 countries never been subjected to such requirements we will meet the objections so far as we can by undertaking that we will not introduce amongst our personnel any persons who have been in Russia since 1917 or any non-Americans unless these particular people are approved by the Soviet. . . . We can also agree that we will remove from our staff anyone complained of by the Central Soviet authorities to our direction where such a complaint is based on even a moral showing of revolutionary or political activities.

On several other points, he remained adamant. He denied the validity of the Soviet argument that allowing the ARA to organize local committees was contrary to Soviet laws. He attacked Litvinov's statement that "food is a weapon" as "far removed from humanitarian action," declaring that it "obviously indicates a desire to use relief for their political purposes and to discriminate between children." He did, however, agree to modify his stand on the selection of areas to be served: "We will willingly in desire to cooperate agree that we will from time to time declare where we wish to establish stations. Refusal upon their part to allow us to do so will result in decrease of this volume of relief."[57] On the following day,

Hoover amended this proviso: "So that they can't say we use food as a weapon, substitute for the last 2 sentences. '[Refusal to allow us to select stations] destroys efficiency and renders adaptation of service to real need of children impossible."[58]

Hoover's consent to some measure of Soviet control substantially counteracted the kind of fear that had surfaced in a Soviet newspaper article. Under the headline, "The Greek and His Gifts," the article declared, "Hoover's verbal guarantee to abstain from political activities is grossly insufficient; the so-called benefactors want to shelter their real work under an armor of extraterritoriality."[59] Litvinov agreed to the substance of Hoover's new proposal but insisted on the absolute right to expel any person whom the central Soviet authorities found guilty of engaging in political or commercial activities, as well as the right to search any premises at which there was evidence of crime in progress. Brown refused to concede these points. The representatives adjourned the day's talks and reported the new impasse to their superiors.[60]

At this point, Brown began to lose confidence in the strategy of pushing the American advantage to the limit. In his report of the day's events to Hoover, he relayed Litvinov's argument that ARA acceptance of the two disputed points was important to Soviet government leaders in "maintaining their sovereignty as a state." Brown admitted that he found this contention "difficult to answer" and recommended acceptance of the Soviet conditions.[61]

Discouraged by Brown's rejection of his proposal, Litvinov went on a round of visits to the Red Cross societies gathered at Riga and inquired about their cash position. The news went out immediately that the Bolsheviks were looking for an alternative to Hoover's help.[62] Litvinov must have submitted a pessimistic report to the Kremlin; on 19 August he received a lengthy analysis of the situation from Chicherin. The Soviet government evidently intended to release the message to the press if the talks failed; the radiogram concluded with a pronouncement that could not have been meant for Litvinov's eyes alone:

If American help to the hungry population does not materialize, the working masses of Soviet Russia and the entire world will realize that this occurred only because the representatives of the American organization, forgetting about the requirements of humanitarianism, showed themselves to be captives of the reactionary White-Guard forces who are leading the attack against worker-peasant Russia.

Chicherin[63]

Chicherin's indictment was consigned, unproclaimed, to Litvinov's file and eventually to the Soviet archives. By the time the message was received at Riga, Brown had in hand a much shorter message from his Chief: "Agree your recommendations. You are authorized to sign. I assume that any American now in Russia will be given full facilities to leave."[64] On 20 August 1921 Brown replied, "Agreed all points this afternoon. Sign eleven A.M. to-morrow. Releasing to press."[65]

The agreement between the ARA and the Soviet government was signed on the following day with all the pomp and ceremony of a historic diplomatic event. The formalities were conducted by the president of Latvia in the presence of officials and reporters from all over the world.[66] Litvinov declared that the "treaty" was as significant as the Soviet-Polish peace treaty signed at Riga earlier that year. He hailed the conference as the first official negotiations between the United States and the Soviet government in four years and expressed the hope that the agreement presaged a more extended treaty between the two countries.[67] Brown was visibly annoyed by the tone of Litvinov's speech. In his own remarks, he omitted reference to Litvinov's comments or to any other subject that might have been construed as political.[68] The politics of famine relief had taken an unexpected turn. The prospective client was openly pressing the benefactor to reverse his policy. Against this shrewd political maneuver Hoover's spokesman had no ready defense. The Chief had given strict orders to avoid politics.

Views from the Inside

A week later Brown sent Hoover a summary of his experiences during the difficult negotiations with Litvinov. He explained his decision to include a statement of the ARA's intention to feed up to one million children. Litvinov had asked for this clause in order to justify to "the Russian people" all the concessions that he had made to the ARA. Brown pointed out to Hoover that the wording of this clause was indefinite and that the commitment was considerably modified by the phrase "within the limits of its resources and facilities," which he had inserted in another clause. He went on to summarize his impressions of the other side.

> They were afraid that we were trying to set up a state within a state, to influence the Russian people toward counter-revolution by the use of "food as a weapon." This dominated the phases of free movement of personnel, choice of local committees and areas of work. I think that before we got through, we convinced Litvinov personally that we were straight, but it took a bit of doing, which is understandable when one considers how, even in countries where we have been operating for the last two years, this phase is not always understood.[69]

Litvinov's description of the general climate of the conference was objective and incisive. In a press interview during the deadlock, he declared: "The trouble is that there has been too much suspicion on one side and lack.of confidence on the other. If you apply my remark to either side you will not be incorrect."[70] On 19 August after the major issues had been settled, Litvinov elaborated on what he considered a great procedural obstacle. The ARA, he said, wanted a quick agreement based on a general acceptance of the principles outlined in Hoover's reply to Gorky. The distrust on both sides, however, made a detailed, specific contract necessary. He claimed that many of the delays were caused by the frequent reference of important questions to Hoover in Washington. If Brown had been given full powers, he concluded, or if Hoover had been present at Riga, agreement would have been reached in a couple of days.[71]

The deputy commissar was correct about Hoover's role in the negotiations. Brown's report contains a vivid description of the clearance process on the American side.

> It may have looked in our wires as though we had lost sight of your original Gorky message and its basic acceptance in Kamenev's reply. This was not so, but it appeared to us that the best method of handling was to elicit their viewpoints, put them up to you, and let you come back with the heavy artillery, which we had every reason to believe would be brought into action. The artillery came through with a bang and contributed very materially toward turning the trick.[72]

In fact, the "heavy artillery" came close to blowing up the conference. The counterbarrage by Lenin and Chicherin was equally intense. A settlement was reached when Hoover finally called a cease-fire. Still, Litvinov's complaint about Brown's lack of final authority must be weighed against the evidence that the Soviet emissary shared his mandate with Lenin, Chicherin, and the entire Politburo. In spite of the delays on both sides, the negotiators took little more than a week to come to agreement. This record has rarely, if ever, been equaled.

Cyril J. C. Quinn, a temporary officer in the wartime army who served as Brown's assistant, noted his impressions of the conference in an informal memorandum that was subsequently sent to Hoover. "It was obvious," wrote Quinn, "that they really desired us to come into Russia and to assist us in carrying out an efficient operation." What the Bolsheviks feared most, according to Quinn, was the independent creation of the local committees by the ARA: "They emphasized time and again that the present state of Russia was one of disturbance and revolt, that there were no neutrals in the country, and that they feared the intention of the people to form counter-revolutionary projects under the guise of our committees." Another point of conflict was Soviet insistence that the ARA confine its activities to areas designated by the central authorities. "The underlying reason is open to the obvious interpretation that for reasons that must have been political they did not desire us to work in the cities of Moscow and Petrograd, but wanted us to confine our relief to the famine areas."[73]

Forty-five years later, Quinn recalled some of the factors that influenced the course of the negotiations. The Soviet leaders were prepared to grant diplomatic immunity to the ARA; the main arguments on that issue and others centered on phraseology. At one point, when the semantic impasse appeared hopeless, the young army officer stood up and said, "Ah, the hell with it!" The deputy commissar gazed at him for a moment and then said very calmly, "Young man, one thing you should always remember—never give an ultimatum."[74] In his written report, Quinn expressed great admiration of Litvinov's dexterity in negotiation, his unusual intelligence, and his persuasiveness. He found this first experience with a high-ranking Soviet official edifying but disconcerting. If the rest of the Bolsheviks measured up to Litvinov in talent and determination, he concluded, the Americans faced formidable competition.

THE RIGA "TREATY"

A British correspondent at Riga commented that "the conference between the American Relief Administration and the Bolshevists has ended in a victory for the Americans, the Bolshevists giving way on all vital points."[75] This was an exaggeration. The extraterritorial rights that Hoover had demanded for his representatives in Russia as protection from the arbitrary practices of the Soviet judicial system were finally reduced to the privileges usually enjoyed by accredited diplomats. The agreement also gave the Soviet government the right to expel ARA workers unilaterally. Another provision which the Soviet regime thought essential to its safety was a clause that granted local and central authorities representation on relief committees set up by the ARA. Finally, the Soviet government won the authority to search ARA premises where there was definite evidence of illegal activity. These provisions made it virtually impossible for the ARA or its legal relief committees to engage in secret counterrevolutionary activities as long as the regime retained the loyalty of its local authorities and of the *Cheka*. To the Soviet government, these safeguards represented a substantial "victory."

The agreement itself consisted of a preamble and twenty-seven clauses that embodied Hoover's original offer as amplified by Brown's additions and modified by the exceptions mentioned above. The Soviet government assumed the expenses of the relief mission, other than the cost of relief supplies at port of entry and the direct expenses of American supervision. The ARA would furnish supplemental food rations to children and to the sick in areas "where it finds its relief can be administered most efficiently and to secure best results." The principal object of the mission, according to the agreement, was to "bring relief to the famine stricken areas of the Volga." Relief was to be carried out "without regard to race, religion or social or political status." The ARA was granted "complete freedom" in the selection of Russian and other personnel, provided that it obtained Soviet approval before engaging Americans who had been detained in Soviet Russia since 1917. The ARA agreed to devote itself "strictly to the ministration of relief" and to refrain from political or commercial activity.[76]

In a supplemental memorandum, Brown stipulated that not more than one hundred Americans would be engaged to staff the mission and that he would notify the Soviet government if more were needed as the operation developed. The ARA agreed to supply travel papers to its personnel when necessary, certifying that the trip was for official purposes. Finally, the memorandum stated that in those districts where the government did not furnish food rations, the ARA would increase its own ratio and thereby reduce the number of children it would feed.[77]

A Soviet legal specialist has described the Riga agreement as a full-fledged treaty since, in his view, it actually set up a "philanthropic state within a state."[78] This picture of the ARA as a sovereign government on Soviet soil is at least overdrawn. The Soviet government did not give up its role as the final authority in the areas to be served by the ARA; it agreed only to the entry of a foreign group with rights and immunities of its own that were set down in writing and enforceable in a practical way. The ARA could cut off the flow of food whenever Hoover decided that the agreement had been violated. The Soviet government resented this curb on its sovereignty and accepted it only under the pressure of grave need. Hoover was similarly affronted by the restrictions imposed on the "sovereignty" of his own organization. The ARA enjoyed complete autonomy in the other countries that it served, even though this arrangement did not always have the unqualified approval of the governments involved. Hoover objected to the limitation of his prerogatives in almost exactly the same terms Litvinov had used in opposing ARA autonomy, each insisting that the other was attempting to use food for political purposes.

The first test was over. The American and Soviet representatives had managed to soften some of their own, as well as their opponents', hostility. What remained of the mutual suspicions and fears was written into the novel "treaty" signed at Riga. In this respect, the agreement satisfied neither side, but it did provide the ground rules for a momentous rescue operation that the Bolsheviks needed and the ARA wanted. It also enabled Hoover to give the order to load the ships that he had already scheduled for the long trip to Russia.

Bolshevik Reactions to Riga

At the time one of the five full members of the Politburo and also people's commissar for war, Trotsky was pictured by editorialists and cartoonists of the foreign press, more or less accurately, as the spirit of militant communism incarnate. Both hopeful and suspicious, he was sufficiently able to control his contempt for "bourgeois relief missionaries" to write that the pact with Hoover held at least a promise of bringing badly needed food to millions of children and of leading to an economic agreement with the United States. He warned that counterrevolutionary elements might take advantage of the special conditions dictated by Hoover and attempt to disguise subversive activity as relief assistance. The Soviet government, he declared, would abide strictly by the spirit and the letter of the agreement and would provide all the assistance necessary to the Hoover organization so long as it did not meddle in politics.

> We do not doubt, comrades, that all local Soviet organs . . . will demonstrate real vigilance and extend real political control to all the local regions in order to prevent adventurists and rogues from using the famine to mount an attempt at counterrevolutionary overthrow in Russia.[79]

Kamenev, the head of *Pomgol,* the official Soviet relief agency, was more subtle.

> The organization which has just concluded the agreement with us has demonstrated beyond doubt that it is capable of rendering real assistance to us. And we know that the Soviet government will abide by the agreement strictly, that this help will be sincere, and that no political considerations or motives, no individuals who might be in a position to utilize famine relief for some kind of political activity will hamper this assistance.[80]

Karl Radek, the leading propagandist of the Foreign Commissariat and a powerful Party figure in his own right, was sardonic about capitalist humanitarianism.

> The Republican American administration has not yet decided to conclude a trade agreement with Russia, but one thing it knows; namely, *if America wants at some time in the future to trade with Russia, she must now come to the aid of the starving.* That is why Mr. Lyman Brown, Hoover's chief, turned up at Riga so promptly. That is why Mr. Hoover, in spite of being overburdened with work as the minister of trade, found the time to interest himself in philanthropic matters.[81]

An entirely different interpretation was offered by Chicherin, who was Radek's superior in the Foreign Commissariat but ranked far below him in the Party hierarchy. For Chicherin, the agreement was a major triumph. The "treaty" with Hoover seemed to augur the end of the diplomatic blockade imposed by the major Western powers. In his first interview after the agreement was signed, he expressed unqualified appreciation in behalf of the Soviet people for the offer of American aid and hoped that the relief program would encourage trade, peace, and better relations between the two countries. Asked about the current Soviet policy on world revolution, Chicherin replied:

> That policy was used by the Government in the first few months of its existence and then only as a war method, the same as both sides used propaganda to weaken their enemies. In peace, the Soviet Government has not had such a policy. . . . In America, the people must distinguish between the Soviet Government and the Third Internationale which has a policy of world-wide revolution. . . . The two organizations are quite separate. . . . M. Zinoviev, who is at the head of the Third Internationale, is the head of the Petrograd Soviet, but he is not in the national government.[82]

That same day, the head of the Soviet government, who was also a member of the Executive Committee of the Communist (Third) International, wrote a letter to Zinoviev issuing specific instructions on the policy to be followed in regard to the Riga agreement.

> It is extremely important that the Comintern, without coming out against the American government, advance a definite slogan that the workers send their contributions exclusively and directly to the representatives of Soviet Russia abroad. Since each and every contribution sent through the bourgeois governments is tied, directly and indirectly, to a greater or lesser degree, to some sort of conditions, the workers must, without fail, agree to send their contributions to us without any kind of conditions, and this difference has tremendous significance to us.[83]

On the following day, a Riga newspaper published an article with a similar message. The Riga negotiations, according to the writer, were unnecessary; all that was needed was to send food, medicine, and doctors.

The bourgeois world exacts conditions but not the working people. The working people do not ask explanations as to the control or the distribution of what is sent to the starving. . . . Under the pressure of this sympathy of the toilers toward Soviet Russia, the bourgeois world and her governments could not but agree to help Russia.[84]

The Russian public was informed about the agreement on 23 August in a column in *Pravda* entitled "Foreign Comments."

To-day the representative of the R.S.F.S.R., Comrade Litvinov, signed an agreement with an American relief organization on rendering help to the starving in Russia. This organization is headed by the American Secretary of Commerce, Hoover. It came into being during the war and functioned in 23 countries. It developed especially wide functions in rendering help to the population of Belgium at the time of the German occupation, and also in German Austria. This organization will control committees on which Soviet authority will be represented centrally and locally.[85]

This was the most neutral description of the Riga agreement that would appear in the partisan press either in Russia or in the United States.

Repercussions in America

Although cabinet discipline did not permit public dissent by members of the Harding administration on the decision to help Soviet Russia, there was, according to Hoover, considerable opposition to the project by a group of department secretaries. Among his firm supporters were the secretaries of state, war, and the navy and the president himself.[86] The State Department's official position was that the Riga pact had no international significance since the ARA was not a government agency.[87] The American high commissioner at Constantinople, however, seemed to share the more widely held opinion that the ARA was not distinguishable from the American government. In a cable to the secretary of state, he suggested a policy for "our famine relief" that reflected an interesting view of the virtues of philanthropy.

I strongly urge that our famine relief work in Russia be maintained

absolutely free of political significations [*sic*] or suspicions of the same.
. . . If we avoid all foreign combinations in our relief work especially
from anti-Bolshevik refugees and demonstrate a big, pure, and
humanitarian effort we will administer the best possible treatment for
the disease of Bolshevism that cannot be cured by political hypnotism
nor military beating of the patient. It is my opinion that America has
the opportunity of a lifetime to render civilization the biggest step
forward of this century.[88]

Hoover needed no advice about avoiding "foreign combinations."
As always, he resisted sharing with rival groups, both foreign and
domestic, what he considered his worldwide franchise for mass
famine relief. Several days before Lenin gave the signal to rally the
world proletariat around its own relief campaign, Hoover moved to
solidify control over famine relief efforts in the United States. On 19
August he released Harding's mandate to the ARA as the only
organization through which American relief was to be administered.
At the same time, he announced the ARA's policy on public campaigns.

It is not the intention of the American Relief Administration to
make any public appeal for funds as it feels that the economic situation in the United States does not warrant such a demand until the
whole employment and business situation is greatly improved. Any
person who desires to contribute may do so through any of the
organizations.[89]

This was consistent with Hoover's skepticism about the value of
piecemeal relief financing and the effectiveness of organizations that
depended on it. But he took a different view of public appeals when
he was negotiating with the Soviet government. More than once, he
told his representative to caution the Bolsheviks about the possible
effect of their actions on relief contributions in the United States. He
used this approach to press for a Soviet deposit in gold against food
losses, for the admission of American reporters to Russia, and, on 22
August, for the release of 120,000 Hungarian and Romanian
prisoners of war.[90]

Actually, the ARA had never needed to solicit nickels and dimes
from the American public. Hoover's announcement indicated only
that he would not join a public campaign in the company of Quakers,
welfare societies, and, inevitably, Soviet sympathizers. Neither would

he support the worldwide campaign undertaken by the international relief societies after his own offer was made public. When he learned that these groups were preparing to enter Russia under an agreement less stringent than that concluded by the ARA, he informed the head of the International Red Cross that the ARA would not cooperate and that he would use the president's mandate to remove the American Red Cross from the international project.[91]

Hoover then turned his attention to American groups that were planning to provide relief to Russia. On 24 August he held a meeting at the Department of Commerce with spokesmen for the American Friends Service Committee, the American Red Cross, the Federated Council of Churches, the Joint Distribution Committee, the Knights of Columbus, the YMCA, and the YWCA. At this conference, the societies agreed to act in accordance with the Riga agreement, to accept assignment of areas by the ARA, to conduct all relations with the Soviet government through the ARA, to serve on the ARA staff at its Russian headquarters, and to place all personnel under the authority of the ARA director.[92]

Other interested groups were more troublesome. Even before the agreement was signed, the left-oriented American Labor Alliance held a mass meeting in a New York theater at which Hoover was denounced for insisting on control of food distribution in Russia. The main speaker, Rose Pastor Stokes, accused Hoover of attempting to overthrow the Soviet government by removing the control of food supplies from its authority.[93] On 24 August the *Nation* revived the matter of Hoover's "bread intervention" in Hungary. The editor and Hoover had earlier engaged in an exchange about an article in which T. T. C. Gregory, a former ARA official, had boasted that he and Hoover had from start to finish engineered the overthrow of Bela Kun's Soviet government in 1919. According to Gregory, the Hungarian army and trade union leaders who led the insurrection were merely pawns of the Americans. Hoover's mild rejoinder that Gregory's version of the event did not "wholly agree" with his own failed to mollify his critics. The *Nation* also blamed Hoover for the delay in reaching an agreement with the Soviet government and approved the formation of "neutral committees" to bring speedier assistance to the starving in Russia.[94] A week later, however, the editor saw the mission as a great opportunity for Hoover to prove his sincerity: "Here are millions in famine, millions living under a form of government which he detests and under a social system which has

ruined some of his own investments." If Hoover could confine
himself to pure humanitarianism, he would "carry out the noblest
tradition of American generosity and add to his own status. We
believe he will; we believe that criticism of political activity of certain
of his agents in the past will put him on his mettle in Russia."[95]

The *New Republic* was less concerned about Hoover's motives than
about the difficulties facing him. Soviet and American suspicions
about Hoover were equally unrealistic, according to the liberal journal; he was well aware of the bitter consequence of intervention in
Hungary. A much more serious problem was "the stupid apathy and
cruel malevolence carefully cultivated in the American people."[96]

A sample of extreme anti-Bolshevik reaction to Riga was an article
that appeared in the *Dearborn Independent,* a weekly magazine
published by Henry Ford for the edification of his employees.[97] This
magazine not only attacked the proposal to feed the Russians but im-
pugned the integrity of the ARA itself. Hoover was outraged that
anyone should accuse his organization of venality or maladministra-
tion. When one of his representatives confronted the editor and
demanded proof of the charges, the editor made vague allegations
about Jewish and Bolshevik activities. Hoover then took up the battle directly with Henry Ford. He insisted that Ford either produce the
evidence or publish a retraction.[98] There is no record of Ford's
response. A midwestern newspaper echoed the *Independent*'s attack
on the ARA and asked why America should "interest itself in
perpetuating a dynasty of darkness that is dying because of its inability to raise its own bread—dying of its own incompetence."[99] The
ARA public relations division was thus faced with the unusual task of
defending Hoover against the charge of trying to save the Bolshevik
regime.

A more serious result of Hoover's agreement with the Bolsheviks
was the renewal of the campaign for recognition of the Soviet government and for the opening of trade relations. On 31 August a labor
leader advised President Harding that the economic crisis in Russia
could not be alleviated by mere charity; what was urgently required
was the renewal of trade with the United States.[100] Senator France,
who returned from Russia on 26 August with Mrs. Harrison, made
no mention of Hoover's part in obtaining her release. He did remark
that he had left the United States convinced that trade with Russia
should be resumed and that his experiences in that country had persuaded him that the Soviet government should be recognized. "There

is little communism in Russia," he declared. "Extreme experiments in that direction proved unsuccessful and the constructive party, of which Lenin is the head, was courageous enough to force an abandonment of Marxian theory and a restoration of certain sound capitalistic policies which are now in effect." It was one of the earliest proclamations that communism in Russia was dead.[101]

From two leading British newspapers came confident and conflicting predictions. The *Times* (London) was somber.

> So long as the Bolshevists remain in power very little real relief is possible. Thousands on thousands will die of starvation, and all that the most earnest humanitarian effort can do will be to save a few hundred here and there. That is worth doing, but the main, the ghastly problem will be left unsolved, and its effects will darken the future.[102]

The *Manchester Guardian*'s correspondent at Riga described the agreement as one of the major political developments of the period. In his view, the agreement allowed a "huge" American organization to come into intimate contact "with the realities of Russia" and thus opened "a way to America playing a greater part in saving European civilization than she has played since the day she entered the war."[103]

A week after the conclusion of the Riga agreement, a group of American correspondents arrived in Moscow. One of the first dispatches informed the American people that the general public in Moscow did not know that the advance party of the ARA was due to arrive that day.[104] The two-way blockade between the Americans and the Russians was finally breached.

—4—

The Unique Encounter

Unlike his representatives at Riga, Hoover was not seriously concerned about what he considered "preposterous" fears and suspicions on the part of Soviet authorities. In his first public statement following the agreement, he announced the appointment of a regular army officer as director of the ARA in Russia and the selection of Moscow and Petrograd as the first areas to be served. The director, Colonel William N. Haskell, was a West Point graduate, had commanded the "Fighting Sixty-Ninth" regiment during the First World War, and had later served as Chief of Staff of the American Second Army. As Allied High Commissioner for Armenia after the Armistice, Haskell had supervised the distribution of ARA relief supplies when that region was on the verge of being overrun by the Bolsheviks.[1]

The appointment of an army officer to head a relief mission was consistent with ARA custom and with the then traditional American belief in the nonpolitical character of the military. The Bolsheviks, however, believed otherwise. In 1920, during negotiations on the relief of occupied Poland, Soviet representatives had taken emphatic exception to the presence of army personnel on the ARA staff. With regard to including Moscow and Petrograd within the famine area, Soviet opposition had surfaced early in the Riga negotiations and had never been fully overcome.

More reassuring to the Bolsheviks was Hoover's revelation that the ARA intended to spend between $1.2 million and $1.5 million a month when the mission reached full stride. At the prevailing level of grain prices in the United States, such expenditure could realistically be expected to supply sustenance for one million children a day, as the separate memorandum of the Riga agreement had promised. The American farmer was pleased by Hoover's ruling that "every dollar to be expended on behalf of Russian children will be spent in this country, and all the food used will be sent from here with the exception of surplus stocks already abroad."[2] Two days after these plans were announced, ARA workers were on their way to Russia. At the same time, a shipment of 3,500 tons of food was dispatched.[3]

As the first contingent of Americans neared Moscow and Petrograd, Lenin decided to dispose of the public famine relief committee once and for all; the agreement with Hoover had made its continued existence unnecessary. Furthermore, according to information supplied by a Bolshevik agent who had penetrated the committee's inner circle, leading members of the group were meeting privately and railing against the regime.[4] In addition, in spite of the government's "proposal" to delay the departure of a delegation abroad, the committee's presidium had voted to send its prominent anti-Bolshevik members on a trip at an early date.[5]

Fridtjof Nansen had unwittingly hastened Lenin's decision. The Norwegian philanthropist had been negotiating with Chicherin for a relief mission under the auspices of the Geneva Conference of International Relief Societies. Since Nansen did not share Hoover's distrust of the Bolsheviks, he did not insist on extraterritorial protection for his personnel or on unilateral control of feeding operations. In other respects, however, the agreement that he signed on 27 August incorporated most of the terms of the Riga compact, including complete freedom in the selection of Russian workers.[6] Before the agreement was actually concluded, Nansen made several tentative appointments. One of the Russians designated was a member of the public famine committee and a former member of the outlawed Constitutional Democrat (Kadet) party.

Lenin was angry and uneasy. If a nonpolitical philanthropist like Nansen could enlist the aid of a known anti-Bolshevik, what was to be expected of Hoover and his army colonel? On 26 August Lenin wrote a detailed directive on the subject and sent it to a member of the Politburo who was eminently qualified to carry it out.

> . . .What are we waiting for now? Can we possibly allow them to make obvious preparations?
> Absolutely unthinkable.
> I suggest: today, Saturday, August 28, dissolve "Kukish" [ironic ab-

breviation of names of leading members Kuskova and Kishkin] by a resolution of VTsIK. Motive: their refusal to work, their resolution. Appoint one Chekist to take over the funds and liquidate the group.

Arrest Prokopovich today for the crime of anti-government speech (at the meeting attended by Runov) and hold on to him for about three months while we investigate that meeting *with a vengeance.*

The other members of "Kukish" must immediately, today, be exiled from Moscow and scattered near one of the rural localities under *surveillance.*

If we wait, it will be a big mistake. By the time Nansen leaves, this thing must be settled. Nansen will be faced with a clear "ultimatum." The game (with fire) will be over.

Tomorrow, publish five lines in a short, dry "government announcement": dissolved for unwillingness to work.

Give the newspapers this directive: tomorrow, start to ridicule "Kukish" in a hundred ways. Ridicule and taunt them with all your might no less frequently than once a week for the next two months.

This will be a heavy blow to them in all respects.

There is no need to hesitate. I advise settling this today in the Politburo.

Foreigners are beginning to arrive; we must clear these "Kukishes" out of Moscow and put an end to their game (with fire).

Show this to the members of the Politburo.[7]

The directive found strong support at the Politburo. According to one report, Trotsky threatened to resign if the committee were not immediately liquidated and its members arrested; he pointed out that Brown had never mentioned the committee during the Riga negotiations.[8]

As it turned out, Trotsky had no occasion to resign. On 27 August the Central Executive Committee of the government (VTsIK) decreed the dissolution of the public famine relief committee.[9] When the non-Bolshevik members convened for their final session, a *Cheka* squad entered the room, announced that the meeting was over and that all members present were under arrest.[10] According to a later account by Ekaterina Kuskova, one of the Chekists informed her that she, her husband Prokopovich, and Kishkin had been sentenced to death by a *Cheka* tribunal.[11] Thus, in a manner reminiscent of the dismissal of the elected Constituent Assembly in January 1918, the Bolsheviks eliminated the last legal group in Russia that presented any semblance of opposition to the regime.

The Soviet press began its campaign of denunciation at once, accusing the famine relief committee of refusing to work and of attempting to "negotiate directly with foreign powers." In a subtle thrust at Hoover, *Pravda* charged Prokopovich with trying to persuade foreign organizations to lay down strict conditions before granting relief.[12] An official *Cheka* report added the accusation that one member of the committee had made contact with the survivors of Antonov's band of peasant insurrectionists.[13]

On 31 August the American consul at Viborg, Finland, informed the secretary of state that the committee had been disbanded. Hughes promptly relayed the message to Hoover. According to the consul: "The Committee was appointed only to interest foreign governments in Soviet non-partisan famine politics, the real power being vested in the famine section of the Central Executive Committee under Kamenev. The non-party Committee, having served its purpose, was therefore dissolved."[14]

On the day that the committee went out of existence, the pioneer contingent of the ARA arrived in Moscow.

THE FIRST ENCOUNTERS

The first American relief workers on the scene were, for the most part, experienced ARA men. Philip H. Carroll, the temporary head of the mission, had not conferred personally with Hoover before proceeding to Moscow, nor had he received detailed instructions from the ARA New York headquarters—no great handicap since neither Hoover nor his staff of experts in New York knew what Carroll would encounter in Soviet Russia. Hoover was, in any case, accustomed to leaving important decisions to ARA officers in the field until violations of broad policy came to his attention. He maintained control over operations through regular inspections and reports by his heads of missions, periodic investigations by his own representatives sent from the United States, and special conferences held at the home office in New York City.[15]

Carroll tried to set up the mission according to conventional ARA principles, which meant organizing joint councils of Russians and Americans to coordinate the distribution of food. In Moscow, he immediately ran into difficulty. After the dissolution of the public famine relief committee, non-Bolshevik intellectuals were reluctant to join enterprises that might fall under official suspicion. And to staff the joint committees with Bolsheviks would have defeated the principle of ARA control for which the American negotiators had fought at Riga. Somehow Carroll managed to find Russians to serve on the Russian-American committees for Help to Children (known in Russian abbreviation as RAKPD). But since the ARA had ultimately to refer frequently to official Soviet organs, the RAKPD groups proved superfluous.[16]

The Soviet government had made no preparations for effective liaison with the ARA. As head of *Pomgol,* Kamenev was charged with direct responsibility for the activities of the ARA. Since no one on a lower level wanted to make authoritative decisions on the many requests presented by the Americans, a great variety of petty matters fell to the busy Bolshevik leader for disposition.[17]

In the field, ARA supervisors dealt directly with the heads of local and provincial governments—a situation that was undesirable for both the ARA and the Soviet government. Communication between the central authorities and local government was slow and erratic. ARA workers encountered officials whose attitudes ranged from friendly to extremely hostile; very few Soviet functionaries had even heard of the Riga agreement. The central Soviet authorities, for their part, were uneasy about direct contact between the Americans and Soviet government agencies. On the first day of operations, a minor incident in which an ARA worker enlisted the aid of a Soviet guard excited alarm that reached the Kremlin.

During the unloading of the *Phoenix,* the first American ship to arrive at Petrograd, an ARA supervisor, Donald Lowrie, noticed that the Russian stevedores were handling the cargo roughly, using hooks that tore open the burlap bags of flour, rice, and sugar and filling their pockets with the spilled contents. Lowrie attempted to stop the pilfering but had finally to ask a guard to arrest one of the offenders. The other stevedores decided to cease work unless their comrade was released. A Soviet official who was summoned explained patiently to Lowrie that the practice was not unusual—that, indeed, he was fortunate in being in charge of cargo that invited minor looting; otherwise the stevedores might take days to unload the ship. Lowrie relented and the unloading was resumed.[18]

Lenin saw Lowrie's action as a brazen affront to the Soviet state;

he sent a letter to the commissar of foreign affairs, advising him to use the full power of the Soviet state to curb the "Hooverites." He suggested action "through the press and perhaps through 'connections' to apprehend and secure the worst ones (like this Lowrie) in order to embarrass them." The letter concluded, "This calls for cruel, *stubborn* war."[19]

The Soviet government responded with measures short of war. On 24 September the Central Executive Committee set up an agency paralleling the ARA to act as intermediary between the relief organization and Soviet government bodies at the central and provincial levels. A. I. Palmer was appointed representative plenipotentiary to the ARA and empowered to issue instructions to all branches of government, including the military, on all matters that pertained to the ARA. His authority included the right to requisition transport and communications facilities, to take legal action against those who failed to comply with his orders, and to register objection to the employment by the ARA of anyone he considered undesirable. Finally, he was authorized to "demand the fulfillment of the obligations contained in the Russian-American Treaty on famine relief in Soviet Russia."[20]

With the appointment of Palmer, Kamenev was able to detach himself from routine supervision of ARA operations. Kamenev had very early taken a favorable view of the American relief workers. The Bolshevik revolutionaries who were in charge of the Soviet relief effort had generally had no previous experience in agriculture, welfare activity, or administration. The arrival of the ARA provided their first real opportunity to "learn from the capitalists." When the first reports about ARA activities in the field began to trickle into Moscow, Kamenev was appreciative.

> The thought cannot be effaced from the memory of the famine sufferers of the Volga that the first who gave them real bread, gave them real milk, was the American organization, and, for this reason, the wall that separates us from America will crumble sooner than will be the case in respect to other countries.

To this generous appraisal, he appended a comment that would become ritual in statements by Soviet spokesmen about American relief.

We, as a proletarian state, cannot, to any significant extent, base our calculations on [nonproletarian organizations]. . . . Those on whom we can base our calculations, however, are the working masses of Western Europe. After the experience of the past two months, we are more than ever convinced that, if it is possible to help famine-stricken Russia (and it is) and if she must be helped (and she must be)—this will be done by the proletariat of Europe and America.[21]

Throughout its stay in Russia, the ARA called upon Kamenev to cut through official red tape in order to obtain such necessities as housing, office supplies, and transportation. He remained a useful friend at court and sometimes acted as the court itself in working out difficulties with minor Soviet officials.[22] Palmer, the first representative plenipotentiary, was a minor functionary with no great Party standing. His authority over local officials was limited, and the ARA had therefore to call upon the harried Kamenev to resolve relatively minor problems. Partly to relieve the commissar of this burden and partly out of recognition of the value of the ARA, the Soviet leadership promptly replaced Palmer with a more imposing figure, Alexander Eiduk.[23]

Eiduk was a celebrated hero of the Revolution. Although neither experienced nor particularly competent in high-level administration, Eiduk did seem to respect administrative excellence. After working with the ARA for about a month, he wrote:

The results of the weakness of our *apparat* in assisting the ARA leads at times to absurdities. For example, there are districts where large supplies of ARA [food] are available, and yet people are dying of hunger in the area only because we are not capable of coping with delivery of provisions. There is always a lack of something; either men or premises or supply plans or lists of children. It must be understood that the ARA is a most efficient organization and we must respond in a like manner. The question is whether we treat the ARA with due consideration. We can give a positive reply to this question as far as the center is concerned. With regard to the districts, however, the answer is in the negative.[24]

Eiduk's "positive reply" was to clear a path for the Americans through the thicket of government regulations. He swiftly arranged for government rations to be issued to the ARA's Russian employees and he granted the Americans permission to carry arms on inspection trips to the remote areas of the country—a rare privilege at the time.[25] Efficiency was not Eiduk's only concern, however. In his first directive, he also ordered strict surveillance of the ARA and its Russian employees.[26]

Soviet representatives below the top level were generally not enthusiastic about the advent of authoritative strangers. In Petrograd, for instance, the representative plenipotentiary was an old-time Bolshevik named Zhukov who openly resented the intrusion of the capitalist missionaries into the historic Red city. Herschel Walker, the ARA supervisor, tried to win Zhukov over by pointing out that hunger in the home of the Revolution made bad publicity for the Bolsheviks, while Zhukov, in return, harangued him about the glories of the Revolution and the communist cause. Neither impressed the other. Zhukov accused Walker of hiring only anti-Communists and declared that the ARA would have to employ Russians sent over by the appropriate trade union. Walker insisted on retaining full authority over the hiring of Russian personnel as guaranteed by the Riga agreement and accused Zhukov of allowing food to be diverted. According to Walker, Zhukov responded to the charge by having the Russian responsible for guarding the food arrested and shot. Walker then realized that he would have to couch his grievances in gentler terms.[27]

Outside Moscow and Leningrad, the ARA organized its districts parallel to the Soviet government's provincial *(gubernia)* structure. At this level, the ARA consulted with the provincial *Pomgol* head (who usually served also as representative plenipotentiary to foreign aid organizations) and with the provincial Soviet Executive Committee *(Gubispolkom)*. In Tsaritsyn (later Stalingrad), the chairman of *Gubispolkom* was also the head of *Pomgol*.[28] In Samara, the representative plenipotentiary was A. Karklin, a member of the central presidium of *Pomgol* and an aide to Stalin.[29]

At the village level, food was distributed by Russian volunteers who worked under ARA supervision through local committees. The ARA worker usually tried to arrange for representation from local government and the clergy in these groups. The political leader was expected to clear away red tape and suspicion so that his area could be fed; the priest knew most of the local inhabitants personally, and the representatives of church and state could be counted on to check each other's judgments concerning the fair distribution of food. The Russians who manned the kitchens, warehouses, and ARA offices were drawn from the thinned-out ranks of the educated, or at least the literate, elements in the community. They were paid by the Soviet government, but the regime looked upon them as "American" personnel as far as class loyalty was concerned. Since the ARA did not make adherence to communism a condition of employment, its Russian personnel included a rather high proportion of members of proscribed classes and parties.[30]

A vivid impression of the Americans' first appearance in the town of Simbirsk appears in an unpublished essay written by a former professor at Moscow University. According to this account, the town had formed a relief committee, but after weeks of meetings and collection campaigns, the committee had accumulated from the impoverished inhabitants only enough money to purchase fifty pounds of grain. Some of the starving fled to Siberia; the rest awaited death. Then one day a party of four young Americans arrived—without food. They questioned the town officials minutely about conditions. When they were gone, the officials complained: "They don't trust us. The Americans asked facts and figures. Then they went to the villages and into the huts. They even questioned the popes [priests]."

About two weeks later three younger Americans arrived. "The Russian wiseacres," writes the professor, "shook their heads: how can they do it from America? How can they provide enough money to feed 'a whole million children? How could three young men, most likely without any experience, not knowing the Russian language, proceed with a task requiring not only the kindness of a dove but also the wisdom of a serpent?"

The young men did not look like American millionaires, still dressed, as they were, in the olive drab of army enlisted men. To complete the disillusionment, they promptly set about "oh, horror —carrying burdens on their own shoulders, loading and unloading trucks." But youthful enthusiasm and energy were insufficient for the work ahead. The administrative machinery in the area had been reduced to "splinters" by inexperienced Bolsheviks. The problem was to enlist the help of the local officials and to resist all attempts to take over control of relief.

According to the account, "the problem was solved in a satisfactory manner in all principal questions." The Americans appointed the secretary of the local Party committee *(Ispolkom)* to their own committee but retained their own authority over all matters pertaining to the accounting, storage, and distribution of food. Within a very brief time, some of the grain that Hoover had begun to store up in June "for just such an emergency" began to flow regularly, and in increasing amounts, into Simbirsk. The timely arrival of Hoover's young men—and food—began to reverse the course of the famine in the town in which Lenin had spent his childhood.[31]

During the pioneer phase of the mission, the Americans in the field improvised techniques of local organization and food distribution without detailed guidance from the ARA Moscow headquarters. As long as no disturbing reports reached the central office, the provincial and village workers enjoyed full authority to implement the ARA's broad policies as they understood them. With the arrival of the permanent ARA staff at Moscow, problems ordinarily settled in the field found their way to the administrative center.

THE ARA CENTER IN MOSCOW

The temporary staff that set up the ARA headquarters in Moscow was composed mostly of old ARA men familiar with Hoover's method of operation and standards of work. In Belgium and elsewhere in Europe during the Armistice period, they had become accustomed to a loosely structured organization. Occasionally, the Chief himself would visit the scene of operations to check that his policies were being effectively carried out. This was not possible in Russia, and none of the ARA officials in Moscow had the stature that insured reflexive obedience.

Hoover may have had this in mind when he chose to bypass the ARA staff in appointing a high-ranking regular army officer as head of the Russian mission: that is, the charisma of high military rank might have been calculated to compensate in some degree for the absence of the awesome and celebrated Chief. To Hoover, Colonel Haskell had satisfactorily demonstrated leadership ability and "complete freedom from any political entanglement under difficult circumstances." Detached from military duty for the duration of his work in Russia, he seemed to the Chief "the ideal man" for the job.[32] But one of Hoover's special representatives reported apprehension among the seasoned ARA men in Russia about the appointment.

I shall be in Russia when Haskell and his party come in and shall see him and try to have him understand *our* way of working. There seems

to be a little fear here that, in accordance with his training and experience, he will lean toward a military type of organization. This
would not be good for the morale of our long-time C.R.B. and A.R.A.
men. I know Haskell and can talk frankly with him.[33]

Frank talk, however, did not smooth the difficulties that arose
when Haskell and his personal staff of seventeen arrived in Moscow.
The informal ARA structure was replaced with the rigid line-and-
staff organization of the army. Haskell's deputy, Captain Thomas C.
Lonergan, was appointed "executive officer" and barred direct contact between "the old man" and the relief staff. Brown notified New
York headquarters from London that Haskell had been advised of
the necessity of some accommodation and that he had agreed to
"change his ways." But Brown believed that more concrete measures
were in order. He suggested replacing Longergan with Cyril J. C.
Quinn, who had served under Haskell in the army, as Brown's assistant later in London, and had taken part in the negotiations at Riga.
To Brown, Quinn was admirably equipped to act as a bridge between
"the Army" and the ARA in Moscow.[34] Hoover accepted the suggestion. Quinn shared the office of executive assistant to Haskell with
Longergan for two months. By the end of March 1922 he had
superseded Lonergan as second-in-command. During Haskell's frequent extended inspection tours, Quinn was in complete charge of
the mission.[35]

As the operation expanded, the demand for American personnel
increased rapidly. Eventually the contingent grew to almost twice the
one hundred that Brown had described to Litvinov as sufficient.
Quinn tried to fill his personnel needs primarily from overseas
sources. These narrowed down to the American Army of Occupation
at Koblenz, Germany, and the corps of Rhodes scholars in
England.[36] Simultaneously, a call went out in the United States.
Thousands of would-be famine fighters lined up outside the ARA
headquarters office at 42 Broadway in New York City. One
successful applicant, Henry C. Wolfe, later a writer on Soviet affairs,
had returned to college after having served in the American Field
Service during World War I. Edgar Rickard, the general director of
the ARA, informed Wolfe that the ARA wanted people who knew
nothing about politics, particularly communism. Wolfe served for
ten months in the hard-hit Samara district with nine other Americans. At the height of operations, these ten supervised the feeding of
about a million Russians.[37]

Out of the pool of unemployed, idealistic, or simply adventurous Americans who wanted to go to Russia, Rickard was easily able to fill out the complement already overseas. A total of 381 Americans served with the ARA in Russia at one time or another. The number of regular army officers on the staff was 26; no more than 19 were in Russia at any given time. The rest of the contingent was drawn from various classes and occupations, including a sizable group of World War I veterans who were overseas at the time performing occupation duty or awaiting shipment home.[38] The ARA New York office was troubled about possible misunderstanding arising from the presence of so many Americans who had been in the army,[39] but the alternative would have been to spend time and money transporting overseas only those Americans who had never been in military service.

The employment of the temporary soldiers of World War I seems not to have lent a military flavor to the ARA operation. The nonregular army veterans made a distinction between themselves and the "Army men." Even after Lonergan's replacement, the civilian majority continued to identify overexercise of authority with the "Army boys."[40]

One of the Haskell's innovations was the total elimination of the ineffectual Russian-American committees. In October 1921 he notified ARA supervisors in all the provinces to disband the RAKPD's and "to take all the Russian personnel directly under their own charge." Hoover approved the move as a necessary step in making the "proper impression among Russian people that this is really an American undertaking."[41]

It was inevitable that the question of control over the behavior of thousands of Russian employees would arise. In most countries, this was no great problem. If an ARA employee was arrested, the courts determined whether the country's laws had been violated. In Soviet Russia in 1921, however, there was no codified system of law, either civil or criminal. According to one study, "It was a time of experimentation, guided in some measure by the Ministry of Justice, but one in which judges and administrators felt themselves essentially free to behave as they wished."[42] The Soviet Constitution of 1918 did contain a bill of rights that granted freedom of speech, association, and assembly, but its closing section excluded from these guarantees "those individuals and specific groups who use these rights to the detriment of the communist revolution."[43] The exclusion was phrased broadly enough to deny protection from summary arrest and prosecution to members of the former "bourgeoisie," such as those employed by the ARA.

But the Riga agreement stipulated that "in securing Russian and other personnel, the ARA shall have complete freedom as to selection." Furthermore, the agreement gave the Americans the right "to set up the necessary organizations for carrying out its relief work free from governmental or other interference."[44] Would the ARA interpret arrests of its Russian employees as governmental interference? A test was not long in coming. Shortly after the ARA arrived in Tsaritsyn, Samara, and Kazan, news of arrests of key Russian employees in these cities reached the Moscow headquarters. The incident in Kazan brought the ARA and the central government of the Tatar Republic into direct conflict.

After the local authorities had arrested three Russian employees of the ARA, the district supervisor, I. W. Wahren, notified the chairman of the Council of Peoples' Commissars of the Tatar Republic that ARA food shipments would stop unless the employees were released and allowed to continue their jobs pending presentation of specific charges. The Tatar Republic submitted to the ultimatum but pointed out that it was doing so not because Wahren's demand was justified but only because the government had "a special respect for the ARA and in particular for the work that the ARA is doing to relieve the starving."

Wahren reported to Haskell that the incident had been settled "in an amiable way" and that his action had convinced the government representatives that "we mean what we say and shall expect them to do likewise."[45] To the Soviet government however, the incident was not settled. Wahren had bypassed the representative plenipotentiary in presenting his demand directly to the Tatar government, and he had threatened to cut off relief on his own authority.

In a long letter of complaint to ARA headquarters, Eiduk accused one of the arrested employees, a Mme. Depould, of appearing at the ARA kitchen "in diamond rings and bracelets and décolleté, and by her external appearance alone evoking the protest and indignation of the hungry crowd of children and their mothers." The overdecorated lady then "expressed herself in a most emphatically anti-Soviet spirit." Upon further investigation, Eiduk claimed, it was learned that her husband, a former baron who had fled from Kazan to join the counterrevolutionary Kolchak army, was "an enemy of the Worker's Government." According to Soviet law, wrote Eiduk, the penalty for being married to a White Guard officer was confinement to a workhouse. Another employee, Solomin by name, Eiduk charged with being "a Russian citizen with an undoubtedly counterrevolutionary past who was heartily distrusted by both the local authorities and the central government." Eiduk also expressed displeasure with the alleged practice of some ARA district supervisors of selecting personnel "exclusively from the ranks of the ex-bourgoisie, which elements are obviously inimical to the starving children whom they cater to, the latter of course in the majority belonging to the poorer classes of the workers and peasants."[46]

In Haskell's absence, Captain Lonergan answered Eiduk's letter. He acknowledged that Wahren had exceeded his authority in threatening to stop relief in Kazan, but he did not agree that the Soviet government had the right to arrest ARA employees without first notifying the ARA supervisor, nor did he see any merit in the complaint about the employment of members of a class that was disliked by the Soviet authorities. Employment with the ARA, wrote Lonergan, was based on ability alone, not on whether the applicant "formed a part of the so-called 'bourgeoisie' or any other class." He warned that "neither directly or indirectly will the American Relief Administration be subjected to such procedure on the part of the Soviet Government."[47]

Eiduk responded that the Riga agreement provided no guarantees to Russian employees arrested for an "offense against the general laws of the RSFSR" but agreed to have all such arrests called to his personal attention so that there would be fewer incidents of this kind. He could not promise that such arrests could be entirely avoided, since the ARA had hired thousands of employees hastily, and there were certain to be "criminals as well as political offenders among them."[48]

Haskell later resumed the argument in more restrained terms than Lonergan. "In choosing our Russian employees," he wrote, "as in the feeding of Russian children, we ask no questions as to race, creed, or political opinion, and we trust that the Soviet authorities will observe the same attitude toward them." On a more practical level, Haskell declared that the arrests would adversely affect Hoover's efforts to obtain $10 million worth of army supplies for Russian relief.[49]

The Soviet authorities temporarily backed off. Orders evidently went out to exempt ARA employees from the periodic drives against the "bourgeoisie." This shift in policy led to an odd incident in Simbirsk. One evening, the *Cheka* raided a meeting of engineers. Before the congregants were led away, the leader of the raiding party asked whether any of the engineers were ARA employees. One man identified himself as such and was promptly released; the rest were taken away.[50]

This early conflict of authority was finally resolved by the collaboration of both sides in a loyalty check program. The ARA submitted to Eiduk lists of prospective Russian employees together with completed questionnaires about their personal histories. After examination of each application by the appropriate Soviet agencies, Eiduk returned the lists, indicating specific objections or approval. A typical objection was one concerning an applicant whom Eiduk rejected "for having been sentenced to two years in a concentration camp." The ARA generally honored such objections.[51]

The Informal American Consulate

From the start of the mission, the American State Department expected that the highly privileged ARA would carry out some of the functions of a consular office. On 2 September 1921 Secretary Hughes notified Brown that the United States government would not participate in the work of the International Commission on Russian Relief since

> . . . this government is in full sympathy with all practicable efforts for Russian relief but believes that American relief should be administered through the private agency of the American Relief Administration. It is thought that full information will be obtained in this way without the risk of complications through government action.[52]

After the ARA set up its central office in Moscow, it served as both a source of information about conditions in Russia and as an unofficial liaison between the Soviet and American governments. The State Department nevertheless insisted on maintaining the ARA's purely private status, even to the extent of denying special passports to Brown and his wife. Brown was understandably annoyed. "My work," he wrote to Herter, "after we remove the camouflage, is certainly to a considerable measure semi-official." He pointed out that the ARA constantly sent trade and economic information to the Department of Commerce, along with political observations and translations of the European press.[53] Much of this information was subsequently transmitted to the State Department.

The kind of information that the ARA sent to the United States early in the mission is typified by Haskell's first report to Hoover on 20 October 1921. "The Soviet government," he wrote, "has a strangle hold on Russia but lacks the support and confidence of the people." He went on to sketch a system of control by a bureaucracy "as severe as the Imperial regime" operating under the direction of a shrewd but narrow-minded leadership and supported by a semiautonomous, powerful, and ubiquitous *Cheka* organization. In spite of the hopeless inefficiency of the local soviets—composed, according to Haskell, of "ignorant representatives of the proletariat"—the government was succeeding in maintaining order throughout the country. The report described the Foreign Commissariat as intent on harrassing the ARA in order "to effect contact with our State Department on any pretext." In most other respects, Haskell found the central Soviet authorities "friendly and helpful." He did note, however, that the Soviet government tried to inject itself into the American relief operation at every opportunity in order to give the peasants the impression that the ARA effort was a function of the Russian government.[54]

On 5 November Haskell sent Hoover a confidential report containing several public statements of a political nature by Soviet leaders and a rough digest of contradictory rumors that were afloat in Moscow at the time.[55] It was the kind of information that was easily available to less privileged observers, but as the ARA became more deeply involved in the complex network of Soviet agencies and developed close relationships with Bolshevik leaders, the range, depth, and accuracy of its information increased. According to available records, ARA reports stayed well within the range that would be considered legitimate by traditional governments in time of peace.

There were, however, several instances in which special privileges granted to Americans because of the relief effort were abused. In November 1921 Thomas Dickinson, who was in charge of the permanent records in the New York office, visited Russia on an ARA fact-finding mission. In Moscow, he asked the manager of the Soviet press bureau for all reports and documents of the Russian government on the famine and relief. He said that his work was not with the Department of Commerce but with the ARA and that it was "strictly limited to the field of famine and relief."[56] Upon his return to the United States, he wrote a series of newspaper articles in which he attacked the Bolshevik regime bitterly, using as evidence the material that he had gathered during his visit.[57] Deeply concerned about the possible effect of Dickinson's behavior on ARA-Soviet relations, Hoover asked the New York office to assure the Soviet government that Dickinson's articles were not authorized by the ARA, that they did not reflect its views, and that their author was no longer associated with the ARA.[58]

Among the Americans who were admitted into Russia because of the relief mission but who were not employed by the ARA were officers serving on board several U.S. destroyers. These vessels were allowed to enter Soviet ports in the Black Sea in order to provide the ARA additional transport and communications facilities. In September 1921 a lieutenant from the U.S.S. *Gilmer* was given the liberty of the port of Novorossisk by the Soviet authorities. Upon his return to the ship, he recorded his observations in a lengthy report which was transmitted through channels to the commander of the U.S. Naval Detachment in the area. Along with political comments ("Small communist oligarchy ready to quit"), the memorandum included a purported description of the number and location of gun emplacements and minefields and a plan for the defense of the city obtained from an informer.[59] Hoover eventually took steps to eliminate such activities. On 24 October 1922 he notified Secretary Hughes that the ARA no longer required the services of the destroyers in the Black Sea, complaining that naval officers had been making investigations that in no way related to ARA work.[60] One month later, Haskell informed the Soviet government that American naval vessels had been ordered to discontinue all visits to Black Sea ports.[61]

The ARA "consulate" became a clearinghouse for all cases involving Americans who were having difficulty leaving Russia. Although the Riga agreement provided for their prompt release, the question was: "Who is an American?" In September 1921 Hughes asked Hoover if the ARA would handle all requests for information about the status of the Russian-born wives and children of naturalized

American citizens.[62] Hoover agreed, and, the ARA thus inherited many of the problems that had been created by the four-year hiatus in communications between the two governments.

In one of the first exchanges with Haskell on the subject of dual citizenship, the head of the Anglo-American department of the Soviet foreign office, Gregory Weinstein [Vainsthein], stated that, according to Russian law, citizens who acquire foreign citizenship without the consent of the government do not cease to be Russian citizens.[63] Haskell admitted that dual citizenship was a long-disputed question of international law but asked that the Soviet government abide by "the spirit of Article 27 of the Riga agreement" in facilitating the departure of Americans.[64] The argument by mail grew heated as Weinstein accused Haskell of attempting unilaterally to settle complex questions of international law; Haskell insisted that he asked only that the Soviet government honor the Riga agreement.[65] Although the Soviet government was not prepared to accept the relief agency as the de facto consulate of the United States in Soviet Russia, it did not want to escalate a disagreement with the Americans at a time when the ARA was to all reports beginning to demonstrate remarkable effectiveness in fighting the famine. It was finally agreed that the American consulate at Riga would certify the citizenship of persons claiming American nationality who wanted to leave Russia. The ARA would then present the certificates to the Soviet Foreign Commissariat, whereupon the proper exit visas would be issued.[66] This highly original ad hoc arrangement served its purpose with only intermittent friction.

Haskell was also engaged in trying to prevent the expulsion of one American who wanted to stay—the Moscow correspondent for the Associated Press. To support his case, Haskell cited Article 21 of the Riga agreement, according to which the Soviet government would "assist and facilitate in supplying the American people with reliable and non-political information of the existing conditions and progress of the relief work as an aid in developing financial support in America."[67] Brown's interpretation of this clause about a month earlier had been that it created no obligations of the Soviet government toward the American press. In reply to an inquiry from Hoover on the subject on 6 September, Brown wrote that he had pointed out the advisability of admitting the press but had made no direct representations on that score. As far as he knew, permission for entry of the press was "completely at the discretion of the Soviet central authorities."[68] When the Soviet government ordered the expulsion of the American correspondent, however, Haskell claimed that the Riga agreement guaranteed press representation in Russia. He asked the Foreign Commissariat to delay the expulsion so that the Associated Press would not be deprived of representation in Russia.[69] On this occasion, however, the commissariat stood firm. The Riga agreement, Weinstein replied, could not "deny to the Russian government the right to take exception to certain representatives of the American press." But Weinstein did not argue the right of the Soviet government to bar all reporters from Russia, nor did this question ever arise during the ARA's stay in the country.[70]

On one occasion at least, the State Department asked the ARA to use its good offices in behalf of a group of Soviet citizens. In late September 1921, news leaked out that the three leading "bourgeois" members of the public famine relief committee had been condemned to death. Maxim Gorky, who had been known to intercede with Lenin in such matters, was out of the country recuperating from an illness.[71] On 22 September the State Department, acting on information received from the former Russian government's embassy in Washington, recommended to Hoover that he intervene to prevent the executions.[72] Upon receipt of the message, Hoover sent through ARA channels a recommendation to the Soviet government that he believed would not compromise the relief mission but that might help to "save these people and establish a position that we may need for our own protection later."

> These reports [of the impending executions] may be purely anti-Bolshevik propaganda and in any event it is a political matter in which a private relief organization can take no interest. On the other hand it seems to us that the authorities should be informed that such action if contemplated will undermine confidence and greatly destroy the sympathetic attitude of the world toward Russian suffering and thereby limit the volume of foodstuffs and supplies. If untrue, it should be promptly denied.[73]

In transmitting Hoover's "advice" to Kamenev, Haskell referred to the committee as "the Famine Relief Society in answer to whose appeal the conference at Riga was called and which therefore receives in the United States part of the credit for the agreement."[74] It was the first intimation by an ARA spokesman that the committee had played any role in Hoover's offer of assistance. Together with Hoover's broad hint about "the volume of foodstuffs," Haskell's pointed reference to the committee found its mark. Several days later, Kamenev informed Haskell that the story about the death sentences was a fabrication. Only ten or twelve committee leaders were still under arrest, and their punishment included "no measures more severe than expulsion from Moscow."[75] There were no executions. The leading members of the defunct committee were exiled to Siberia and later permitted to leave the country.[76]

The ARA and Ukrainian Autonomy

In November 1921 Hoover's special representatives Frank A. Golder and Lincoln Hutchinson applied to the Soviet government for travel papers in connection with an exploratory trip to the Ukraine. Although, according to a treaty signed in December 1920, many of the commissariats of the Ukrainian government had been taken over by the RSFSR, the Commissariat of Foreign Affairs was not among them, and the Ukrainian Soviet Socialist Republic was declared an "independent and sovereign state."[77] The request was refused. According to Eiduk, five of the provinces mentioned in their itinerary were "fully assured of a normal harvest." Ukrainian authorities at Kiev and Kharkov were surprised that the ARA wanted to visit these localities since "no one is starving there." Furthermore, Kiev was under martial law, and the government feared that the presence of "foreign official persons" would create difficulties. The government's position in general was that the ARA should not split its forces but should confine its efforts to the Volga area.[78]

In his reply to Eiduk, Lonergan made no distinction between the Ukraine and Russia. Paragraph Two of the Riga agreement, he declared, gave the ARA the right of entry, exit, and movement throughout Russia. The inspection trip was necessary in order to investigate conditions under the terms of the Food Draft Agreement of 19 October 1921, which allowed the ARA to designate the areas of Soviet Russia that would be served by the program.[79] This plan provided for the shipment of food packages to individuals by the

ARA. American and European donors paid the ARA for the amount of food they wanted to have sent to specific beneficiaries; the ARA took care of everything else. After further consultation, Eiduk notified Lonergan that he saw no obstacles in the way of such a trip and that he was issuing orders "to supply the gentlemen with all the necessary documents and means for their trip."[80] Armed with these credentials, Golder and Hutchinson set off for the Ukraine.

They were cordially received by the provincial government at Kiev and were able to set up food package stations with no difficulty. At Kharkov, however, they met with a distinctly cooler reception.[81] The head of the Ukrainian government, Christian Rakovsky, was not available for interview. The Vice-President, Nikolai Skrypnik, told them that the Ukrainian Soviet Socialist Republic would be glad to receive American assistance provided that an appropriate agreement could be arranged. The ARA representatives were astonished. They said that they were under the impression that the Ukraine was part of Russia and that any agreement with the latter automatically included the former. "You are poorly informed," replied Skrypnik. And there the matter rested.[82]

The ARA team continued its investigation of the Ukraine, but the setting up of relief operations was delayed for over a month while Russian and Ukrainian authorities discussed protocol. In the meantime, a Soviet periodical reported that some of the most fertile areas of the Ukraine were struck by a famine that had reduced their inhabitants to eating food substitutes. To compound the disaster, peasants who had fled the Volga region were now streaming into starving villages in the Ukraine.[83] Hutchinson reported that "over a very considerable area conditions are as serious as in any part of the Volga basin."[84]

While Haskell reported that Russian officials regarded the issue raised by the Ukrainians as relatively minor, Rakovsky kept insisting that a separate treaty would have to be negotiated with his government and that it was a matter of "great political importance." In the end, Rakovsky won. On 10 January 1922 Haskell and Rakovsky concluded an agreement that was substantially the same as the one signed at Riga.[85] Two weeks later, Eiduk notified the ARA that the Ukrainian government had ratified the pact and had appointed him representative plenipotentiary for the Ukrainian Republic.[86] The independence of the Ukraine had been preserved through a clause in the preamble that read: "Whereas, the Ukrainian Soviet Republic declares itself not a party to nor obligated by the [Riga] agreement and the Russian Socialist Federative Soviet Republic concurs in this declaration of the Ukrainian Soviet Republic. . . ."[87] The ARA could now proceed with the feeding of the Ukraine. It was not an easy undertaking. By April, over one-third of the population was facing starvation.[88]

In the first five months of operations, the ARA established itself in Russia as a highly effective relief agency and as an unofficial representative of the American government. After the first awkward encounters, both sides improvised procedures that meshed with little friction. The Soviet central authorities were impressed with the confident efficiency of the young American relief workers and with the results of their first efforts. On 7 September 1921 the ARA fed the first group of Russian children at a hastily furnished kitchen in Petrograd. Four days later, the Moscow staff opened a child-feeding station in a restaurant. On 17 September kitchens were in operation in the heart of the famine region, and by 1 December ARA relief teams had fanned out beyond the Urals, into the nearer reaches of Asia, and southward to Astrakhan on the Caspian Sea. More than a half-million starving children were fed daily at some three thousand ARA kitchens in 191 towns and villages.[89] It was evident that Hoover's goal—the rescue of one million children—would be fulfilled, but it was equally obvious that the famine was still spreading. Both the ARA and Soviet authorities in Moscow realized that the fate of a large section of the Russian population depended on decisions that would be made in the United States.

—5—

Expansion of the Mission

RELIEF AND POLITICS—THE HOME FRONT

The reports that Hoover received from Russia during the first few months agreed that his original goal of feeding one million children would have to be changed if a horrible tragedy were to be averted. His special representative, Vernon Kellogg, recommended doubling the program.[1] Colonel Haskell warned that "millions of Christian people in Russia face certain death before the 1922 harvest unless material outside assistance is forthcoming."[2] On 8 December 1921 he sent an urgent appeal to Hoover.

> Somewhere between five million and seven million people in this area must die unless relieved from outside Russia. . . . As a Christian nation we must make greater effort to prevent this tragedy. Can you not ask those who have already assisted this organization to carry over eight million children through famine in other parts of Europe to again respond to the utmost of their ability?[3]

Haskell was probably unaware of the fact that the Chief had already arranged to tap the resources of the United States government. On 6 December President Harding recommended that Congress appropriate funds for the purchase of ten million bushels of corn and one million bushels of seed to supply the ARA in Russia. On 10 December a bill requesting $10 million for that purpose was introduced in the House of Representatives.[4] Hoover's "private" relief effort was now officially in the public domain.

Hoover could have avoided recourse to the legislative branch only by launching a nationwide appeal for funds, but he was still opposed to a public campaign for contributions to Russian famine relief. On one occasion he censored a cable from Walter Brown that recommended a public appeal in behalf of supplying medicine and clothing to famine victims. Hoover explained his action in a letter to the ARA New York headquarters.

> I have deleted the parts of the cable that conflict with our own policies and it might be worth while to send it out. . . . I think you better consider altogether whether we want to send out an appeal for the purpose of buying medical supplies and clothing and if we are not going to make such an appeal I see no use in sending out any statement on the subject because it will only involve us in responsibility for money that is handled by other people.[5]

Rather than stimulate widespread public activity of uncontrollable groups, Hoover preferred to limit the appeal for funds to Congress and its committees. The risks were smaller and the chances of realizing a substantial yield much greater. There was also the strong possibility that a large congressional appropriation would have a beneficial effect on farm prices and ultimately on the economy as a whole. On the first day of hearings before the House Committee on Foreign Affairs, Hoover and Governor James P. Goodrich asked that the amount requested by the president be doubled to $20 million, Goodrich argued, "You would not want, and I should regret to see, this country start in and not do the job right because of the lack of two or three million dollars."[6]

No one on the committee took exception to the increased amount. According to a former assistant secretary of agriculture, the price of corn had been depressed by the accumulation in farmers' hands of a surplus of only 5 percent of the total production. The movement of part of this excess supply could be expected to have a salutary effect on the price of corn and possibly other farm products as well.[7] To Hoover, the effect of the appropriation on the national economy was not immaterial. When Representative Tom Connally said, "Let us not dilute our generosity with any selfish purposes," Hoover replied:

> I have a feeling we are dealing to-day with a situation of a great deal of depression and have a proper right to inquire not only whether we are doing an act of great humanity, but whether we are doing an act of economic soundness. To me, after assessing our ability to give, no other argument is needed beyond sheer humanity.[8]

But the passions aroused by the "Red scare" had not yet subsided, and it was possible that Hoover's bill might be mutilated or even destroyed in open ideological controversy. To insure swift passage of the appropriation, Hoover's agents alerted congressmen from the farm belt and leaders of agricultural groups about the imminence of a bill for the purchase of grain.[9] The committee cooperated by holding open hearings for only one day and on very short notice.[10] Opposition forces never had the opportunity to mobilize. Only one witness raised the question of bolstering a Red government; the rest were Hoover men and spokesmen for farm groups.

Samuel Gompers, president of the American Federation of Labor, wanted reassurance that the appropriation would not furnish "aid and comfort" to the Bolshevik regime and that all funds would be under the strict control of the ARA. Representative Connally replied that the testimony had already disclosed the fact that the Soviet regime, "instead of being a government of vultures, was aiding and helping to distribute this food, and it actually made contributions to the other Provinces." Gompers assured the committee that his mind was "disabused" on that score even before he came to the hearing and that he was actually appearing in favor of the bill.[11] The committee adjourned and went into executive session, to which Hoover and his associates were invited.[12]

Within a week the bill was reported to the floor of the House with a favorable recommendation by the committee. Debate was spirited but brief, and the bill cleared the House by 181 to 71. But almost as many members were registered "not voting" as voting for it.[13] This augured trouble in the Senate, where the rules allowed anti-Hoover and anti-Soviet members to luxuriate indefinitely in obstructive eloquence.

On 20 December Senator Tom Watson of Georgia took the floor to present the most bizarre argument that would be offered against the appropriation. Russia, he claimed, had enough wheat; she had never asked the United States for help. The entire business was arranged for the exclusive benefit of the ARA. "Charity is a business, a profession," the senator asserted. What Russia really needed was not charity but recognition. "We are committed," said Watson, "to the principle that all government rests on the consent of the governed. The Russians like this form of government. They sustained it with their blood as well as their treasure and their service. We have no right to dictate to Russia."[14] From time to time, the senator yielded to colleagues who offered an interesting variety of objections to the bill, but none of these senators represented a corn-growing region.

In summary, here are some of the arguments presented:

Congress had refused to pass a request for $10 million for the development of Muscle Shoals, a project that would have kept thousands in employment.

Russia owes the United States $192,601,297.

Russia has an army of one-and-a-half million men.

The Russians do not even know how to mill corn; they don't like it, won't eat it.

Four million American veterans are in distress. Tens of thousands "are slowly but surely dying for lack of gratitude and lack of attention."

The Constitution forbids the imposition of taxes for the welfare of anyone except the people of the United States.

The defenses of the country would be weakened by placing $20 million at the disposal of the Red Army.[15]

The "pro" senators presented a host of mutually contradictory arguments. The senator from Idaho cited the bravery of the Russians during the war and described the relief effort as a step forward in reconciling the two countries. One senator from Utah pointed out the benefits to the farmer, the moral value of the bill, and its usefulness in counteracting Bolshevik propaganda. The other senator from Utah argued that the relief mission would weaken the Soviet regime and provide the "entering wedge to drive from power the men who are today directing the affairs of Russia."[16]

Those who spoke against the bill seemed determined to prevent passage in its original form. They translated their objections into amendments. When the bill came to a vote, it was passed without a roll call. Within two days, the appropriation cleared the House-Senate Conference Committee. The differences between the two versions were resolved by the simple expedient of removing all the extraneous Senate amendments. On 22 December the conference bill was approved by both houses and was immediately signed into law by the president.[17] From the time of its introduction in the House of Representatives until approval by the president, exactly twelve days had elapsed. With even less commotion, Congress approved the transfer of surplus supplies of the War Department and other agencies to the ARA for distribution in Russia.[18] The president was equally compliant. Before the passage of the bill, Hoover had prepared an executive order authorizing the establishment of a purchasing commission headed by himself to handle all transactions in connection with the appropriation. On 24 December the president signed the order.[19]

At this point, a strange interdepartmental battle developed. During the course of the debates on the bill, it occurred to the Treasury Department that the United States Grain Corporation (USGC) was holding some $12 million on deposit in its own name in a private bank. The USGC had been set up during the war as a government-owned corporation to purchase grain for the U.S. Food Administration. Later it was authorized to act as purchasing agent for the official American Relief Administration. When the latter was superseded by the private ARA, the USGC went into slow liquidation—a process that was still under way when Congress was considering the appropriation bill. The Grain Corporation possessed by this time $12 million in addition to the $7 million officially granted to the ARA.[20]

Secretary of the Treasury Andrew Mellon was surprised that the USGC had not notified him about the extra money. On 19 December he asked for return of the $12 million so that funds could be expended in the normal manner through checks drawn on the Treasury. Edwin Shattuck, president of the USGC and also an officer of the ARA informed Mellon that it had always been the corporation's practice to maintain its own bank deposits in order to carry on its business operations and that this practice had been continued during liquidation. Unconvinced, on 27 December Mellon renewed his request for custody of the funds, since "the entire capital stock of the U.S. Grain Corporation is owned by the United States, and that, of course, gives the United States a direct interest in its funds." Shattuck refused to relinquish the money.[21] Mellon reluctantly acknowledged defeat. In a curt letter to the secretary of commerce, he mentioned the discussion with Shattuck and enclosed a statement which the Treasury Department would issue to the press. The statement explained the situation in detail and observed "This situation is the natural result of the organization of Government corporations independent of the usual accounting control."[22]

According to one provision of the appropriation bill, the president was to submit a full accounting of expenditures to Congress by 31 December 1922.[23] In the meantime, Hoover was free to purchase, allot, and distribute food for Russia without serious interference from Congress or the Treasury.

Hoover and the Soviet Gold "Contribution"

Soon after the ratification of the Riga agreement, Hoover decided to augment the resources for fighting the famine by obtaining a contribution from the Soviet government itself. At first, he strongly "suggested" that the Soviet government use some of its gold reserve to purchase grain in the Balkan countries, or, if this were not possible, to buy grain in the United States at cost through the ARA. "We wish to force their hand to do their share in adult feeding and prevent blame on us," he wrote to Brown on 26 August 1921.[24]

The Soviet government agreed to place $4.5 million in gold at the disposal of the ARA and gave assurances that the grain purchased with these funds would be distributed impartially. The ARA, in effect, was to act as middleman in a cash transaction between the Soviet government and American grain wholesalers. For such a departure from the official no-trade policy of the United States government, Hoover needed the approval of the State Department. Dissatisfied with the arrangement, Hughes notified Hoover that "mere Bolshevik assurances" were not sufficient, that the only real guarantee of fair distribution of the food would be total control by the ARA under the Riga terms.[25] Apparently convinced that he could persuade Hughes to agree once a firm agreement was reached with the Soviet government, Hoover prepared to clear the next hurdle. On 26 October he asked the Treasury Department if it would allow this single exception from the government's embargo on Soviet gold.[26]

As negotiations dragged on, however, Hoover did not press State or Treasury for approval of his plan. While Congress was still considering the appropriation bill, Hoover cabled Brown to inform Leonid Krasin, the Soviet commissar of foreign trade, who was in London with the Soviet trade delegation, that the impending appropriation put an entirely different light on the question of Soviet gold, that the American grant would "no doubt be contingent upon the Soviets' enlarging the program of purchases through the A.R.A. to ten million dollars for distribution solely in the Volga area."[27]

The Soviet leaders had no reason to doubt that Hoover spoke for the American government. Thus on 29 December Brown informed Hoover that Krasin had agreed to the new terms and that the Soviet government had undertaken to expend the $10 million within ninety days of contract. Two days later, Brown and Krasin signed the agreement.[28] The arrangement was, in effect, the first national grant on a two-for-one matching basis.

With the contract in hand, Hoover notified the Treasury Department, "With the President's approval I have undertaken to accept $10,000,000 in Bolshevik gold for the American Relief Administration. . . . I would indeed be greatly obliged if you could tell me how we can get forward with this."[29] But neither State nor Treasury was disposed to give its approval to the *fait accompli* presented by the secretary of commerce. The matter was finally settled in Hoover's favor at a meeting of the cabinet.[30]

Neither Congress nor the public was immediately informed about the new international agreement. On 22 January 1922 Herter advised the ARA New York office to delay publication of the agreement since both the State and Treasury departments·

> . . . would probably be embarrassed by this exception. If the information filters out slowly I feel that it would be preferable to having it come out all at once. Even at the present moment neither the State Department nor the Treasury has copies of our Agreement as the Chief has asked me not to send them unless requested to do so.[31]

The Soviet legislature did not have to wait for the information to "filter out slowly." Lenin had informed the Congress of Soviets about the gold contribution on 23 December 1921.[32]

Hoover and the Interested Groups

Hoover's activities always attracted the attention of a wide variety of interest groups. In the case of the appropriation bill, a number of economic associations leaped to his support. William C. Redfield, president of the American-Russian Chamber of Commerce and former secretary of commerce, informed Hoover that he was prepared to bring pressure on Congress to approve the transfer of surplus materials to the ARA. This proposal was the forerunner of the larger appropriation bill. "We are here to help," wrote Redfield, "and if you or anyone authorized by you will pull the wires we are prepared to jump."[33]

Even before Hoover gave the signal to "jump," Redfield outlined several reasons for backing Hoover's proposal in a letter to a congressman.

The first reason is humanity. The second reason is that of our own domestic trade. . . . Russia will some day come again to her own. Already the signs of returning political and public sanity appear. When she recovers, she must turn for guidance and supplies of every kind for reconstructing her new life to that nation which has been supremely her friend in her times of trial. . . . Nothing could be more certain to react largely and favorably upon American business than unselfishness at this moment.[34]

At the committee hearings, the lobbyist from the American Farm Bureau Federation made a similar prediction: "In addition to saving the lives of starving people in Russia, there will be a comeback—bread cast on the waters has always had a tendency to come back to the giver."[35] In the face of solid support of the bill by these interest groups and others, the bombast of Senate die-hards rang in vain.

After the bill passed, the staff of the Commerce Department was kept busy handling requests from congressmen for consideration of their constituents in placing orders for food. To a congressman who had served on the committee that approved the bill, Hoover wrote that bids were already out for evaporated and condensed milk (which the congressman's state produced in abundance).[36] He informed a representative from Iowa that the ARA was prepared to purchase a substantial amount of powdered milk from an Iowa company "if this milk can show proper qualities for our feeding abroad."[37] Three weeks later, Hoover notified the representative that the ARA had placed an order for 169,000 pounds of dried milk from the company in question.[38]

The economic groups that stood to benefit from the appropriation were not alone in their support of the bill. The measure won the approval of an unusually wide array of normally conflicting groups. The United Committee of Russian Organizations, representing the more conservative émigré groups, sent its congratulations to President Harding.[39] Liberal, anti-Hoover opinion, as expressed in the *New Republic,* called a truce in its running battle with the secretary and described the appropriation as one of the "precedents of a new international order based on humanity and good will. Its significance is heightened by the fact that the beneficiaries are living under a government which President Harding, Mr. Hoover, and almost every member of the Senate and Congress abominates."[40] Even the *Nation,* which as late as 21 September had called the famine reports "exaggerated," commented that "America seems to be awakening at last to the reality of the Russian famine."[41]

Beyond the wide spectrum of supporters were the anti- and pro-Soviet intransigents. A Minnesota congressman forwarded to Hoover a telegram from the former minister of the Republic of Finland to the United States: "Could you speak to Secretary Hoover in order to get help for Karelians and discontinue any relief action for Bolshevists unless they give up their wars, unlawful methods, and propaganda." Christian Herter replied: ". . . That is a matter which I am sure Mr. Hoover would feel lies in the province of the Department of State and not in his."[42] From the pro-Soviet side, however, came pressures that Hoover believed lay entirely within his province. Against the radical groups that rose with new vigor to rally support around their own Russian relief campaigns, Hoover mounted a determined attack.

One of the first groups to implement the principle of "unconditional workers' assistance," prescribed by Lenin in his directive to Zinoviev, was an organization called the "Friends of Soviet Russia" (FSR), the first and most successful of the communist "front groups." Launched in New York City shortly after Lenin's appeal to the world proletariat in August 1921, the FSR spread rapidly to most of the major cities and industrial towns in the country. For the first time since the onset of the "Red scare," the Communist movement in the United States found itself with an issue that carried enough appeal to elicit a substantial response. Collections for Russian famine relief began to amount to quite respectable figures.[43] Not all the funds collected, however, reached the famine victims. As the FSR freely admitted, a sizable contribution was made to the magazine *Soviet Russia* to advance "relief propaganda" and "knowledge about

Soviet Russia."[44] The campaign literature featured lengthy denunciations of "bourgeois" relief organizations like the ARA, as well as eulogies of the workers' and peasants' government.[45]

The ARA systematically collected samples of FSR propaganda material and passed them on to Hoover in Washington. Hoover's power to curb the FSR's activities was, of course, limited. The FSR's campaign was perfectly legal. Hoover was determined, nevertheless, to exercise all his influence to put a stop to the flow of propaganda that emanated from the relief "front group." At that time, Hoover's influence was considerable at the world headquarters of the Communist movement. On 28 October 1921 Herter sent some of the most blatant FSR propaganda pieces to Brown.

> The Chief thinks it might be a good idea to pass these on to Haskell and let him show them to the Soviet authorities, at the same time pointing out to them that this sort of material only cuts down the total amount of relief which will go to Russia through the A.R.A., and that it will probably be in their interests to call a halt to it.[46]

For several months, there was no Soviet response to Hoover's warning. Shortly after the passage of the appropriation, however, Haskell reported to Herter that when he showed the FSR material to Eiduk, the latter "almost hit the roof and said that he would see that it was stopped at once." Krasin remarked that if the Soviet government had a representative in the United States, such matters could be handled expeditiously.[47] In any case, however, the FSR not only continued but expanded its independent, anti-Hoover campaign. Its letterhead carried the slogan: "Our principle: We make the working-class appeal. Give not only to feed the starving but to save the Russian workers' revolution. Give without imposing imperialist and reactionary conditions as do Hoover and others."[48]

At least five of the seven members of the FSR's executive committee were known Communists.[49] It soon became expedient to merge the activities of various "front" groups into a large committee that would attract the support of public figures who were not connected with the Communist movement. The "front" set up to include all the other "fronts" was dubbed "The American Federated Russian Famine Relief Committee," which dedicated itself to "sending relief supplies direct to the Russian Soviet Republic."[50] The workhorse of this committee was the FSR, which managed in six months to transmit $400,000 to the larger group.[51] To add to the confusion, a third group called the "American Committee for Russian Famine Relief" (ACRFR) was organized by a group of congressional figures through the initiative of an international relief free-lancer named Walter Liggett. Although this group contained some of the members of the federated committee, it was not a Communist "front." Liggett's Committee (as the ACRFR came to be known in ARA correspondence) succeeded in garnering eight senators, ten congressmen, ten bishops, and a sprinkling of state governors as sponsors. The leading members were allied in their support of recognition for Russia, concern about the famine, and opposition to Hoover. At the head of the list was Hoover's unrelenting political enemy, Senator Joseph France.[52]

Hoover applied the Red label to all three groups. Drawing freely on inferential material supplied by the Department of Justice, he sent identical letters to those representatives and senators on "Liggett's Committee" whom he thought he could sway. He mentioned the committee's associations with the "Friends of Soviet Russia" and with a Dr. Dubrovsky, the head of the Soviet Russian Red Cross. He claimed, however, that the "Bolshevik association" did not disturb him as long as it did not serve as "cloak for propaganda."[53] In response to a request for information from the governor of Idaho, Hoover quoted a telegram from the Department of Justice in which the other two committees were described accurately as "officered and managed by well-known communists or sympathizers."[54]

In his campaign against pro-Soviet activity, Hoover worked closely with Attorney General Harry F. Daugherty. On 25 November 1921 Hoover suggested to Daugherty that he interview Marguerite Harrison, because she had information that could prove useful in countering Red propaganda in the United States. Mrs. Harrison, he pointed out, had been active with the Intelligence Division during the war. The attorney general sent his appreciation of Hoover's "interest and courtesy" and arranged for the meeting.[55] At a later date, the Department of Justice returned the favor by transmitting to the Department of Commerce a résumé of its file on one of the most determined opponents of Hoover's Russian relief policies.[56]

When the battle between Hoover and the pro-Soviet relief committees approached near hysteria, a New York newspaper commented: "It is conceivable that some of the Bolshevist partisans in this country may have said foolish or prejudiced things. But what difference does that make? The anti-Bolshevist partisans are not less mad. . . . The attack on these organizations is consequently as infamous as it is absurd.[57] To Hoover, however, there was nothing infamous about fighting domestic "Reds," even though their efforts to raise money for Russian relief were meeting with some success. And to Lenin, who saw famine relief as a continuation of politics by other means, an independent campaign by the American "proletariat" for unconditional relief of Soviet Russia was far from mad.

Hoover's animosity toward relief groups that resisted control by his own organization was not limited to left-wing or pro-Soviet committees. He was constantly haunted by the fear that independent groups would deviate from the policy vis-à-vis the Bolshevik regime that he had set down for the ARA. The broad outline of this policy is revealed in a letter he wrote to a businessman who objected to feeding Russians.

> We must make some distinction between the Russian people and the group who have seized the Government. I have obviously no more sympathy with this group than you have. . . . If the proposals I have made extended to the restoring of economic life in Russia, and in general to stabilizing the situation for the benefit of the Bolsheviks it would be deserving of your criticism, but no such proposals have been made.[58]

To feed a population and at the same time to avoid restoring its economy was a difficult undertaking. Hoover's efforts to restrict famine relief activity to those who would try to carry out such a policy led him far afield of ordinary philanthropy. When the Quakers insisted on making a public appeal for Russian relief, Hoover accused them of succumbing to the propaganda of the flour millers, of outright falsification, and finally of "association with radical groups."[59] On 13 February 1922 he wrote to the Friends Service Committee, "I cannot conceive a greater negation of all that Quakers stand for than a regime that carries on its banners 'religion is the opiate of the people.' "[60]

In spite of Hoover's efforts, the relief groups continued to conduct public campaigns and to attack Hoover personally when the conflict sharpened. In a moment of extreme frustration, he informed the head of the Quaker committee:

You will realize that I went into the Russian situation with great unwillingness, under pressure that I was not doing the right thing unless I
lent my influence to it. . . . From a personal point of view, I have every
reason to regret that I ever touched a situation that is so pregnant with
mud and personal vilification from all sides as this appears to be.[61]

Up to this point, Hoover had not expressed publicly any qualms
about having undertaken the relief project. A certain regret on
his part, however, is altogether believable. His reputation as a
philanthropist, as well as his domestic and international policies,
were being steadily undermined by forces which he had himself
released.

Relief and Recognition of Soviet Russia

With the opening of access to Russia through famine relief, new
pressures arose for the reversal of the U.S. nonrecognition policy.
Even within official circles the feeling was expressed that some sort of
change was called for. The American ambassador to Italy, for instance, was convinced that limitless economic and political opportunities now awaited the United States in Russia, opportunities
which European nations would not hesitate to exploit while bending
every effort to keep the United States frozen in its posture of
aloofness from the Soviet regime. "Russia will play an amazing
role," he wrote to the State Department.

If we intend to have the slightest influence on the part Russia will play,
whether that influence is to be practical or idealistic, economic or
political, we must not allow other nations to stir our public opinion or
press upon us policies prepared for us in the cuisine of their propaganda or by their influence upon any members of our Government.[62]

The ambassador denied, however, that he was advocating a reversal
of the State Department's policy on recognition or trade relations.
    The ARA in Europe confirmed the fear that other nations were
trying to curb the expansion of American influence in Russia. A State
Department official in London advised Secretary Hughes that
France and Great Britain were acting to prevent America from
"gaining a strong position in Russia." Citing Walter Brown as his
source, the official reported that the British Foreign Office had
hinted to news correspondents that they should minimize the effects

of the ARA's relief program.[63]

Some of Hoover's own representatives believed that the United States should take the initiative in ending the estrangement from Soviet Russia. Lincoln Hutchinson, whom Hoover depended on for reliable advice, wrote to Brown on 9 November 1921 that he was unable to understand "why the United States should not abandon its 'holier-than-thou' attitude and frankly recognize [the Soviet regime] as a *de facto* government."[64] Governor Goodrich, another Hoover representative, reported that the Bolsheviks were "inflicting upon the people of Russia a system of government they do not approve" and added that he could not see "any hope of a counterrevolution or any sudden change in government." In spite of this, Goodrich recommended recognition of Russia as an effective instrument for moderating and finally replacing the Bolshevik regime.[65] In a magazine article that appeared shortly afterward, however, Goodrich offered a description of Russian public opinion that differed entirely from the version he had given Hoover.

> I was surprised at the lack of criticism of the Soviet Government, expecting the people would be sullen, despondent, and bitter in their condemnation of its acts. It may be that the free expression of opinion has been suppressed; yet often I was with men and women who had suffered much, with no one but Americans present, and I rarely detected any bitterness in their speech. Rather they seemed to accept the hardship they had endured as a necessary accompaniment of a political upheaval such as Russia had passed through, evidently believing that in no other way could the old order be destroyed.[66]

Hoover, however, saw no reason for official rapprochement with a regime he regarded as illegitimate and transitory. In a letter of introduction that he wrote for a prominent Russian émigré, Hoover declared, "He represents the democratic group in Russia, and their hope is that they can keep some sixty thousand professional Russians who are outside Russia alive until the Bolsheviks disappear."[67] Hoover regarded the relief of Russia not as a prelude to recognition but as a substitute for it. On 6 December 1921 he wrote to Hughes: "At the present moment, although other powers have recognized the present Russian government and we have refused to do so, yet Americans are infinitely more popular in Russia and our Government more deeply respected by even the Bolsheviks than any other." He forecast that the relief mission would continue to enhance this "kindliness of relations" and eventually create a situation that would "enable the Americans to undertake the leadership in the reconstruction of Russia. . . ."[68]

Hoover's strategy of substituting relief for recognition is reminiscent of his attempt to sidetrack the Bullitt agreement through the Nansen proposal in 1919. This time, however, he could not push this approach too far without endangering an ARA operation already in progress and without lending weight to the accusation that he was using relief for his own political ends. Thus, he remained publicly silent on the subject of recognition, while his enemies, and even some of his friends, promoted the policy that he had never ceased to oppose.

RELIEF ADMINISTRATION
AND THE SOVIET SYSTEM

The congressional appropriation resolved the worst problem that faced the ARA in Russia. Under the terms of the Riga agreement, the Americans were permitted to feed only children. Because of the ARA's limited resources and Soviet suspicions concerning Hoover's intentions, no other arrangement was possible at the time. Thus, during the first four months of operations, hundreds of thousands of children were fed daily at ARA kitchens while their parents starved. The suspicions of the Soviet leaders were somewhat allayed by the efficient and strictly neutral manner in which the pioneer relief group set up stations and began its job of feeding children. "This cursory glance at the work of the A.R.A.," wrote Eiduk in *Izvestia* on 8 December 1921, "warrants an optimistic view of this organization. There is actual food, there is real aid." On 30 December, a week after passage of the appropriation bill, the ARA concluded an agreement with the Soviet government to feed adults in the famine areas.[69] Over the next four months, the tempo of relief activity by the ARA rose to a peak. Both sides in the strange partnership were faced with problems that arose out of the inevitable clash of authority.

Relief and Dual Authority

In vast areas of Russia and the Ukraine during the winter of 1922 life was reduced to obtaining food to survive. Social and intellectual activity declined as all classes hoarded their last energies for the struggle for a piece of bread and a piece of wood to sustain their families. Authority over "who gets what, when, how" had been delegated to the ARA by the Riga agreement. "No wonder," wrote a sympathetic Russian observer in Kiev, "that the A.R.A. became the *idée fixe* of everybody, especially of the intelligentsia. The starving population did not think of anything else, did not hope for salvation from any other side."[70]

New conflicts in authority arose during this period. On 3 April 1922 Cyril Quinn complained to the ARA headquarters at London that one Russian employee was under arrest in Tsaritsyn, eight in Samara, and one in Moscow. Since the ARA employed at the time thousands of Russian citizens who were members of "suspect classes," it would appear that the settlement reached after the Kazan incident in November had been generally effective in smoothing over the basic conflict. Quinn, however, saw the arrests as part of a larger pattern of obstruction by central Soviet authorities.[71]

The trouble in Samara arose from the hostile attitude of Representative Plenipotentiary Karklin. In January 1922 Karklin demanded the right to screen all outgoing ARA telegrams. In March, he allegedly interfered with the establishment of food warehouses.[72] Lonergan, executive assistant to Haskell at the time, went to Samara himself to remind Karklin about his obligations and about the rights of the ARA under the Riga agreement. Karklin thereafter refrained from direct intervention in ARA activities, at least in regard to matters of administration and warehouses.[73] Later in the month, however, D. G. Savkin, one of Karklin's subordinates in the Pugachov District, ordered the arrest of five Russian employees on charges ranging from giving food cards to members of the bourgeoisie to "committing an offense against the proletariat" by refusing employment to a female applicant because of her lack of education. All those arrested were subsequently released, but two of the offenders were sentenced to five years' deprivation of civil rights, including the right to hold a responsible government position.[74]

Early in April 1922 Quinn mentioned the Samara arrests to Eiduk, who responded that "all active members of the Socialist-Revolutionary Party were being arrested and [the ARA] happened to have employed them."[75] The defense of any individual Russian employee who belonged to the Socialist-Revolutionary party thus involved ARA opposition to central government policy. Failure to protect ARA employees, on the other hand, meant tacit cooperation

with the Soviet regime in a repressive campaign and opening the way
to Soviet control of food distribution by means of subtle intimidation
of the Russian employees.

Haskell decided to bring the basic issue to a head by firm action in
the less complicated case of the single arrest in Tsaritsyn. At an
earlier date, Haskell had objected vigorously to the detention of a
Mr. Arzamasov on flimsy evidence. On 3 March Eiduk answered by
reaffirming Soviet authority over Russian citizens.

> I am sure, my dear Colonel, that you will report the content of my
> letter to Mr. Bowden [the ARA supervisor in Tsaritsyn] and impress
> upon him the impermissibility of condemning to death 30,000
> children . . . on account of the arrest of Mr. Arzamasov even though
> the latter were not guilty.[76]

The appeal to sacrifice a possibly innocent man for a larger
humanitarian purpose did not work. After waiting more than a
month for Arzamasov's release, Haskell notified Eiduk that he was
suspending all feeding at Tsaritsyn pending satisfactory settlement of
the problem.[77] The threat produced the usual satisfactory result but
not without a protest from Kamenev. Haskell denied that the ARA
had any intention of protecting criminals or counterrevolutionaries
but insisted that he would continue to oppose "unwarranted and un-
justified arrests" by local officials that worked to the detriment of
ARA operations.[78]

This left open the matter of the government's campaign against
Socialist-Revolutionaries. On 23 May 1922 Quinn reviewed the
Samara arrests and requested the removal of the Soviet official
responsible for the action.[79] On 13 June Eiduk sent a confidential
telegram to Karklin, issuing the necessary order.

> After a lengthy conversation with the A.R.A. director I have come
> to the conclusion that Comrade Savkin must be removed from work in
> the Pugachov *uezd* [district]. We cannot jeopardize the work of feeding
> tens of thousands because of one man. Please recall Savkin as soon as
> you get this. Use him for any other work except with A.R.A. Wire ex-
> ecution.[80]

The arrest of the ARA employee in Moscow had nothing to do
with the drive against dissidents. For some time the staff in Moscow
had known that one or more of the Russian employees in the head-

quarters office also served the Soviet secret police—the GPU. As a matter of mutual convenience, the American workers placed all papers that were certain to be ransacked in one corner of a desk drawer so that they could be perused with the least disorder. When Haskell inquired about a female employee who had been arrested, he was informed that she had been jailed for some dereliction of her duties as a GPU agent. Eiduk claimed, however, that the secret police did not know she was employed by the ARA; "I consider the matter closed," he wrote. Under the circumstances, Haskell could only agree.[81] In most other instances, however, the ARA was able to protect its Russian employees.

The ARA and the Railroad Crisis

By March 1922 the ARA New York staff had dispatched to Russian ports a flood of relief supplies that could not be absorbed by the Soviet transport system. Thousands of tons of food remained locked in freight cars stalled at stations and sidings far from the famine areas. Railroad workers who had not received their own food rations for weeks refused to transport ARA food until they themselves were fed. Government officials began to requisition American food by the carload to meet the needs of their own departments. *Pomgol* entered the competition for empty freight cars to transport seed to the famine areas. In the scramble for rail facilities, the priority that had been promised for ARA relief shipments was all but forgotten.[82] Finally, Haskell turned over 4,500 tons of corn to the railroad workers on condition that the Soviet government return a similar amount to the ARA within two months, the loan guaranteed by a Soviet deposit of an equivalent value in gold in London.[83] The broader problem, however, was more complex.

Quinn interpreted the delays in ARA shipments as part of a deliberate policy designed to promote American recognition of Soviet Russia. In a report to London headquarters, he tried to relate the arrests in Samara, Tsaritsyn, and Moscow to the transport delays and corn requisitions. "In this connection," he wrote, "it is interesting to note that at our last meeting with Mr. Kamenev, he stated very definitely that since the United States did not recognize Soviet Russia, there was no possibility of our having complete freedom and liberty of action in our relief work in Russia."[84] Quinn's suspicions were reinforced by Eiduk's indifference to his complaints and by Kamenev's unavailability for discussion of the problems.[85]

The transport problem, however, had deeper roots than this. The Soviet railway system had been steadily deteriorating for years in spite of the most determined efforts of Bolshevik leaders. Trotsky's method of resolving the difficulty through stern regimentation of the railway labor force had aroused a bitter controversy with Lenin at the Tenth Party Congress; but Trotsky was defeated, and so, presumably, was his draconian approach to transport efficiency. The appointment of Feliks Dzerzhinsky, the head of the security police, as commissar of transport, however, signified that coercion had not been entirely abandoned as a means of meeting railroad schedules.[86] The failure of the crippled transport system to respond promptly to the change in management affected all sectors of the Russian economy as well as the American relief operation.

Hoover knew of the increasing decay of the Soviet transport system. In 1919, he had made outside supervision of Soviet railways a condition of granting relief. In 1921, he tried to convince the International Relief Societies Commission that the relief of Russia was impossible without total rehabilitation of the transport system. Now he was confronted with the problem. When his European director presented the delays in ARA shipments as simply one phase in the Soviet campaign for recognition, Hoover advised him to "wait developments before taking summary action."[87] The information that he had received from Haskell only the day before, on 14 April, indicated that the ARA's transportation difficulties would be resolved without involving the organization in discussions about America's recognition policy.

On 10 April Haskell decided to find out whether the failure of the Soviet authorities to answer his complaints was negligence or deliberate policy. To this end, he sent an uncoded message to Hoover recommending the cessation of all food purchases in the United States and the suspension of all further shipments pending a demonstration on the part of the Soviet government that it really wanted the ARA to continue its work in Russia. The message had scarcely been dispatched when Eiduk telephoned to arrange a conference for the next day.[88]

At the meeting, Haskel and Quinn confronted Eiduk and Kamenev with the outstanding grievances. Kamenev readily admitted that the requisitioning of ARA supplies was "criminal" and would cease immediately. Eiduk said that he had already arranged that no ARA employees would be arrested without his consent and that an obstructive official in his office had been dismissed. In regard to the transport problem, Kamenev gave assurances that ARA shipments would enjoy the same priority as important government freight. He reaffirmed his government's confidence in the ARA, stating, "They are convinced that no one else could handle the situation under the present trying circumstances."[89]

On 12 April Kamenev telephoned Haskell, confirmed all the guarantees made at the conference, and agreed to furnish in writing a statement setting forth the powers and limitations of the Soviet representatives in the districts. He also arranged a meeting for that day among himself, the ARA directors, and the heads of the railway system, including Dzerzhinsky himself. At this meeting, the commissar of transport answered Haskell's complaints calmly and courteously. He explained in detail the great difficulties facing the railroads, promised to expedite ARA shipments, and gave his personal guarantee that there would be no further requisitions of ARA supplies. At Haskell's insistence, he agreed to allow ARA traffic personnel to arrange routing of relief shipments directly with Soviet railroad officials.[90]

Haskell was skeptical about the promises made at the meeting; he held off recommending the resumption of food purchases. During the following two weeks, however, Dzerzhinsky and his staff drew up specific plans together with the ARA traffic directors to loosen the freight jam and speed relief supplies to the famine districts. At these meetings, Dzerzhinsky repeatedly reminded his subordinates that it was inadvisable to make promises they could not fulfill.[91] Haskell was reassured. On 27 April he notified Hoover that the transport problem had been resolved and recommended that the purchasing program be resumed.[92]

The conference between the Soviet and the ARA transport officials did not result in the rehabilitation of the Russian railroad system. While the American traffic managers' advice was probably helpful, the prompt movement of the mountains of ARA food that had piled up resulted primarily from the assignment and enforcement of high priority to relief shipments. The willingness of the Soviet government to submit to this rearrangement of one of the key branches of its economy suggests the value that it placed on the relief mission. In a letter to Haskell on 15 April 1922, Kamenev frankly acknowledged the dependence of the government on the ARA: "The Government and the Russian nation will never forget the generous help that was offered . . . the more so because that country is not in a position to cope with the natural calamity, prostrated as it is by the World War and the Civil War."[93]

It is extremely unlikely that the Soviet regime had deliberately stalled American food shipments and ordered the requisitioning of ARA supplies to impress on the Americans the desirability of recognizing Russia. Because of weaknesses in management, control, and facilities, Soviet officialdom was simply not prepared for the rush of American supplies. The fact that it took the head of the *Cheka* to overcome the chaos that ensued was not lost on the ARA director, who, from time to time, thenceforth invoked Dzerzhinsky's name when local authorities became obdurate. When, for instance, Soviet officials in Minsk refused to allow the ARA to move into the building assigned to it, Haskell asked Eiduk to have "Mr. Dzerzhinsky or other proper Moscow official" instruct the Minsk authorities in their obligations.[94] The peculiar efficiency of the head of the *Cheka* thus became a valuable asset to the American administrators as they tried to mesh their operations with the Soviet system.

Expansion and Involvement

The growth of the ARA feeding program aroused demands by a variety of Soviet agencies for expansion of ARA services. A local board of health in Mari asked the ARA Medical Division to take over the construction of a new water supply system.[95] The medical staff of a hospital in Kiev requested the American relief organization to "take charge of the hospital and use it as it wills." "The hospital may be taken from the Commissariat of Public Health, in whose charge it is," wrote the doctors, "and given in lease to the A.R.A."[96] The ARA did not avail itself of this unusual opportunity to obtain a medical concession in the Ukraine. It did, however, assure the survival of the Bolshoi Ballet by providing sustenance for its students.[97]

The competition for ARA assistance began almost with the arrival of the first contingent in Russia and included top government organs. On 25 October 1921 the Kalmyk Representation of the People's Commissariat for Nationalities bypassed the Soviet relief commission and petitioned the ARA directly for aid in alleviating "the terrible conditions" of its population.[98] The Mari Representation was more cautious. On 26 October it asked permission of *Pomgol* to communicate with the ARA about a relief program for children.[99] By January 1922 all such requests were channeled through the office of the Soviet representative plenipotentiary. Thus, on 9 January the petition of the Kirghiz Republic was received by Eiduk and passed on to the ARA.[100]

The ARA was permitted, if not actually encouraged, by the central Soviet authorities to take over the feeding of vast areas as its special responsibility, at least as far as the peasants were concerned. The government used its own meager resources to feed what it considered its own constituency. According to the offical Soviet report on the famine, "Beginning in April, when the foreign relief organization began to disburse its help widely to adults, the attention of *Pomgol* was concentrated on giving food relief to union members, government workers, and to feeding the sick."[101] Among the groups omitted were unemployed intellectuals, members of the clergy, and small tradesmen who had not yet been absorbed into private commerce through the New Economic Policy.

University students were included in the government's ration schedule but at a low level of priority. A former professor at the University of Kazan recalled that the ARA provided one hot meal a day for the students, supplementary rations for the employed faculty, and subsistence rations for professors whom the authorities had expelled as "irreconcilable."[102] The Soviet famine report states, "In the university cities, A.R.A. maintains dining-rooms for needy students. Thus, just in Odessa, A.R.A. gave out 107,496 meals in the student dining-rooms in only two months."[103]

The ARA responded to the pleas of institutions, homes, and hospitals by reorganizing sanitary facilities, setting up and supplying hospitals, ambulances, dormitories, and shelters for children.[104] Epidemics in the famine regions were brought under control by a program of mass inoculation under American supervision.[105] The Soviet authorities watched benignly as ARA activities spread into fields not directly connected with food distribution, but, almost inevitably, the American relief organization became involved in government policy itself. On 18 February 1922 Haskell asked the government whether food was being shipped out of the Ufa area. He said that he would not deliver supplies into a region capable of exporting produce. Eiduk denied that such shipments had taken place.[106]

On 18 April the ARA supervisor in Samara complained that the government was not providing sufficient food to the Red Army soldiers assigned to guard relief shipments, and asked ARA headquarters to compel the government to increase the rations.[107] On 11 May the ARA representative at Rybinsk informed Haskell that laborers unloading freight cars were causing long delays in relief distribution. The workers were not under the control of the provincial transportation department but of their own union. As a result, work was slow and discipline impossible to maintain. Finally, the workers went out on strike, and all relief work came to a halt. Quinn complained about the stoppage to Eiduk. On 12 June Eiduk notified the ARA that the strike had been settled by the shipment of additional funds to meet the laborers' demands.[108]

Not all ARA complaints related to problems of food distribution. On 30 June Haskell informed Karl Lander, who replaced Eiduk as Soviet representative, that a union leader had made disparaging remarks about the ARA at a public meeting. Haskell asked for an official repudiation of the insult in the local press. "Furthermore," he wrote, "the individual who has made the unfortunate speech in question should be discredited and punished to show the good faith of the Russian government."[109] In Simbirsk, the ARA district supervisor requested and obtained government action in counteracting "inspired" rumors that ARA food would eventually have to be paid for by the population. The local press published an announcement signed by the supervisor and the Soviet representative stating that the food was an American gift paid for by a congressional appropriation and private donations. A thousand posters with that message were printed and distributed throughout the area.[110]

Soviet appreciation of the ARA's accomplishments was mixed with resentment of its obtrusive presence in the tightly controlled system. When the American staff arrived in Moscow, the local officials requested that all personnel register with the house commandants and report the arrivals and departures of all visitors. In November 1921 Eiduk was still fighting vainly to obtain compliance with this rule.[111] Learning in December that a Russian employee had removed the photographs of Marx, Lenin, Trotsky, and Zinoviev from the walls of an ARA kitchen in Moscow, Eiduk insisted that the ARA restore the portraits and take steps to prevent future "desecrations" at American feeding stations. The ARA accommodated him.[112]

A constant source of irritation was the status of the ARA's Russian employees in Moscow. The countrywide trade union structure had been developed not only as a symbol but as a vital support of the proletarian state. And in 1922 the unions still enjoyed a measure of autonomy as protectors of the rights of workers, although this role was somewhat diminished by the resolutions of the Eleventh Party Congress.[113] Evidently the representative plenipotentiary was subjected to pressure by trade union leaders in Moscow to eliminate the American island of open-shop employment in the capital city, but the ARA resisted recognizing trade union authority over its employees.

On 22 July 1922 Lander informed Quinn that "the question of standardizing the conditions of labor of the A.R.A. employees can no longer be deferred." He pointed out that 75 to 80 percent of these workers belonged to trade unions and insisted that the ARA acknowledge the local union committee as the workers' representative. Lander also demanded that both he and the union committee be notified about the hiring and firing of any employee. Quinn rejected both demands outright as violations of the Riga agreement.[114] In September, Quinn reinforced this stand by discharging a member of the union committee. Lander warned Quinn that this violated existing labor laws under which a worker could not be discharged except for unfitness to perform the work required or for conviction of a crime. Quinn was adamant, and the ARA headquarters and kitchens in Moscow remained nonunion shops.[115]

Soviet officials in Moscow were more tolerant of the privileged Americans than were local liaison representatives. An ARA inspector described the difference in attitudes in a memorandum.

It is the common experience of A.R.A. men that the farther you get from the center, either of the Soviet government itself or of the *Gubernia* or A.R.A. District Headquarters, the greater generally are the difficulties with the local authorities. What might seem reasonable to Lander in Moscow will be disputed by the second-rate representatives sent out by Moscow to the District.[116]

In Orenburg, for instance, the Soviet representative allied himself with local officials in harassing the ARA. According to the ARA district supervisor, the Soviet representative demanded that the ARA feed the Red Army in spite of the specific prohibition in the Riga agreement. The provincial office of the GPU insisted on scrutinizing all ARA correspondence with the central government. The editor of the local railway newspaper was discharged for printing a favorable article about the ARA. The other newspapers in the area remained completely silent on ARA activities. The ARA supervisor reported that the local administrators for *Pomgol* sometimes refused to distribute seed wheat to members of the local ARA committees.[117]

Rumbles of discontent on the part of local officials occasionally broke out into the open in the press. In the summer of 1922, a provincial weekly newspaper commented sarcastically on the "burden of work and worries of the A.R.A." The article criticized the rations given to ordinary people and added: "But the priests of Mariupol eat much better than before. And you say the A.R.A. gives nothing. It gives—how can you say it gives nothing? But to whom?"[118]

During the period of rapid expansion of the ARA's program, both sides tended to smooth over minor difficulties, and the peculiar system of dual sovereignty operated surprisingly well. The government reluctantly accepted the Americans' minor derelictions from the Soviet way of life; the ARA treated the recalcitrance of local officials as a minor nuisance. Disagreement about the food package program, however, pointed up a conflict between the values of two authorities that could not be easily resolved. The Soviet regime saw the ARA-directed remittance program as an instrument for the survival and resuscitation of the last non-Communist groups in Russian society. To the ARA, the packages donated to specific beneficiaries by friends and relatives abroad represented badly needed supplementary assistance. To the sizable section of the population that was not adequately provided for by either the ARA or the government programs, the packages from abroad frequently meant survival itself.

An early clash about remittances to designated groups ended in an agreement whereby the Soviet government was given representation on all directing committees and the ARA agreed not to turn over shipments to any individuals or groups other than those specified by the donor.[119] Even this arrangement, however, ran into difficulty in the case of recipients who were under attack by the regime for one reason or another. On 22 April 1922 the ARA tried to clear a shipment to Patriarch Tikhon of the Russian Orthodox church for distribution, according to the directions of the donor, "at his discretion to the needy and starving people in Russia." Although Eiduk had permitted an earlier shipment to the patriarch, he withheld approval of this and of all others addressed to Tikhon. The patriarch had been arrested at the end of April and charged with advocating resistance to the confiscation of church treasures.[120]

Lander was more cooperative than Eiduk, in most matters, but could not accommodate the ARA in regard to the Tikhon shipments. On 24 June he wrote the ARA supervisor of remittance shipments: "I regret to inform you that I cannot give my approval for delivery of food packages to Patriarch Tikhon on account of the latter's disloyalty and manifestly hostile attitude toward the Government of the Republic, which found expression in open violation of her laws and precepts." In July, Lander agreed to a compromise arrangement. Recognizing that it would be inexpedient to cancel the shipments altogether, he consented to the delivery of the packages to Tikhon's successor for allocation as indicated by the donors.[121]

The Soviet government did not conceal its ideological objections to the remittance program. Kamenev described the program as a source of difficulty because, in the opinion of the government, it brought relief to the bourgeoisie at a time when the ARA was decreasing its assistance to the proletariat.[122] A similar view was reflected in the Soviet report on the famine.

> Out of a total of 393,273 packages received by July 1 of the year, 60 per cent of A.R.A. packages were received by intellectuals, professors, and city residents, leaving 40 per cent for workers and peasants of the countryside and rural areas.
>
> By nationality, the packages were distributed thus: 50 per cent of the total went to Jews, and moreover, not to the poorest ones but to members of the petty bourgeoisie and tradesmen, the remaining 50 per cent to the other nationalities of the R.S.F.S.R.[123]

The figures were accurate. Package contributions and direct relief to Jews, particularly those in the Ukraine, were organized by the American Jewish Joint Distribution Committee (JDC). Half of the general relief funds collected by the JDC was distributed to non-Jewish recipients because only under such an arrangement did the Soviet government permit the Jewish agency to render any assistance at all to Jews. The only other sizable group that benefited from the remittance program consisted of the friends and relatives of Russian émigrés.[124]

The program was allowed to continue only under the closest government surveillance. By agreement with the ARA, all packages valued at over fifty dollars were submitted to the Soviet authorities for approval before delivery. During the period of expansion of the general ARA relief program, this approval, with the exception of the Tikhon shipment, was routinely granted. In this area as in others, agreement by both sides on the broad goal of feeding the starving maintained the precarious balance of powers.

SOVIET LEADERS AND THE EXPANSION
OF THE MISSION

Lenin's initial suspicions about the relief mission abated as the first glowing reports about its work in the famine regions reached the Kremlin. An optimistic Marxist interpretation replaced fear of a new "broad intervention." By establishing themselves as the first to render real help in fighting the famine, the American capitalists, it seemed to Lenin, were seizing the initiative in the race for the Russian market. Hoover's proposal to act as agent for the Soviet government in the purchase of seed from the Balkan countries reinforced Lenin's belief that he meant business—literally. Although on 1 September 1921 Lenin asked Molotov to present this proposal to the Politburo for immediate decision, the Politburo never even discussed the matter.[125]

The next opportunity for expanding the relationship with the ARA came in October in connection with the proposed remittance program. According to the draft agreement, the ARA would be responsible for supplying and shipping the food packages to Russian ports. The Soviet government would transport the parcels at its own expense to ARA warehouses, where recipients would pick them up. The ARA retained the right of refusal to sell food drafts or to deliver parcels to any individual or organization. The Soviet government, however, could refuse to allow delivery only in cases where it had "good and sufficient proof of misuse or speculation."[126]

Opposition to this agreement arose at a Politburo meeting from which Lenin was absent. Stalin apparently convinced the other members that the relief of specifically designated beneficiaries was of no value to the regime. At his suggestion, the Politburo wrote to Lenin on 18 October stating that since the program was a matter of trade and not charity, the government should exact payment for the delivery of the packages to the ARA warehouses.[127] Lenin, however, seemed determined to encourage the Americans to broaden their mission. On 19 October he replied:

> If indeed that is the goal—trade, then we ought to gain that experience, for they are giving us real assistance for the starving and the right of control, and the right of refusal in three months. Therefore, it does not follow that we should take payment for the food and clothing. Establish such control, with the approval of the Politburo, that will combine the hope and capability of supervision over everything.[128]

The remittance agreement was signed in its original form the same day.[129]

Optimism about a new relationship with the United States seemed to dominate Lenin's thinking during this period. He refused Chicherin's suggestion that he resign from the Executive Committee of the Communist International in order to placate Western European opinion. ". . . In my opinion, no compromises or steps are called for. *HOOVER* is really a *plus*," he wrote Chicherin on 16 October.[130] Several days later he advised: "Agreements and concessions with the Americans are super-important to us: with Hoover we have something worthwhile."[131]

The congressional appropriation convinced him that America represented Russia's only real hope for assistance from the capitalist powers. On 23 December he told the delegates to the Ninth All-Russian Congress of Soviets:

> We have been able to collect approximately 300,000 rubles. This is a negligible amount, and in this we see how selfishly the European bourgeoisie has reacted to our famine. . . .
>
> I must inform you that in recent days we have achieved a very considerable success in our struggle against the famine. You have no doubt read that in America twenty million dollars has been appropriated for help to the starving in Russia—on the basis of which the A.R.A. (the American organization for help to the starving) ordinarily gives assistance. Several days ago, we received a telegram from Krasin informing us that the American government proposes to guarantee formally the delivery of food and seed for those 20 million dollars within three months if we agree to disburse from our funds 10

million dollars (20 million gold rubles) toward that goal. We immediately agreed to give that amount and transmitted this by telegraph. So, evidently it can be said that within the first three months we are guaranteed 30 million dollars' worth of food and seed for the starving. This is, of course, little; it by no means wipes out the calamity that has befallen us. This you will understand. But, in any case, this is at least help, which will undoubtedly ease the desperate need, the desperate famine.[132]

Three days later, Lenin told the Congress of Soviets, "Now our main hope is in the agreement proposed to us by the American government."[133] Any distinction between the ARA and the American government was fading; even more noteworthy was the shift in Lenin's attitude toward the ARA since the time of the Riga negotiations. Whatever he may have felt on first receiving Hoover's suggestion for a "contribution" in gold, his speech to the Congress of Soviets was remarkably free of resentment on this score. The entire speech, in fact, seemed to reflect an earnest desire to cast as favorable a light as possible on the American initiative.

Trotsky had no functional connection with famine relief, and the ARA staff reported no personal contact with him. When the mission reached its peak, Trotsky still saw it as a device designed by the American bourgeoisie to test the possibilities of the Russian market. To Anna Louise Strong, a pro-Soviet American correspondent, he declared:

> American capital is situated in a more favorable position than European capital. In spirit, the Americans are empirical; they always try to verify each impression by sight, touch, and taste. The A.R.A., which has given such invaluable help to the starving masses of Russia, at the same time played the part of a highly-qualified feeler, sent forth by the American Government into the very heart of Russia. Better than any other country, America has seen us as we are and now we have only to wait until public opinion of the wealthy classes of America digests the information received and forms its conclusions and consequences.

Soviet Russia would have to wait, he concluded, until the capitalist politicians understood "the necessity of adapting themselves to the Soviet juridical system concerning property instead of awaiting the apocalyptic hour of its fall."[134]

For Hoover, such an understanding would have meant a retreat from his position of 21 March 1921 that there was no possibility of normal trade with a country "under a government that repudiates private property."[135] Nothing that he subsequently said or wrote ever suggested that he had changed his mind. Trotsky's confidence in the imminence of a reversal in American policy was apparently inspired by the extent and success of the ARA effort. His earlier cynicism about "philanthropic missionaries" was absent from this interview. According to one report, however, his general attitude toward the United States had not changed. On 23 April 1922 Goodrich informed Hoover that within high Soviet government circles, Trotsky was considered to be basically hostile toward America.[136]

Kamenev, a leading member of the Politburo as well as head of the government relief commission, continued to work closely with the ARA. When other duties prevented him from personally overseeing the Soviet liaison office, the ARA's difficulties seemed to multiply. Haskell did not always insist on prompt, meticulous performance on the part of Soviet officials, but when a situation became intolerable, he would summon Kamenev and threaten to curtail relief. On one such occasion, according to a Hoover investigator, "Kamenev threw a fit and begged him not to think of sending the wire, saying, 'It would ruin us if the A.R.A. withdrew relief now.'"[137] "Us" may have referred to Kamenev's relief agency, to the Bolshevik regime, or to the famine victims; Kamenev felt the weight of responsibility for all three, and appreciated the ARA's considerable help in lightening the load. On 15 February 1922 he asked a special representative of the ARA to convey his personal gratitude to Hoover and acknowledged that "the help given by America far exceeded the efforts of the combined civilized world." It was his hope, he added, that the ARA's experience in Russia would convince the United States that Soviet Russia was "a country with a great future and vast possibilities of development."[138]

Stalin's near-paranoiac suspicions about foreign organizations were not allayed by the accomplishments of the ARA or by the prospect of a new relationship with the United States. On the eve of the passage of the appropriation bill, he warned:

> But it must not be forgotten that the trading, and all other sorts of missions and associations that are now pouring into Russia, trading with her and aiding her, are at the same time the most efficient spy

agencies of the world bourgeoisie, and that, therefore, the world
bourgeoisie now knows Soviet Russia, knows her weak and strong
sides better than at any time before, a circumstance fraught with grave
danger in the event of new interventionist action.[139]

Stalin had political resources in addition to his influence in the
Politburo that could be used against intrusive foreigners. Through
his leading positions in the Organization Bureau and the Secretariat
of the Party Central Committee, he controlled the assignment and
transfer of key personnel throughout the country. The unanimous
view of former ARA workers polled forty-five years later was that
provincial and local Party officials were by and large hostile toward
the relief mission.[140] Whether this reflected spontaneous animosity or
specific directives is uncertain. What is clear is that Stalin's
suspicions were not reduced by the good works of Hoover's food
missionaries. The record yields not one favorable comment about the
ARA by Stalin.

Bits of evidence suggest that Zinoviev, another member of the
Politburo, remained hostile toward the presence of the ARA in
Petrograd during the period of expansion. In one report, Goodrich
singled out Petrograd as a trouble spot. Local authorities complained
about the ARA supervisor Walker's refusal to work through existing
Soviet relief organizations and about the strain that the increased
number of relief kitchens placed on transportation facilities.[141] During an inspection visit by Rickard and Brown in June 1922,
the Petrograd officials tried to sieze an ARA bakery; they
were stopped only by Soviet troops under orders of the central
government.[142] Whether Zinoviev provoked or knew anything about
this incident is unkown; but he was in charge of the city's government at the time and, according to Walker, considered the presence
of the ARA in Petrograd an insult to the Revolution. In any case, the
ARA staff regarded him as anything but a friend of the relief mission.[143]

In April 1922 Aleksei Rykov and Mikhail Tomsky were elected to
full membership on the Politburo. Rykov, who later succeeded Lenin
as chairman of the Council of People's Commissars, firmly supported the New Economic Policy's emphasis on better commercial
relations with the capitalist world. His influence on other Soviet officials, according to Cyril Quinn's recollections, was considerable
and could generally be counted on to promote cooperation with the

ARA.[144] Tomsky had no direct contact with the American relief group. As the foremost spokesman for the trade unions, he probably resented the ARA's insistence on keeping its Russian employees in a special category outside the jurisdiction of the unions, but he did not intervene openly in the dispute.

At this time, Nikolai Bukharin was a candidate member of the Politburo as well as editor of *Pravda,* which in 1922 carried several violent criticisms of the ARA. On 11 May, for instance, *Pravda* stated that the manager of the ARA's food package division had ordered all employees to report for work as usual on 1 May—a day officially observed as a state holiday in Soviet Russia. One worker was discharged for disobeying the order. The writer commented:

Let this serve as an example that proves that the Americans, like the other European capitalists, are not here to rescue the starving, to improve the condition of the workers. Oh, no. They are preparing chains and a noose for them. Therefore, workers, be on guard. Since we are forced to work together with bourgeois Europe and America because of the destruction and economic conditions, we must be on guard, and, at the first attempt to slip handcuffs and a noose on us, we must do the same in return.[145]

Eiduk was evidently embarrassed by the unrestrained attack on his "partners" in the rescue enterprise and came to the ARA's defense in *Izvestia.*

There was a time—and we can now look back to it without compunction or sadness in a spirit of emotional neutrality—when our joint effort with the A.R.A. was somewhat clouded by a film of mutual distrust, which was quite natural, given the environment of the exceptionally peculiar interplay between the Soviet Republic and America. The importance of the problem with which both we and the A.R.A. are confronted and the tremendous moral responsibility involved in our common work, however, have brought us together at closer range, and the effective work which has clearly emerged has smoothed the rough patches of the road . . . .

I would like to emphasize also one more important aspect of the work of the A.R.A.—the political role played by this organization in our favor abroad. The prominent leaders of the A.R.A. and many of its members and co-workers are constantly in close touch with America and Western Europe. Their stay within the territory of the Soviet Republic affords them the best facilities to study at close range things as they are in Russia. . . . When they go beyond the frontiers of Russia, these observers present public opinion in foreign countries graphic, impartial, and unvarnished information. I can cite many instances of this. The times of silly, insipid, and outrageous yarns about Russia are gone. I shall note especially in this connection the copious information presented by Governor Goodrich of Indiana, who is soon expected back in Russia. As a special case in point, I shall refer to Mr. Truesdale, an A.R.A. correspondent, who spent several months in Russia. I shall mention now Colonel Haskell, a truly reliable source of information on all new developments in Russia. He is quite a magnet for foreign correspondents and really up to date on all current events. . . .

In closing, I would like to say a few words about a minor incident that arose evidently due to a misunderstanding. The other day, *Pravda* published a story about an alleged "American" here in Moscow who objected to the A.R.A.'s employees' observing May 1 as the International Labor Holiday. Now, as a matter of fact, it was not the Americans who opposed this but one of their employees who acted on his own out of lack of circumspection and discretion in handling such a delicate matter involving political tact. We cannot but believe Colonel Haskell that generalities drawn from this particular case do not reflect the true nature of the entire matter.[146]

If this was intended as a hint from higher echelons that *Pravda* should view the indiscretions of the Americans with greater understanding, its editors failed to get the message. On 8 June the Party newspaper charged the same ARA supervisor with violating Soviet labor law in firing two women, one pregnant and the other convalescent.

Why are all these violations allowed? Are the Russian workers employed by the A.R.A. under the protection of laws defending labor in the Soviet Republic? Or must those who work for American organizations be subjected to American laws for the protection of labor.[147]

In August 1922, when ARA relief work was at its peak, *Pravda* criticized the staff in charge of the remittance program for providing the administrative personnel of a formerly American-owned company with food packages sent by the expropriated owner, describing the gifts as an American move to regain ownership of the factory.[148]

Since Bukharin was at least technically responsible for what appeared in *Pravda,* it may be surmised that he was not among the Bolshevik leaders who experienced a change of heart about the ARA. In the case of Karl Radek, however—the other candidate member of the Politburo—a transformation in attitude was clearly evident. On 25 October 1921 Radek had excoriated the capitalist world for allowing "millions of people to die of starvation when they had plenty with which to help them," entirely omitting mention of the ARA relief. "Such a world," he concluded, "must be destroyed."[149]

Later on, however, according to Cyril Quinn, Radek became quite friendly with the ARA directors in Moscow and joined Kamenev in supporting the ARA in discussions at the ruling center.[150] In December 1922 Hoover's special representative, Frank Golder, reported:

Radek and I have become quite chummy and he was over for dinner at the Pink House to-night and talked most interestingly to the boys. . . . We are going to keep him supplied with American books of political importance and if there is no other fund your servant will foot the bill. It is exceedingly important for us to keep in good relations.[151]

One of the topics discussed over dinner was the disagreement among leading Bolsheviks about whether to allow the ARA to come to Russia. Radek said that some leaders were afraid the Americans would learn too much about Soviet Russia. Others argued that this was unavoidable and entirely necessary if normal relations with the United States were to be renewed. Radek said that he had joined other leaders in refuting the view that Hoover's goal was to discredit the Soviet regime. They argued that since Hoover was an organizer, his chief interest was "in construction and not destruction."[152]

The heads of such important commissariats as finance, foreign affairs, and trade shared Lenin's hope that the ARA's expanded program presaged a new era in Soviet-American relations. As American assistance increased, however, and the Harding administration showed no signs of initiating closer relations with Russia, Foreign Commissar Chicherin began to suspect that the U.S. relief offer was primarily humanitarian. "America is a riddle," he wrote on 28 January 1922. Everything seemed to be pushing her toward closer ties with Soviet Russia, but in spite of the efforts of "a group of brilliant Republican senators such as Hiram Johnson and Borah," the Republican administration was not moving in that direction. Chicherin noted that "former tsarist diplomatic circles and bourgeois emigrants" still exerted strong influence in Washington. As long as this went on, he commented, the superb assistance rendered by the ARA "is obliged to assume a purely philanthropic character."[153]

Krasin, the commissar of foreign trade, saw the relief mission as a major breakthrough in the Soviet campaign to end the country's political isolation and to reenter the world of international trade. In June 1922 he expressed to a Hoover representative his deep appreciation of the efficiency and value of the ARA's work in Russia.[154] Later that month, Goodrich wrote to Hoover about his meeting with a group of government officials consisting of Commissar of Finance Grigori Sokolnikov, Kamenev, Litvinov, Rykov, and Krasin. All those present, including Goodrich, had shown a keen interest in using the ARA to arrange some kind of rapprochement between the United States and Soviet Russia. The Soviet officials seemed willing to meet American terms as outlined by Secretary Hughes in his note to Litvinov of 25 March 1921.[155] The Hughes note had reaffirmed Hoover's declaration of 21 March that there was no basis for trade relations with Russia until the Soviet government presented evidence that its economic system had undergone a fundamental change in regard to "the protection of persons and property."[156] Goodrich was convinced that the American relief mission was pushing the Soviet government toward undertaking such a change.

During the spring and summer of 1922, the pro-ARA partisans among the top Bolshevik leaders were on solid ground. By May, 5 million Russians, including 3 million adults, were receiving daily ARA rations; in August, the total number fed rose to 10.5 million. At this time, approximately 180 Americans were supervising 18,073 ARA kitchens in twenty-five provinces from the Ukraine to Asia. Almost 5,000 institutions, including 1,837 hospitals, were being supplied with medicine and other necessities.[157] On 14 July 1922 the director-general of the ARA, Edgar Rickard, announced, "As a result of [the ARA's] efforts, the famine is dead and the Russian people live."[158] Two months later, the Soviet government declared, "As a result of [the government's] extraordinary measures the backbone of the famine has been broken."[159]

As it turned out, the celebration was premature. And since the only real consensus that had been reached was on the necessity of working in harmony to defeat the famine, the belief that the crisis was over was bound to affect the unique rivalry-partnership. The Bolsheviks' ambivalence toward the relief mission had never been fully resolved. In some Soviet officials, an inner battle raged between ordinary common sense awareness of the importance and success of the ARA effort and dogmatic denial that the bourgeois world was capable of real concern for the fate of the masses, especially those who had thrown off the capitalist yoke. Dr. Herschel Walker observed:

> The government's appreciation of the A.R.A. is very difficult to describe. . . . In a personal talk with a government official in an intimate manner, the official would undoubtedly express his true mind and say that the A.R.A. is doing a great deal of good and saving many children that would otherwise have died of starvation. However, the minute he thinks of his government or the present ruling party, his attitude toward the ARA changes, and he says that the bringing in of food is only a cloak to hide their desires, either commercial or political, and that the amount of food brought in, expressed monetarily, is nothing for so rich a country as the United States.[160]

This ambivalence was personified in the division among the top Soviet leadership. Only Lenin could command continued cooperation with the Americans once the famine crisis was overcome. But in May 1922 he suffered his first stroke. On 6 June Haskell wrote to Hoover that Lenin was dying, that the end would come "any day, certainly within a few weeks," and that it was impossible to predict whether Trotsky and military communism would take over or whether there would be an acceleration of the movement to the right.[161]

Lenin survived the stroke but was incapacitated for weeks. Kamenev acted as chairman of the Council of People's Commissars during the long periods of Lenin's illness in 1922 and 1923. During this period, Stalin consolidated his hold on the Party organization. The economic and diplomatic agreements with the United States that Lenin had expected were not materializing. In a literal sense, too, the climate in Russia had changed: all signs indicated a good harvest.

—6—

The Politics of Retreat

THE DIFFICULT DECISION

In April 1922 Hoover seemed "firmly resolved" to withdraw the relief mission from Russia within six months. Weather conditions appeared normal, and since there was every indication that the Soviet government would soon enter into trade relations with other countries in Europe, Hoover could see no reason to continue "charitable assistance" beyond the next harvest.[1] But as the ARA historian pointed out at the time, cutting off relief was certain to arouse great controversy. Other relief organizations would insist that the emergency was not over. The Soviet government would corroborate this and belittle the effectiveness of the ARA. ARA people in the field would be equally pessimistic since they would tend to "see only the small picture." Correspondents from hostile newspapers and other eyewitnesses would spread horror stories that would contest the statistics compiled by the ARA. Finally, there would be critics who would argue that the decision to terminate relief was political, that the organization was continuing its work in Austria, Poland, and Czechoslovakia, where conditions were not as bad as in Soviet Russia.[2] The ARA's European director put the matter bluntly. Any move to end operations in Russia, wrote Brown, would lend support to "radicals and counter-revolutionists, the 'I-told-you-so' press and politicians in the U.S.A."[3]

Hoover did not need reminding that disengagement had perils; but to continue relief when the emergency was over violated what he considered the basic principle of famine relief. "Relief must be confined to averting actual starvation," his second-in-command,

132

Edgar Rickard, declared to a group of mining engineers. "The American Relief Administration [is] not concerned in the provisioning of any country."[4] The Chief had, indeed, fashioned the ARA as a rescue team and not as a social welfare agency. In fact, he was skeptical about the ultimate benefits of nonemergency relief, even when it was dispensed by groups other than his own.

Hoover's top staff agreed that the famine crisis was over. During April and May, assessments of the food situation in Russia were solicited from all the district supervisors and forwarded to New York headquarters. Without a single dissent, the supervisors agreed that ARA assistance would not be needed after the harvest.[5] In June, Goodrich, Rickard, Herter, Brown, Haskell, and Quinn unanimously confirmed this judgment and concluded that any food sent into the area of operations after the harvest would, in effect, be appropriated by the Soviet government in the form of taxes. They further agreed that outright termination of the mission, rather than a reduction in scale, would be best. Haskell wrote:

> Continuation on a reduced scale will mean criticism from all radical elements of Russia and America because of not doing enough, et cetera, and . . . all conservative groups will criticize the American Relief Administration for supporting the Soviet government beyond the famine emergency. . . . We request your final decision.[6]

Hoover promptly notified the secretary of state that "the great famine in Russia is over with the present harvest" and that it was time for the ARA to quit. He suggested that the American Red Cross take over a reduced relief program in Russia in order to "maintain the fine spirit imported into Russia" by the ARA. Continuing assistance in this manner would have a "lasting effect on the relationship [between] the two peoples." Otherwise, he wrote, the departure of the ARA would mean abandoning the field to "irresponsible organizations, chiefly of communistic inspiration, incapable of efficient or honest management and administration of supplies filled with misrepresentation both of the American and of the Russian people."[7]

The plan never materialized. On 12 July he told his top aides not to assume that he had decided to withdraw the ARA from Russia. That determination would be made at a top-level conference of ARA officials in New York. In the meantime, the staff was to proceed with "demobilization from general famine relief . . . as rapidly and rigidly as possible," since the ARA had "no resources to continue [on the] present scale a moment beyond the arrival of the new harvest."[8]

On 30 July ARA field directors met with the headquarters staff in New York to discuss the future course of Russian relief. The conferees included, among others, Hoover, Haskell, Rickard, Goodrich, Brown, and Herter. The decision was to continue the mission to Russia after the harvest but on a greatly reduced scale. Hoover had evidently concluded that the risks involved in maintaining the ARA in Russia were less than the dangers presented by an abrupt withdrawal. It was a surprising reversal of the position adopted a month earlier. The plan adopted in New York contemplated closing out the feeding of adults by 1 September. Assistance to children would be restricted to areas of acute need, with particular emphasis on large cities, where the capability of the Soviet government to take care of the victims of war and famine was seen as doubtful. The food remittance program was to continue as before.[9]

The compromise between prompt termination and a full-scale relief program created new problems. To the Bolshevik leaders, the ARA's operations in Moscow and Petrograd and the food remittance program had always been the least palatable aspects of the mission. To continue these programs while curtailing overall assistance placed an additional burden on ARA supervisors, who already sensed "ingratitude" on the part of Soviet officials. As the general situation improved in Russia, the need to accommodate the Americans diminished.

The New York decisions were officially put into effect on 12 September 1922. According to a directive sent to all district supervisors, adults were no longer to be included in the relief program; the number of children to be fed at ARA kitchens was reduced to one million.[10] A week later, the individual ration was reduced by one-third. On 30 September rations for hospital personnel were discontinued because Haskell considered the Soviet hospitals greatly overstaffed. At the same time, he instructed that food was to be turned over in raw form to local institutions but segregated from other supplies, identified as ARA rations, and distributed as such.[11]

Along with the reduction in aid, the 12 September directive ordered a radical change in the method of operations. The ARA would no longer try to maintain itself as a completely insular body but would use its resources to strengthen and develop local institutions, such as hospitals and children's shelters. According to the directive, this program would help soften the shock of eventual withdrawal. It was anticipated that the ARA would remain in Russia at least through the winter but not after the harvest of 1923.

THE SECRETARY OF COMMERCE
AND THE RUSSIAN MARKET

During the spring and summer of 1922, representatives of the Soviet and European governments met at Genoa and then at The Hague to explore the problems connected with restoring Russia to membership in the international trading community. The United States refused to attend either conference. To a certain degree, America's aloofness reflected the secretary of commerce's belief that as long as Russia clung to its "foolish system," it would remain in economic slough and therefore have no products to trade.

Ironically, Hoover's own efforts in fighting the famine were contributing substantially to economic recovery in Russia. The easing of the food crisis gave the Soviet government breathing space in which to implement the New Economic Policy. With the legalization of private trade in consumer goods and a free market in farm products, the country's economy was beginning to revive. Although the partial restoration of property rights was far from the "radical transformation" of the system that Hoover posed as an absolute necessity for economic revival, the new approach at least promised better things to come. "A decided change has taken place," Rickard told a group of mining engineers in New York on 4 May 1922, "and will continue to take place, looking toward a more sensible form of government control." He cited the abandonment of the *Cheka* and the codification of criminal law as moves in the right direction, but he concluded that there was not yet real protection of property rights in Russia and therefore no basis for recognition of the Soviet government.[12]

As secretary of commerce, Hoover was impelled to explore, however cautiously, the possibilities of trade with Soviet Russia under existing conditions. In response to an inquiry by Secretary of State Hughes on the advisability of admitting a Soviet trade representative named Matvei Skobelev to the United States, Hoover wrote:

Generally, if the Soviet government wishes to open a purchasing agency in the United States we should agree. Manifestly we cannot agree to their opening an agency that is intended to promote revolution or carry forward transactions that even indirectly promote these ends.

Hoover added that if the Soviet leaders intend only trade, it should be tried. He suggested that the public be informed about the case of Ludwig Martens (an unofficial Soviet representative who was deported in 1920 for subversive activities' to serve as "a warning to our commercial public in their transactions."[13]

Hughes was more hesitant about allowing a communist representative to enter the United States. He noted that since Martens' deportation, no agent of the Soviet government had been admitted and that "the experience with Mr. Martens creates a certain presumption in favor of adherence to this precedent." Hughes proposed further investigation of Skobelev's past activities, but he did not rule out relaxation of current American policy. "This Government desires . . . to place no avoidable obstacle in the way of the consummation of such legitimate trade between the United States and Russia as may prove practicable in the existing circumstances."[14]

The two leaders of nonrecognition opinion within the administration seemed to be moving reluctantly toward some sort of commercial relationship with Soviet Russia. The channels of communication with the Soviet leadership opened by the ARA offered the most practical means to explore the subject.

The Proposed American Commission

At this time, James Goodrich was the most ardent advocate of renewed American-Soviet relations within ARA circles. On 20 June 1922 he suggested setting up a commission of American experts to make a survey of the Soviet economy.[15] In September, Haskell discussed the project with Kamenev, who said that he would welcome such a commission but that other high government figures saw the proposal as an affront to the dignity of the Soviet state. "It must be remembered," he told Haskell, "that Russia was one of the large nations of the world, that, after all, they were not a lot of wild animals and that they were responsible to a very proud and patriotic people whose sovereignty would have to be respected." He then described the kind of opposition that the plan faced. Trotsky, for instance, maintained that such an investigation was superfluous, that the ARA already had some two hundred of its people in the field conducting precisely such a survey. Haskell replied that the ARA's investigations were concerned only with relief matters and were not economic or political in character.[16]

Trotsky, however, was correct. The reports filed by ARA directors, supervisors, inspectors, historians, and special representatives were not restricted to relief but encompassed most aspects of the Russian scene in which an economic commission might be interested. The Soviet government knew of these investigations—indeed, made them possible by expediting all the necessary arrangements. To create another investigative agency appeared to the Soviet leaders as another device designed to humiliate the regime and delay the establishment of normal relations. In a scathing editorial on 19 September *Izvestia* defended the government's refusal to countenance a "one-sided commission." The United States was denounced for maintaining a "dog-in-the-manger" policy on trade with Russia. Furthermore, the writer declared, American relief did not give the United States unlimited rights in Russia.[17] For *Izvestia,* it was an unusual slap at the ARA.

Frank Golder nevertheless continued to probe the possibilities of an American commission. On 20 September he passed on to Hoover Krasin's suggestion that a comparable Russian commission be permitted to visit the United States. During the course of the conversation, Krasin had confided to Golder that the Soviet leaders preferred an association with the United States to one with any other country and had shown this by exempting American factories from expropriation.[18] On 2 October Golder reported that he had no news of further progress on the proposed commission but stated that it would be advisable to send such a group into Russia at the earliest possible moment.

> Conditions here are bad and are now growing worse, but I feel it is merely the darkness before the dawn. Our friends the Communists will be forced to give up tinkering and undertake really constructive work on a private ownership basis or on such conditions as capital can accept. By the time our Commission has fully informed itself the Soviet government will be ready to talk sense and then we can get down to business.[19]

The efforts of Goodrich and Golder to pave the way for a resumption of trade through a fact-finding commission failed. Nevertheless, Hoover's representatives kept the lines open to the

Soviet leadership in an effort to determine if it were really possible to "get down to business" with the Bolshevik regime.

The ARA and the Urquhart Concession

Department of Commerce and ARA officials kept Hoover informed on the progress of the negotiations between the Soviet government and Hoover's former business associate, Leslie Urquhart, for a far-reaching concession in Russia. The Urquhart concession was seen in international financial and government circles as a test case advanced by the British government to determine the usefulness of the Anglo-Russian Trade Agreement of 1921. According to a report transmitted to Hoover in December 1921, however, Urquhart was a far from reliable instrument for testing Soviet sincerity. One of his associates in the Russo-Asiatic Corporation was quoted as saying that:

> Mr. Urquhart had great hope but little expectation that he would be successful, and that he went through with it after the preliminary negotiations in order to demonstrate in a practical manner to the British public the impossibility of making honorable engagements with the Soviet authorities, or engaging in any business enterprise in Russia under their present regime.

The report went on to describe an interview in which Urquhart declared that he had no desire to sign a contract with the Russians but that he hesitated to refuse for fear of possible reprisal by the Soviet secret police, who, he claimed, kept him under strict surveillance at all times and thus inhibited his freedom of choice during the negotiations.[20]

In spite of Urquhart's dubious credentials as a forthright petitioner in the cause of Western capital, Hoover followed the course of his year-long quest for a concession with keen interest. On 2 June 1922 Goodrich reported that he had met with Urquhart in Paris and spent an entire morning discussing the Russian situation with him. According to Urquhart, the American government was well advised not to participate in international conferences with the Soviet government; in a very short time the United States would be in a position to exert "decisive influence" on Soviet affairs independently.[21] On 13 June a

member of the ARA staff in Moscow informed New York headquarters about a conversation between Rickard and Urquhart during
the ARA director-general's visit to the Russian capital. Urquhart
was reported to have told Rickard that American relief was still
desperately needed and that the ARA could "draw heavily on that
fact in putting over any deals we might care to make."[22] On 30
August Herter transmitted to the State Department the terms of the
tentative agreement reached between Urquhart and the Soviet
minister of foreign trade. According to Herter, the information had
been obtained from a member of the corporation.

The property involved in the concession was the vast tract in
Siberia that Hoover had managed with huge success when he was a
director of the Russo-Asiatic Corporation before the war. The terms
of the contract included a substantial reimbursement to the British
firm for losses incurred during the period of confiscation, the grant of
a 99-year lease on the firm's former property, immunity from Soviet
labor laws, and exemption from all export duties. These benefits
were granted to the corporation in return for a royalty of 7.5 percent
in lieu of all local and national taxes. The "member of the corporation" commented that "this is less than we had to pay under the
old regime at Kyshtim."[23]

On 30 September Haskell notified Hoover that, according to
Krasin, "the conditions laid down for Urquhart are entirely satisfactory and were accepted without complaint."[24] One week later,
however, the Soviet press announced that the agreement had been
rejected by the Council of People's Commissars because of strained
relations with the British government. "It can be argued," declared
Pravda, "that Urquhart is only a private individual and that he is in
no way responsible for the actions of the British government. This,
however, is not the case. Mr. Urquhart is the real 'master' of
capitalist England and its ruling oligarchy."[25] From London, Golder
commented:

> In this morning's paper, I notice also that Urquhart's concession
> has been turned down as I had feared. I think the turn-down of the
> concession was due rather to the influence of the Left wing rather than
> to international politics, the last merely was an excuse, but I may be
> mistaken.[26]

Hoover's warning to Urquhart in March 1921 that the Soviet

government would have to move much farther to the right before profitable concessions could be established was fully vindicated. In 1923, Hoover's tireless opponent, Senator France, accused him of having used reduction of ARA relief as a threat to support his former associate's quest for a concession. This charge is not supported by the sequence of events in 1922. The final decision to curtail relief was made in July, almost two months before the signing of the Urquhart agreement. In his reply to Senator France, Hoover cited a telegram dated 28 August 1922 that was written at his dictation and delivered to the Soviet authorities by the Moscow office of the ARA.

> Press reports purported made in Berlin by representatives of the Russo-Asiatic that I had some interest in their business absolutely untrue. Please inform Chicherin that if such representations were made to him they were no doubt for purposes of influencing his judgment. My interests were sold years before the Bolshevik revolution and I have no property interests or claims on Russia in any shape or form.[27]

Hoover's uncomplimentary reference to Urquhart's representative may have been interpreted by the Bolshevik leadership as a hint that the American secretary of commerce did not favor preemption of Russia's resources by British interests and that Moscow could reject Urquhart's bid without fear of an adverse effect on American relief. It is doubtful, however, that Hoover's actions influenced Soviet decisions on the Urquhart concession. According to an observer who was in Chicherin's confidence in 1927, Lenin had changed his mind three times about the concession before vetoing it for reasons quite unrelated to Hoover or to American relief.[28] In any case, Hoover had fulfilled his obligations to the American business community in carrying out by remote control a tortuous research on the hazards of foreign business ventures in Soviet Russia. The fate of the Urquhart concession served to confirm his original judgment that the Bolsheviks were not yet ready to enter into serious trade relations.

OVERSIGHT AND INFLUENCE IN RUSSIA

When Hoover undertook the relief of Russia, he looked upon the Soviet government as the temporary guardian of a nation in acute need of assistance. He was willing to extend help upon formal application by the guardian, and the first horrifying reports of the famine provided sufficient certification of need. When he decided to carry on a reduced relief program after the harvest of 1922, he gave up his role as famine-fighter and assumed the more prosaic responsibilities of a welfare agency specializing in supplemental assistance to dependent children. In recognition of this change, he relinquished some of the traditional prerogatives of the ARA, such as total independence and isolation of its functions from those of the government. At the same time, however, he assumed some of the rights that a social welfare agency normally exercises in respect to indigent clients. This involved inquiry into the available resources of the guardian and their disposition, and protection of the interests of the dependent children. Inevitably, these new responsibilities injected the ARA into vital areas of Soviet policy-making at a time when American relief was still desirable but no longer critical.

The Export Controversy

A major conflict between the ARA and Soviet authorities was presaged by a report delivered by V. G. Mikhailovsky, director of the Statistical Department of the Moscow Soviet, on 1 August 1922. Mikhailovsky told a gathering of representatives from the top government economic agencies that there was no home market for the expected grain surplus because of the virtual absence of manufactured goods to offer the farmers in exchange. The best solution was to sell the surplus in the foreign market, where the prospects of a good profit were assured by the high price of American grain. This move would restore Russia's position in the world grain market and raise the level of the domestic economy generally.

The proposal was vigorously opposed by some of the conference participants. They argued that it was premature to talk about exporting grain when a substantial part of the country was experiencing a shortage of food. "Our wheat exports," said one opponent, "should not be promoted against the hungry stomach of our Russian peasant and worker." Mikhailovsky replied that there was no legal way to deprive the prosperous peasant of his surplus and distribute it to his less fortunate neighbor. If this produce were not sold abroad, it would pile up in the barns and be of no use to anyone.[29]

Within the following two months, ARA representatives at the major Soviet ports substantiated rumors that preparations for such export grain shipments were well advanced.[30] Hoover was confronted by a difficult problem. Could the U.S. secretary of commerce continue to ship American grain to a country that was planning to dispose of a grain surplus in competition with American producers? To the head of the ARA, the question appeared in a different light. Was not a welfare client obliged to exhaust all available resources before accepting charity from a relief agency?

Hoover first broached the latter question in regard to the crown jewels, then in the possession of the Soviet government, and church treasures that had been confiscated, ostensibly to augment the government's relief fund. On 26 September 1922 he asked Haskell to demand from the Soviet government an accounting of the value of these resources.[31] On 25 October he raised the subject of the surplus grain. "The first obligation of a government," he wrote, "is to prevent starvation of its people and only when every resource of the government has been exhausted can there be a rightful or successful call for . . . charity."[32]

In response to Hoover's first demand, Lander presented Haskell with a balance sheet that indicated an expenditure of less than $1 million for relief representing the bulk of the proceeds from church confiscations.[33] Kamenev had previously assured Haskell that the value of the church treasures had been greatly exaggerated.[34] On the more important subject of grain exports, Kamenev revealed to Haskell on 6 November that the government expected to ship approximately $50 million worth of grain abroad.[35]

Although American assistance had diminished considerably by this time—the ARA was feeding about one million children daily—the Soviet government was reluctant to see the mission terminated entirely. On 9 November Kamenev met with Haskell to find some way to reconcile Hoover's demands with Soviet economic policy. His government, he told Haskell, expected to realize only $10 to $15 million from the export of grain, and the money was urgently needed to finance the purchase of machinery to operate the country's mines. The government was willing, however, to pledge the crown jewels and some of the confiscated church property to obtain a loan in that amount if these assets could be guaranteed against foreign claimants. The proceeds would then be used for famine relief and for the purchase of cotton needed by the textile industry. If such a loan could be negotiated, the Soviet government would prohibit all grain export until the next harvest.[36]

Predictably, Hoover rejected out of hand the suggestion that he take the initiative to ease the Soviet government's financial difficulties. On 18 November he vented his outrage at the Soviet export plans.

> . . . The A.R.A. . . . must protest against the inhumanity of a government policy of exporting food from starving people in order that through such exports it may secure machinery and raw material for the economic improvement of the survivors. Any such action imposes the direct responsibility for the death of millions of people upon the government authorities.[37]

This stern condemnation of Soviet policy was sent to Haskell for communication to the appropriate authorities. The cable was not released for publication, nor did it include a threat to end, or even diminish, ARA assistance. In the absence of such pressure, Soviet leaders decided to go ahead with their plans.

Despite the obvious incongruities of the situation, there was logic behind the Soviet stand. The collapse of the Genoa and Hague conferences had foreclosed all possibility of obtaining credits for the purchase of badly needed tools and machinery on which the rural and industrial economies depended for recovery. The necessary capital could be raised only by selling grain abroad. There was also a practical reason to refrain from trying to acquire the grain surplus for famine relief through arbitrary requisition or exorbitant taxation. The bitter 1920–21 experience had demonstrated that such measures were ultimately counterproductive; their readoption might lead to another famine in 1923, in which case Hoover could reasonably accuse the Bolsheviks of having brought on a new catastrophe by destroying the peasants' incentives. Whether he would come to the rescue of Russia again was doubtful.

The Soviet government won its gamble because Hoover's concern for his charges in the famine area was not the kind of responsibility that he could shed with an indignant cablegram. Reports of extreme privation poured into the Moscow headquarters from ARA supervisors in the Ukraine and the Volga region. In December 1922, when Haskell proposed an expansion in relief to include three million children, Hoover agreed.[38]

The increase in ARA shipments over the next five months was dwarfed by the amount of grain exported from Russia. By May 1923 Olga D. Kameneva, the leading member of a new Soviet relief commission, reported that some 400,000 tons of farm products had been shipped abroad so far that year. Recovery of the economy without the export of wheat, declared Kameneva, was "absolutely unthinkable." She acknowledged that some of this grain came from areas adjacent to famine regions and that the simultaneous export and import of grain represented a waste of transportation facilities. But she attributed the paradoxical situation to the policies of "foreign relief organizations." These groups, she claimed, would have been more effective if they had used their money to buy grain within Russia for their relief programs but that since their purposes were not strictly humanitarian, the Soviet government was unable to persuade them to alter their policy.[39] Hoover, apparently, was equally powerless to alter the Soviet government's policy in respect to the exportation of grain.

The ARA and Soviet Tax Policy

On 14 September the ARA district supervisor at Tsaritsyn complained to the Moscow office that the government had assessed the rural district of Nikolaevsk an amount that exceeded the total crop of the area. "While it may very well be that we have nothing to say with regard to the government's program," he wrote, "it is our business what is done after the tax is collected."[40] The ARA inspector sent to the scene to investigate notified the central office on 4 October that the supervisor's estimate of the crop and of the needs of the population was accurate but that his figures on the tax collections were "a bit out of proportion." He commented, however, that "the essential and apparently undeniable fact is that any tax whatsoever on the district is unjust and even criminal."[41]

Applying New Economic Policy principles of private property and free trade in grain while portions of the country were still starving had placed the Soviet government in a peculiar dilemma. Even within the famine area, there were some relatively prosperous districts in the fall of 1922, and in the less fortunate districts there were some relatively prosperous peasants. The government was reluctant to levy a steep progressive tax on the more productive areas and peasants for fear of removing incentive to sow the fields. Thus, the new tax in kind fell on all districts and peasants except the entirely destitute. From Pugachov, which was described as the worst locality of the worst province after the 1922 harvest, came reports by ARA representatives that government officials were intimidating peasants in an effort to extract exorbitant grain taxes.[42] An article in *Izvestia* on 5 October 1922 confirmed that such districts were not immune from taxation. Without a trace of irony, the writer announced that the famine area was required to pay only one-half of the supplemental tax levied for famine relief.[43]

The ARA Moscow headquarters noted these apparent dislocations and registered its concern about the government's tax policies. On 13 December the ARA asked Soviet authorities to supply detailed information on the amount and disposition of the grain tax collected during the year, the official estimate of the crop in areas receiving ARA relief, and the outcome of the government's export plans.[44]

In Samara, ARA representatives intervened more directly in behalf of the poorer peasants. At the height of the famine, when all the inhabitants were in great need, the owners of horses did not object to free use of their property for the transportation of relief supplies. After the harvest, however, the better-off peasants found more profitable use for their horses and refused to make them available to the ARA. They also put pressure on the local government to close ARA stations, which were cutting into the private trade in grain by distributing food free. The authorities reacted favorably to the demands of the more affluent peasants because the central government had ordered a drive to reduce the number of foreign relief installations.

The ARA was thus placed in the odd position of defending the poorer peasants against the free-enterprise policies of the Communist government. The American relief workers mobilized the poor of the area and, in at least one instance, the local militia as well, in requisitioning the horses of the more prosperous peasants for the transportation of grain from the ARA warehouses to the kitchens. The district supervisor noted sardonically, "It is rather difficult to convict an organization of bourgeois activities which so drastically requires communist cooperation of all peasants and the aid of the rich to the poor. . . ."

An ARA inspector who visited the area in February took sharp issue with this violation of the hallowed principles of private property. In his report to Moscow, he condemned the temporary expropriation of the wealthier peasants who had "by hard work, superior ability, and thrift, kept their heads at least above water." A more constructive course of action, he wrote, would have been to tax the entire village for the cost of transportation. This, he declared, would be beneficial "from the point of view of education in self-government."[45] Several months later, he took a closer look at the consequences of the government's "reversal of attitude toward rich and poor peasants." He found that the government's regulations for the distribution of seed discriminated against peasants who were too poor to own a horse. He commented:

> Now that the government has abandoned them, there seems to be nobody in the wide world to help the poorest peasants except the American Relief Administration; and out in the districts it often comes to a strange anomaly—the A.R.A. inspector says to the representatives of the Communist government when village difficulties arise over transport etc., "We're helping your poor for you—come now, squeeze the rich again!" to which the government representative replies, in effect, "We can only give you very limited support in your difficulty, because we are trying to build up a class of strong peasants and we cannot afford to burden them for the benefit of the weaker peasants, who can be of no help to us."[46]

While Soviet leaders resisted ARA pressure to change official policies, Hoover was engaged in countering the adverse effects of the relief mission on his own policies. This included, ironically enough, limiting the influence of Russian relief on American attitudes toward Russia.

REACTIONS ON THE HOME FRONT

The ARA's judgment that the famine was over—an estimate in which the Soviet government concurred—harmonized with Hoover's policies at home. The announcement that the crisis had passed would presumably remove the basis for public appeals and campaigns by "irresponsible groups." The picture of peaceful cooperation between

Americans and Bolsheviks—an image that Hoover had himself fostered by suppressing all news about conflicts with the Soviet regime—would fade as interest in American relief died out. Thus, one powerful support for the movement in favor of recognition of Russia would be seriously undermined. Discussion of official policies toward Russia would again be confined to smaller and more manageable groups within government.

But the ARA staff had foreseen that any decision involving Hoover and Soviet Russia would arouse public controversy. The anti-Hoover forces, lacking influence at the centers of power, reached out to the public through leaflets, the liberal and radical press, mass meetings, and pro-Soviet relief committees. As a result, more people joined the attack on Hoover and on administration policy toward Russia. To Hoover, this was an ominous development. Before the Russian mission, he had successfully projected an image of disinterested, even heroic, dedication to the cause of fighting famine. The *Nation* freely acknowledged his virtuosity in the public relations area when it congratulated the Soviet leadership for displaying "a genius for publicity which only Mr. Hoover in the Western world can rival."[47] Now, in 1922, he was faced with the bitter prospect of having to defend what was undoubtedly his most successful achievement in famine relief against a new attack elicited by his decision to curtail relief.

Hoover's public relations office was the States Organization Division of the ARA, which, with the assistance of the Historical Division, devoted itself to fostering a favorable image of the ARA and its Chief. Under the direction of George Barr Baker, this division undertook the task of responding in kind to more violent attacks and to marshaling unanimity on broad policy within the ARA. As Hoover's difficulties multiplied during the last stage of the mission to Russia, Baker's office was increasingly called upon to defend the Chief's policies and to carry the attack to the enemy.[48]

Except for a few eccentrics like Henry Ford, conservatives in the United States generally agreed with Hoover's policies toward Russia. On occasion, however, even loyal supporters on the right took exception to what they now regarded as his overtolerant attitude toward the Soviet regime. One of the few active conservative organizations in the 1920s was the National Civic Federation headed by Ralph Easely. The federation was dedicated to the fight against old age pensions, pacifists, radicals, and recognition of Soviet Russia. In December 1922 Easely wrote Hoover that he was "upset" by a Hoover statement concerning the possibilities of opening trade relations with Russia, seeing in this statement an intimation that one could do business with the likes of Chicherin, Lenin, and Trotsky. Hoover dismissed Easely's criticism as a "misimpression."[49]

Much more difficult to handle was a relatively small, diverse group to the left of Hoover that was constantly alert to any move of his that might be interpreted as anti-Soviet. In private communications, Hoover characterized these Left-liberals, socialists, and Communists as "pinks and reds" without discrimination. On such issues as recognition, relief, and Hoover, there was unanimity among these groups, if on very little else. These were the "irresponsible groups chiefly of communistic inspiration" that Hoover feared would take over Russian relief if he ended the ARA mission abruptly in 1922.

In the forefront of the battle against Hoover and his works was Paxton Hibben, a former secretary of the United States legation in Colombia, former director of a private relief mission in the Near East, and director of the American Committee for Relief of Russian Children.[50] On 8 November 1922 Hibben opened the attack on the ARA for reducing its relief program in Russia. In an article in the *Nation,* he declared that Russia faced another year of famine and that over seven million people were in immediate need of assistance. Their plight, he maintained, was in no way attributable to Soviet policy but to a shortage of draft animals, agricultural machinery, and seed grain. Hibben claimed that the Soviet government had been "over 100% effective" in its own efforts to secure grain for the spring planting but that the ARA had retarded the sowing program by failing to meet shipping schedules.[51]

Hibben's estimate of the number of Russians facing starvation was evidently based on a forecast contained in a dispatch from Walter Duranty published on 16 October. Duranty, a *New York Times* correspondent who enjoyed the confidence of both the ARA staff in Moscow and the Soviet government, had written that Russians and Americans in the Soviet capital generally agreed that seven to eight million people would be starving in March 1923.[52] On 20 October Kamenev told Haskell that, according to the official government estimate, over eight million people, though not actually threatened by starvation, would need outside assistance by 1 January 1923. Haskell was skeptical. This pessimistic estimate did not tally with the calculations of his own staff, nor was it consistent with Soviet plans to export wheat.[53] In any case, neither the ARA nor the Soviet government believed that a new famine on the scale pictured by Duranty and Hibben was imminent.

Several months later, Hoover's opponents on the left, and some of more moderate persuasion as well, sharpened the attack by charging that Hoover's policies on both recognition and relief were based on venal interest. At a mass rally for recognition of Soviet Russia held in New York City on 7 January 1923, a prominent labor attorney declared Hoover the evil genius behind the administration's non-recognition policy; he was obstructing change because he wanted to promote British penetration of the Russian market through the Urquhart concession (he failed to mention that Hoover had severed his connection with the British firm well before the inception of the ARA). When Hibben addressed the meeting, he labeled Hoover and the National Civic Federation "professional opposers of recognition of Russia." In refuting the moralistic arguments advanced against recognition, Hibben contrasted the United States, with its "race wars," "murderers," and Ku Klux Klan, with Soviet Russia, where "people may criticize the government to their heart's contents . . . and still view the world with no [prison] bars to intervene."[54]

Opposition to the ARA's reduced relief program spread to more conventional groups, such as the major charitable societies. During the famine crisis, these agencies had submitted to Hoover's control of their activities in Russia. The announcement that the famine was over, however, released them from reluctant fealty to Hoover and his policies. In September 1922 the National Information Bureau, the clearinghouse for coordination of public appeals by major philanthropic organizations, conducted its own investigation of conditions in Russia. In January 1923 the bureau submitted its report to the ARA for examination prior to publication. The gist of the investigating committee's findings was that eight million Russians would be starving by August if no foreign relief were forthcoming. The report attributed the existing difficulties in part to late shipments of seed by the ARA. It minimized the possibility of grain exports by the Soviet government but approved such a policy in principle. The report concluded that American assistance was urgently needed to prevent suffering and death and that this aid should not be predicated on approval of Soviet political or economic policies.[55]

The report read like a manifesto of dissent from the ARA's own findings and policies. To Hoover and his associates the most grievous sin was the constant reference to the benefactors as "these American organizations." The ARA New York office saw the report as a frontal attack on Hoover's relief policies and responded accordingly. A staff member drew up a critique of the report for delivery to Allen Wardwell, its principal author, characterizing it as "the best piece of Bolshevik propaganda which I have yet seen." Evidently the reviewing officer for correspondence decided that this was not the most appropriate way to approach the highly respected National Information Bureau. The critique was never sent. Instead, the substance of the ARA's objections was delivered by telephone, presumably in more sober language.[56]

Hoover's reaction to the report was more restrained. "It is so involved," he wrote to Goodrich, "the innuendo is so carefully disguised and it is so painful an effort to prove that everyone helped relieve the Russian famine except the A.R.A. without plainly saying so, that I am convinced nobody will ever understand it."[57] In the meantime, however, he took steps to make sure that the National Information Bureau clearly understood the consequences of issuing such a report. On 23 January he held a meeting at his home attended by representatives of the ARA, the National Information Bureau, and several of the large foundations. He told the gathering that the ARA would not object to a public appeal for funds if the Soviet government would agree not to ship any grain abroad. He described his own efforts to prevent such exports, citing the correspondence with Kamenev.

Wardwell argued that it was unfair on any grounds to withhold from the American public the information that eight million Russians were facing starvation. Hoover then declared that if an appeal were launched on this basis, he would be forced to defend the integrity of the ARA by releasing the correspondence with the Soviet government, including his denunciation of the export policy. The meeting ended with no agreement on the general situation in Russia but with a clear understanding that no appeal for funds would be made.[58]

The bureau published its report, incorporating a number of amendments suggested by the ARA New York office.[59] Hoover did not release the record of his controversy with the Soviet authorities over grain exports. The philanthropic agencies did not launch a public appeal for Russian relief.

DIVISION WITHIN THE RANKS

Haskell, Hoover, and the Bolshevik Regime

Hoover's choice of Colonel Haskell to head the Russian mission was based partly on the latter's background of noninvolvement in politics. It was, moreover, reasonable to assume that a regular army officer would conform to the American tradition of subordination of the military to civilian authority in all matters relating to policy. Thus, Hoover had every reason to believe that Haskell, like all other ARA administrators, would refrain from taking public policy stands not specifically authorized by the Chief.

When Haskell first arrived in Russia, his hostility toward the Bolsheviks was deeper than Hoover may have desired. His first report from Russia described the Soviet regime as a tyranny that held control without "the support or confidence of the people." He charged that the famine was due solely to the Soviet government's former requisition policy; the Bolshevik's attempt to attribute the disaster to drought or military intervention was, according to Haskell, "ridiculous."[60]

As time went on, however, Haskell's animosity toward the Soviet leadership subsided and gradually gave way to respect for the hardworking Bolsheviks with whom he came into regular contact. By February 1922 he was no longer convinced that the famine was caused by Soviet economic policy alone. "The Russian famine," he wrote to Hoover, "is a natural one undoubtedly intensified by the aftereffects of former economic policy." He noted that the central authorities were generally helpful in "breaking down local red tape, setting aside local regulations, and demanding local cooperation for our work." "The Riga agreement," he added, "is being adhered to absolutely."[61]

Haskell's public appreciation of Soviet government efforts in behalf of the ARA accorded with Hoover's general policy of preserving the image of a smooth, neutral relief operation free of conflict with the regime. The home office took no objection to Haskell's effusive expression of gratitude to the Russian leaders in an interview with an American correspondent in July 1922. After describing the wholehearted cooperation of the ARA's Russian employees, Haskell said, "Moreover, putting aside all politics, I must say that the leaders

of the Soviet government have kept their agreement and have scrupu-
lously provided everything we need." He paid special tribute to
Dzerzhinsky for having straightened out the railroad problem.[62] Two
months later, during a celebration of the first anniversary of the
ARA's arrival in Russia, he took the occasion to express his hope
that a new understanding between the two countries would emerge
out of the famine aid program and that normal relations would soon
be established. He said that Herbert Hoover was among the rapidly
increasing number of friends of Soviet Russia in America and that
nothing could prevent a reconciliation between the United States and
Russia.[63]

Haskell's optimism was based almost entirely on the ARA's
friendly relationships with "more reasonable" Soviet leaders. He
believed that their conversion to a more moderate outlook had been
considerably advanced by contact with the Americans and that the
establishment of closer relations between the two countries at this
point was not only feasible but necessary as a means of transforming
the Soviet regime. Thus, on 12 February 1923 he informed Herter
that he wholeheartedly favored a visit to America by such figures as
Radek, Krasin, and Litvinov, since they "invariably come back with
more reasonable ideas and always convinced that they have got to
suppress the agitators in Russia and get on more friendly terms with
America."[64] The home office disagreed. When the American commercial attaché informed Herter that Krasin had expressed a desire
to come to the United States, Hoover's assistant replied that Krasin
was "completely untrustworthy and unreliable" and that it would
not be fruitful to encourage such a visit at this time.[65]

Increasing difficulties with the Soviet government did not affect
Haskell's views on the broader aspects of Soviet-American relations.
On 20 February 1923 he complained to the New York office about
growing Soviet hostility toward foreign relief agencies and reluctance
of the central authorities to meet their financial obligations to the
ARA. On 6 March, however, he sent Hoover an analysis of conditions in Russia that amounted to a plea for economic assistance to
the Soviet government. Haskell declared that this clearly exceeded
the province of the ARA but that if foreign financial aid were not
forthcoming, the consequence would be "misery and suffering by
millions over a long period of years." According to Haskell,
Kamenev had read and approved the contents of this cable.[66]

Haskell's appeal for general assistance to Soviet Russia was a clear violation of ARA canon since it advanced a policy entirely contrary to the Chief's. In releasing the cable to the press on 8 March Hoover excised the offending passage.[67] But the *Nation* had obtained a copy of the original early enough to publish its contents two days later in an editorial under the headline, "Hoover Stabs Russia."[68] On 11 March *Izvestia* published the full text of Haskell's message and indicated Hoover's expurgation. Within the week, the same Soviet newspaper published an article in which Lander singled out Haskell for high praise as "an adherent to the idea of friendship between Russia and America."[69]

On 23 March Hoover spelled out his own views about financial aid to Russia. In a letter to an officer of the International Committee of the YMCA, he analyzed conditions in Russia after the famine and the possibilities of alleviating the general poverty. He agreed with Haskell that recovery would be slow and painful without foreign assistance. But he concluded that neither recognition nor a renewal of trade relations would stimulate a "flow of foreign savings, business, or skill into Russia." Foreign capital, according to Hoover, would not be available to Russia until its institutions were altered fundamentally to assure "security and freedom of initiative." The NEP reforms, he declared, were not "sufficient to improve the conditions of large industry, because the impulses which are the real basis for the attraction of capital and brains for reconstruction have not been restored." As far as reconstruction assistance was concerned, Hoover saw in Russia "an ample field for those who can devote themselves to such work, for the terrible suffering of a great people groping for freedom from centuries of wrong must enlist the sympathy of every well thinking person." Characteristically, he added the warning that such work should not be "exhausted in propaganda"; it should be carried out by "responsible" organizations such as religious groups.[70]

There is evidence that disagreement on future relations with Russia reached into subordinate levels of the ARA. In November 1922 Harold H. Fisher, director of the ARA Historical Division in New York, proposed the creation of an "American Friends of Russia" committee to educate the public on the dangers of recognition. Herter agreed with the plan "from A to Z."[71] The Moscow director of the Historical Division, John R. Ellingston, took an entirely opposite view on recognition. In May 1923 he wrote to Fisher, "I long ago wrote you that I thought we ought to recognize the Soviet government for the ultimate good of both peoples, Russian and American."[72] Like Haskell, Ellingston believed that the general trend in Russia was toward the liquidation of communism. "As to the international situation here," he wrote to Fisher later that month, "the time is most propitious to force these people over to the right, and for America to auspiciously begin some sort of relations with them." Unlike Haskell, however, he was convinced that the ARA had pursued this task too timidly and was therefore wasting a unique opportunity to influence a great historical development.

> Complete condemnation of [the Bolsheviks] and the spirit behind the Russian revolution is, it seems to me, no more just, although just as natural, as British condemnation of the French revolution, and I suspect that no one in America 50 years from now will regret the Russian revolution or feel that its big results were other than good. It seems to me that we do not give them chances enough, that our attitude has been too frightenedly inimical. That I think is the one criticism which can be brought against the relations of the A.R.A. in the past with these people—it is the result of a lack of vision on the part of the chiefs of the show here.[73]

Ellingston's bold and somewhat benign view of the Bolshevik Revolution and its leaders could hardly have been more at variance with the outlook of his Chief. Hoover was relatively unchanged by the experience of day-to-day supervision of the relief mission. His refusal to make distinctions among the Soviet leaders severely limited his capacity to exploit the differences among them and nudge the regime "further to the right." Haskell, on the other hand, was forced to make such distinctions in his everyday dealings with the government. His success in enlisting such leaders as Kamenev, Krasin, Radek, and Dzerzhinsky as "friends of the A.R.A." helped him overcome "Communist" obstruction at critical times. Through this experience, he became convinced that a broad viable relationship between Soviet Russia and the United States could be achieved on the basis of the friendships that the ARA had established with the "good" Bolsheviks. Hoover's cautious probes into the possibilities of doing business with the Soviet regime left him unpersuaded that the "fine spirit" he had introduced into Soviet Russia through the ARA had effected any significant change in the communist system or its leaders.

During the period of reduced relief activity in Russia, Hoover and his home staff tried to minimize the impact of the mission on American attitudes toward the Soviet regime. At the same time, the ARA continued its efforts to make a lasting impression on the Russian people. The reaction of the Soviet leadership was almost automatic.

—7—

Disengagement in Russia

The Soviet government decided to end its own emergency relief program at the same time that the reduction in ARA assistance was scheduled to go into effect. On 8 September 1922 Kamenev told Haskell that *Pomgol* would shortly be abolished since "it was not [the government's] intention to feed great numbers of people and create chronic paupers, but rather to make everyone get to work and to feed only the displaced children, orphans, refugees, sick, etc." Haskell noted, "In fact, the policy of the Government [is] almost exactly in line with the American Relief Administration."[1]

The Soviet central authorities were undoubtedly encouraged in taking this step by such reports as the one featured in *Izvestia* on 16 August. "From Famine to Harvest—One Step" was the headline over a story written by the newspaper's correspondent in Samara.

> Only a few months ago the province of Samara was in the cruel grip of famine. . . . Only a few weeks ago official information was being received from the province describing how the starving peasants were feeding on substitutes, spring grass and roots.
>
> At the present time, this is no longer the case, and, in two rural districts, Melekes and Stavropol, there is even a surplus from the harvest.
>
> All the nightmares of starvation have faded into the past. . . . The spirit of the peasants has risen, they are helpful and energetic, and, under the influence of a good harvest, and the aid that was extended to them, their attitude toward the Soviet power is most congenial.[2]

The correspondent's celebration was premature. On 29 August the ARA representative in the Pugachov district of Samara reported to his district supervisor that "the population of this district will be absolutely dependent upon outside aid for its food within two or three weeks. The crops have been practically a failure."[3] Several days later, the Soviet representative plenipotentiary complained to Quinn about the proposed reduction in ARA relief in Samara.

> As you know, the situation in Pugachov district is, perhaps, worse this year than last. . . . In other districts which have been stricken by drought, locusts, etc., over a score of rural areas in the northern part of the *gubernia* [province] were left without bread. . . . In view of the above, I most urgently request that you reconsider this drastic reduction of your feeding operations in the *gubernia* of Samara.[4]

Despite such disturbing reports, the ARA and the Soviet government proceeded simultaneously with their respective plans to curtail relief. By a decree of the All-Russian Central Executive Committee issued on 12 September 1922, *Pomgol* was abolished and replaced by a Central Commission for the Struggle against the Consequences of the Famine *(Tsentralnaya Kommissia po Borbe s Posledstviami Goloda,* abbreviated as *Posledgol).*[5] On the same day, the Moscow Soviet dissolved its own *Pomgol* committees in the province and directed its presidium to take up "the struggle against the consequences of the famine." The resolution of the Moscow Soviet included expressions of gratitude to the "American Commission" for having donated eighty million gold rubles for the hungry and for having contributed its services "without any political intent."[6]

Almost immediately, the Soviet government undertook a variety of measures to eliminate one of the most disturbing "consequences of the famine"—the position of influence and esteem that the ARA had come to occupy in Russia.

POSLEDGOL VERSUS THE ARA

The campaign to reduce the privileges and immunities of the ARA was launched on 1 October 1922. In a letter to Haskell, Lander outlined a series of changes in the operations of "all foreign relief agencies." Henceforth, all such groups were to share in the payment of administrative expenses incurred in rendering relief. Except in cases where the need for immediate relief was acute, they were forbidden to open their kitchens in localities where government institutions were in operation. Clothing distrubution centers, student kitchens, assistance to teachers and professors would now be administered by corresponding state organizations, cooperative societies, and trade unions under the general coordination of *Posledgol.* Individual recipients of relief parcels would be required to pay all customs and transportation fees. The distribution of parcels addressed to groups would be managed in close cooperation with trade unions, which were to be granted preference in ordering and purchasing remittances.[7]

Haskell saw the directive as a unilateral abrogation of the Riga agreement and therefore as a form of indirect pressure on the ARA to withdraw altogether. On 2 October he notified Lander that the ARA had already reduced its operations voluntarily, that there was no reason to impose arbitrary restrictions on the ARA, and that the Riga agreement must remain "in full force and effect." He demanded that Lander submit by 12:00 on 4 October the answers to two questions. Did the Soviet government want to end the food remittance program as it was currently operating? Did the Soviet government intend to "maintain the sanctity" of the Riga agreement? If ARA assistance were no longer needed, he would immediately cancel all outstanding orders for food and start closing down all ARA operations.[8]

Lander responded by retracting his letter, explaining that it had been written "in the order of a great urgency, after office hours." He declared that the new conditions did not apply to the ARA, that the government appreciated its efforts to reduce expenses and contemplated neither a revision of the Riga agreement nor a withdrawal of any of its guarantees. Any future alteration of the "form or methods of work," Lander wrote, would be instituted only through mutual agreement between the ARA and the Soviet government. Two days later, Lander informed Haskell that "in our government circles, the question of repudiating or revising the guarantees given to the A.R.A. on the basis of the Riga agreement has never been raised so far."[9]

Haskell accepted the surrender. He informed New York, "Lander came to my office and was very humble." According to Haskell, Lander's original letter had been the result of pressure from the trade unions to take control of the ARA's operations. "It was a test," wrote Haskell. "When we stood pat, the government decided it is better to have us in Russia, and turned down the unions. I think you will agree with me that the events of the last three days have served to clarify the atmosphere and to increase the strength of our position."[10]

Within a month, however, the Soviet government changed its mind and refused to exempt the ARA from the new restrictions on foreign relief agencies. On 31 October orders went out from Olga Kameneva to all subordinate branches of *Posledgol* to impose regulations on foreign open kitchens, "which must result in closing most of them." All foreign relief supplies were to be delivered to Soviet children's institutions, departments of education, and children's relief committees.[11] The new policy was put into effect promptly. Within the week, Haskell complained to Lander that local Soviet officials were obstructing the operations of ARA open kitchens. "I assure you," warned Haskell, "that I shall not submit to dictation, either directly or indirectly." For once, Lander did not apologize for the action of subordinates. He denied the charge of obstruction but defended the right of local officials to have their own opinions about open kitchens under foreign management.[12]

Lander's rebuff signaled the beginning of a campaign to abrogate the "surrender" of 4 October. When Haskell sailed for the United States at the end of November to confer with Hoover, Soviet authorities increased pressure on the ARA to close down its independent installations.[13] At the same time, the government took steps to eliminate all the other activities and privileges of the ARA that Soviet leaders now considered too expensive, too conspicuous, or in any way inimical to their own authority and policies. On 27 November Lander notified Quinn that the ARA would henceforth be responsible for paying the salaries of Russian employees in the historical, publicity, communications, and inspections divisions and for all expenses connected with the unloading of remittance packages. On the same day, Lander suggested that the ARA reduce its operations in Petrograd and Moscow. Several days later, he complained about the sale of empty food sacks by the ARA, declaring that all such "commercial activity" was prohibited by the Riga agreement.[14]

In December, the government asked the ARA Moscow contingent to move to more modest quarters or pay a premium for what Lander considered "luxurious housing."[15] ARA workers were notified that they had to pay cash in advance for all telegrams.[16] The number of railroad cars available for travel by ARA personnel was sharply reduced.[17] A particularly oppressive restriction for Americans unaccustomed to the rigors of the Russian winter was a ban against the importation of alcohol for distribution outside the control of the Commissariat for Public Health.[18]

Quinn delayed action on new Soviet demands and insisted on the reversal of restrictive orders that had already been put into effect. In regard to the sale of empty sacks, he reminded Lander that the government had never before objected to this practice and that the proceeds were used to purchase more food for the hungry. Lander finally agreed to permit these sales but requested that the containers be offered first to government institutions rather than to private buyers.[19] Quinn accepted the compromise.[20] He tried to contest other reinterpretations of the Riga agreement using the argument, "I was present during the negotiations," but Lander held firm.[21]

Finally, Quinn took the matter up with the New York office. On 28 December he reported that the attitude of the Soviet government toward the ARA had stiffened after Haskell left for the United States. He asked whether he should yield to some of the Soviet demands, adding that, in his opinion, such a retreat "would be a very unsatisfactory policy."[22] In a separate cable to Haskell in Washington, Quinn described the mounting Soviet pressure but assured the director: "Don't worry. We understand thoroughly that our job is to keep the show going, but some indications of the result of the discussions in Washington will help us immensely in our task."[23]

The decision that emerged from the Hoover-Haskell conference was sent to New York headquarters on 23 January 1923 for transmission to the ARA at Moscow.

> The Chief feels Moscow ought to be advised that inasmuch as we are positively going to pull out of there on April or May first, we better avoid conflict over this question by undertaking ourselves to pay the cash budget overhead, provided the Soviet authorities will allow us to sell foodstuffs in Russia sufficient to bring in the amount necessary for this purpose. We should make up our minds finally and positively that we are going to pull out of Russia at this date, and we simply want to maintain as much peace as possible up to that time. We should not extend our program beyond the point absolutely necessary to save human life. The Chief feels that the Soviet authorities are trying to crowd us out of Russia and will endeavor to put us in the wrong; so we need to keep peace temporarily and make arrangements for our final exit.[24]

It was a difficult assignment for the workers in the field. By

January, there were increased demands for the ARA's services in the former famine areas. As the number of children fed at ARA open kitchens rose rapidly to over one million, Quinn retreated as slowly as possible in the face of Soviet pressure to close the installations. After the date that Hoover had set for the "final exit," two million more children joined the ARA food lines.[25]

The Rearguard Action

The Soviet government did not move immediately to help the areas that had been vacated by *Pomgol*. On 14 October 1922 an *Izvestia* correspondent openly criticized the government for dismantling its famine relief apparatus while the threat of famine still hung over "many regions of Russia." "Most threatening," he declared, "is the situation in the southern part of the Soviet Ukraine."[26] The government nevertheless kept up the pressure on the ARA to close its kitchens in that area. On 1 December Quinn agreed to confine ARA relief in the Ukraine to Soviet "closed institutions," such as children's shelters, hospitals, and convalescent homes, but he reserved the right to maintain open kitchens wherever the ARA district supervisor deemed necessary. "We cannot agree," he informed the Representative Plenipotentiary of the Ukrainian Republic, "to the representative of the U.S.S.R. [Ukrainian Soviet Socialist Republic] dictating on matters relating to the administration of our relief operation."[27]

The Ukrainian authorities decided to take more drastic action. On 4 January Lander passed on to Quinn a formal decision by the Ukrainian Congress of Soviets to discontinue all ARA operations in four provinces. Two days later, he insisted that Quinn respond immediately to this order, reminding him that the resolution "has to be obeyed not by myself alone but by all government institutions in the Ukraine." On 13 February he informed Quinn that he was surprised to learn that the ARA was still feeding children at its own kitchens in Kiev. He warned the acting director that he must close these kitchens immediately and that he would not intervene with the Ukrainian government in case of trouble.[28] It was not until Haskell returned from the United States that the ARA finally acceded to the demands of the Ukrainian authorities. On 24 February Haskell notified Lander that the ARA had decided to shut down its installations in the provinces indicated.[29]

As the strange contest between zealous benefactor and reluctant client continued, the ARA found allies among local authorities. In December 1922 Quinn countered a request by Lander to cease operations in the Black Sea-Kuban area by citing an urgent telegram from the representative of the Tsaritsyn Soviet pleading for the continuance of the relief program. Lander replied that it was natural for each region to insist on receiving aid as long as possible: "This explains why the determined steps taken by us to have the A.R.A. withdrawn from the above district resulted in great excitement among the local authorities, who had not expected us to act so decisively on the request expressed by them some time ago." Lander reaffirmed the decision to discontinue ARA relief; the telegram from Tsaritsyn was no longer relevant, he declared, because of the improvement in the government's own relief program in the area.[30]

In Samara, the "consequences of the famine" during the winter of 1922-23 were remarkably like the famine itself. On 31 January 1923 *Izvestia* reported the grim news that the province's harvest was only 30 percent of the normal yield. "A shortage of 70 percent" remarked the writer. "This is a matter for reflection."[31] The ARA district supervisor was equally pessimistic: "As was to be expected, the second part of the winter is sharpening the famine. Stores of grain are running out."[32]

Again, the local authorities appealed directly to the ARA to countermand the central government's instructions to close down the American installations in the area. Quinn responded by refusing to comply with Lander's request to withdraw from the Syzran rural district of the province. The estimates of the *Posledgol* representative in Samara were wrong, Quinn maintained; according to the head of the local government, the crop realized in the area fell far short of the amount reported by the *Posledgol* provincial headquarters.[33]

Lander reacted sharply. "I presume," he wrote to Quinn on 1 March, "that as the Representative of the Russian government, my request should mean more to you than the statement of a local authority."[34] Nevertheless, with the help of the local soviet of Syzran, the ARA continued to press for continued relief. On 9 March the ARA director in the area forwarded a statement from the official Soviet representative with foreign relief organizations in the Syzran-Simbirsk district to the effect that at the request of the local soviet executive committee, he was formally petitioning the ARA to remain in the district until the next harvest.[35] The ploy was successful. The

ARA continued relief operations in the district until 21 June 1923.[36]

The remittance package program ranked high on the Soviet government's list of undesirable activities. The regime saw the ARA's policy of delivering parcels to all designated recipients without discrimination as a subtle form of support of religious groups, non-Communist intellectuals, the remainder of the former nobility, and the new class of petty tradesmen that had sprung up under the New Economic Policy. Ukrainian officials particularly resented the tremendous flow of packages to Jews from relatives who had emigrated to the United States.

The campaign against the remittance program got under way in December 1922, when the authorities refused to permit delivery of packages to an unprecedented number of groups and individuals.[37] Previously, the government had allowed such groups as the exiled public famine relief committee to send ARA food packages to Russia. To assure delivery, the committee designated *Pomgol* as the distributing office.[38] On 9 December 1922 the Soviet representative to the ARA Remittance Division demanded that the relief organization discontinue all transactions with the public famine relief committee and with all other groups that were illegal in Russia.[39]

In February 1923 the Soviet government intensified its drive against the remittance program. The Commissariat of Post and Telegraph abrogated the special exemptions from import duties and delivery charges.[40] On 24 February Haskell complained to Lander that designated recipients of bulk shipments were being intimidated and even arrested and that parcels were being delayed as much as seven months. He singled out the local government of Elizavetgrad, a town in the western Ukraine, for having published an order that prohibited, under pain of arrest, the delivery by any independent committee of any foreign freight to individual Jews.[41]

Finally, at the beginning of March 1923, the ARA decided to end the struggle to maintain the remittance program. In his official notification to Lander, Quinn explained that the price of food in Russia had fallen so low that the shipment of parcels from abroad was no longer worth the expense. The sale of remittances, he wrote, would be discontinued within a week, and delivery of parcels to Russia would end on 15 June.[42]

At one point, Kamenev tried to head off the drive against the ARA. In an article published in the Party press, he remarked that during his visit to Lenin, the ailing Bolshevik leader had shown a keen interest in the attitude of Herbert Hoover and the progress of the ARA.[45] But by the fall of 1922, Lenin's influence on Party decisions had shrunk considerably.[46] And to the more irreconcilable Bolshevik leaders, the bourgeois charity mission was an offense against the dignity of the Soviet state and a living challenge to their ideological convictions.

Haskell attributed the inconsistencies in Soviet attitudes toward the ARA to political maneuvering within the top Bolshevik leadership and to Kamenev's inability to control this kind of contention during Lenin's prolonged absences.[47] The head of the ARA Historical Division in Moscow reported to the home office that Litvinov blamed the "extreme left communist wing" for the growing hostility within the Party toward the mission.[48] In fact, however, even the "sensible" Soviet leaders found it increasingly difficult to reconcile wholehearted support of the mission with their deeper commitment to the communist cause. Along with the other Bolsheviks in the leadership, they were impelled toward a Marxist interpretation of capitalist philanthropy. Thus inhibited, they could venture only sporadic assistance to the ARA when the Party propagandists went on the offensive.

THE DELAYED REACTION

As the ARA gradually retreated from its far-flung relief posts, the Soviet government moved to displace the bourgeois benefactors from the "hearts and minds" of the Russian people. To those who had been watching the novel competition, it was not an unexpected development. In one of his earliest dispatches from the famine area, the *New York Times* correspondent had remarked:

> . . . the famine has thrown Russia open, for the first time since the revolution, to a body of independent, non-socialist foreigners. Still more, these foreigners are in a sense competing with the Russian authorities in the race to save lives on the Volga. Their coming has put the Soviet government on its mettle.[43]

It was an uneven contest. The superiority of the ARA's tested techniques and experienced personnel had been obvious from the start. Soviet relief administrators had publicly expressed admiration for the efficient Americans and urged their own workers to emulate them. But as the successful, highly publicized benefactors began to gain increasingly wide popularity in Russia, Soviet appreciation became admixed with deep concern. An ARA official noted with some exaggeration as early as April 1922:

> . . . I think that their insolence toward us just now is partly due to the fact, of which they are just becoming cognizant, that the people in the territory where we are feeding are deeply grateful to us, admire us, and depend on us. The contrast between us and their government is too striking. From the government they have never had anything but broken promises, from us they always get what they were promised. In such a situation it is obvious who will get their affection.[44]

The end of the famine emergency energized a delayed reaction against the disturbing foreign influence. Disparaging comments about the ARA's "real" purpose began to crop up in the Party press. Gradually, the government moved to undermine the status and popularity of its adversary. It was a delicate operation. While there was still hope of winning the Harding administration over to a reversal of its nonrecognition policy toward Russia, the Soviet leadership could not risk an open break with the ARA. Its propaganda campaign against the ARA was therefore erratic, and its uneven course confused the ARA staff in Moscow.

At one point, Kamenev tried to head off the drive against the ARA. In an article published in the Party press, he remarked that during his visit to Lenin, the ailing Bolshevik leader had shown a keen interest in the attitude of Herbert Hoover and the progress of the ARA.[45] But by the fall of 1922, Lenin's influence on Party decisions had shrunk considerably.[46] And to the more irreconcilable Bolshevik leaders, the bourgeois charity mission was an offense against the dignity of the Soviet state and a living challenge to their ideological convictions.

Haskell attributed the inconsistencies in Soviet attitudes toward the ARA to political maneuvering within the top Bolshevik leadership and to Kamenev's inability to control this kind of contention during Lenin's prolonged absences.[47] The head of the ARA Historical Division in Moscow reported to the home office that Litvinov blamed the "extreme left communist wing" for the growing hostility within the Party toward the mission.[48] In fact, however, even the "sensible" Soviet leaders found it increasingly difficult to reconcile wholehearted support of the mission with their deeper commitment to the communist cause. Along with the other Bolsheviks in the leadership, they were impelled toward a Marxist interpretation of capitalist philanthropy. Thus inhibited, they could venture only sporadic assistance to the ARA when the Party propagandists went on the offensive.

The ARA was not without weaponry to mount its own defense. On 25 October 1922 the Moscow office issued leaflets to the field branches for distribution with food packages. In this manner, relief recipients were informed about Hoover's philanthropic accomplishments, Gorky's appeal, the extent of American relief in Russia, and the fact that the food had been paid for by the American people and given "freely and unconditionally to the Russian people." The leaflet gave full credit to the Soviet government for providing the funds for the storage and transportation of the relief shipments.[49]

The ARA was the last independent agency in Russia that was permitted to circulate its own public relations messages. At best, however, this was a meager resource compared to the sprawling propaganda apparatus at the disposal of the Soviet government. But the visible presence of the remaining American relief stations and the remembrance of the free food given out at the kitchens that had been closed were leaving an indelible imprint on the consciousness of millions of Russians.

An incident that occurred during the Christmas season of 1922 provided the Soviet press with an opportunity to present the ARA in an unfavorable light. A number of American relief workers tried to smuggle Christmas gifts out of the country in the ARA's diplomatic pouch. The contraband included jewelry, furs, and art miniatures, all of which were subject to a heavy export tax. For the first time, Soviet authorities requested permission to open the pouch. The pouch was opened in Quinn's presence, and the contraband articles were revealed. After a brief investigation. Quinn discharged five ARA workers.[50] About two weeks later, *Izvestia* exposed the incident under the headline, "How They Are Helping." The writer claimed that rumors about such activities by Americans had been circulating ever since the ARA had arrived in Russia. He concluded with a passionate indictment of the transgressors: "This is the way they are helping the starving. This is the way representatives of 'civilized' America behave in 'barbarous' Russia."[51]

According to an American correspondent who had close connections with Soviet leaders because of her open sympathy with the regime, both the incident and the article had been deliberately planned to counteract what she called the "wide, if shallow, popularity" of the Americans. "It was no folly," she declared; "it was clear intention, now that relief was almost over, to show the Russian people the wolf of capitalism under the sheepskin of charity. They showed it."[52]

At Quinn's insistence, Kamenev promised to write an article in *Izvestia* absolving the ARA as an organization of any wrongdoing. When the article failed to appear by 21 December, Quinn was convinced that the original story had been officially inspired.[53] But Kamenev had evidently responded to Haskell's suggestion, relayed from New York, to "muzzle the press for the time being unless they have got something more important to holler about."[54] Nothing on the subject appeared in the Soviet press until 22 December, when *Izvestia* published a letter from Lander exonerating the ARA staff of any blame in the incident. "On the contrary," Lander wrote, "the top administration of the A.R.A. in Russia, in the person of the assistant to the Director of the A.R.A. in Russia, Colonel Haskell—Mr. Quinn—readily met the demands of the Soviet authorities in opening the pouch, uncovering the guilty people, and punishing them."[55]

Kamenev's failure to lend his name to the exoneration of the ARA made it clear that the ARA would have to withstand any new assaults on its reputation without the open support of its most highly placed "friend at court."

Communist Reappraisal of Capitalist Philanthropy

While the ARA remained in Russia, the Soviet government generally confined its propaganda campaign to a reinterpretation of the value and purposes of American relief. The reappraisal of capitalist assistance was, for the most part, intended for the relatively small audience that was interested in Marxist analysis of current events. Possibly the purpose was to reassure confused Party members that the bourgeois relief effort had little real significance in the struggle for the loyalty of the working class. To the ARA staff, which dutifully collected and sent to the New York office all Soviet comments on its work, the ideological reassessment of its efforts was proof positive of the government's ingratitude.

To deprecate the significance of foreign relief assistance, the government exalted the role of the international proletariat in fighting the famine. The organization with the largest working-class membership (and the longest title) was the International Workers' Committee for Aid to the Starving in Russia (*Mezhdunarodny Rabochy Komitet Pomoshchi Golodayushchim Rossii*—abbreviated to *Mezhrabpom*). Lenin himself had ordered the creation of *Mezhrabpom* at the time of the signing of the Riga agreement. It operated under the jurisdiction of the Communist International as the coordinating agency for a relief campaign among the world proletariat.

Although the amount of relief supplies actually collected by the organization was far from impressive—some $2.5 million worth—it was extremely successful in arousing sympathy for Soviet Russia and organizing pro-Soviet groups throughout the world.[56] Under the guidance of the talented young activist Willi Münzenberg, *Mezhrabpom* enlisted the support of trade unionists, artists, writers, and scientists, including such notable figures as Käthe Kollwitz, Albert Einstein, Martin Andersen-Nexö, George Bernard Shaw, Alfred Whitehead, Anatole France, Henri Barbusse, and Paul Vaillant-Couturier.[57] The campaign conducted in the United States through an affiliate, the Friends of Soviet Russia, was a source of particular pride to Münzenberg. In a report to the Fourth Congress of the Communist International, he declared:

> The campaign for aid to the starving afforded us, for the first time, the opportunity to carry out work in North America in wide union circles, and to unite them for aid to the starving under the control of the Communist Party. In this manner, we succeeded, for the first time, in attracting wide masses to discussions about the Soviet Union and about the proletarian revolution. . . .[58]

A representative of the Communist International acknowledged in *Izvestia* that the actual aid provided by *Mezhrabpom* was relatively minor.

> The financial means of the international proletariat are so small when compared with those of the philanthropic section of the world (and especially the American) bourgeoisie that it would be ridiculous to claim from these slaves of capital the same assistance that can be expected from their "masters." The aid rendered by *Mezhrabpom* is not help in the ordinary sense. It is only a new method of class war.[59]

Since the amount of food dispensed by the ARA was far greater than that distributed by all the other foreign organizations put together, Soviet commentators had to set up novel standards in downgrading ARA assistance. On 23 September 1922 *Izvestia*'s special correspondent in the Volga region declared, "Of all the foreign organizations, the one that meets with the greatest sympathy of the population is the International Union for Aid to Children, then the German and the Swedish Red Cross, and, least of all—the most powerful of the foreign organizations, the A.R.A."[60] No reason was given for the low degree of public appreciation of the ARA.

This denigration of the ARA by invidious comparison was evidently part of a concerted campaign in which even Kamenev was constrained to take part. In a report delivered to the All-Russian Central Executive Committee on 29 October, he ranked the ARA first in regard to quantity of help rendered but only fifth on the basis of quality. The ARA and other "bourgeois" organizations, he explained, had confined themselves to "pursuing the one aim of saving lives among the Russian population," while groups like *Mezhrabpom* had expanded their activities to include the economic reconstruction of Russia.[61]

Perhaps the most unusual reinterpretation of the American relief mission was the one worked out by Krasin in an *Izvestia* article on 10 March 1923. The commissar of foreign trade wrote that he had been puzzled at first by Hoover's offer to fight the famine but that an article by a Soviet economist had finally led him to a proper understanding of America's motives. The key, according to Krasin, was the rapid development of the United States as the world's leading industrial power. Since so many Americans were leaving farms to take jobs in factories, the country would be confronted with a severe shortage of food. Russia, on the other hand, had enough cultivable area not only to make up this deficit but to serve as "the granary for the entire world." It was for this reason, he wrote, that the United States had come to the aid of Russia.

To the commissar of foreign trade, this was an encouraging development.

> For us, for the economic reconstruction of Russia, this direction of America's national economy is of great consequence. It provides the best assurance that, however hostile to Soviet principles the leading American politicians may be, America is bound to seek our friendship, and, sooner or later, the moment will come when American capital will cooperate in the economic reconstruction of our country.[62]

Evidently Hoover saw no need to rebuild Russia as a future source of food for the United States. The following day's issue of *Izvestia* carried a full account of Haskell's controversial cable of 6 March and of Hoover's deletion of the passage in which Haskell had appealed for foreign assistance in the reconstruction of the Soviet economy.[63] The U.S. secretary of state seemed equally unaware of what Krasin saw as the clear economic needs of American capitalism. On 25 March Hughes reaffirmed the United States' policy of not resuming relations with Russia until the Soviet government stopped disseminating revolutionary propaganda.

Pravda promptly denounced Hughes for failing to represent the real interests of the American bourgeoisie. According to the Party newspaper, a growing number of capitalists were alarmed at the harmful effect that the administration's Russian policy was having on their dividends. The writer advised Hughes to forego "the methods of a capitalist agitator" and come forth with the "serious offers of a businessman." Almost as an aside, *Pravda* added:

> When the capitalistic farmer, deprived of a market, is forced to burn his bread and the industrial capitalist to reduce production, a reason is easily found for humanitarian activity, charity, etc., especially when such activity is connected with an opportunity to become acquainted with the Russian market and with precise information on the general condition of our economy, not to mention other benefits and advantages. We therefore fully understand the humanitarianism of the American government. This humanitarianism had very definite material roots, had "an economic foundation," as we would say in scientific slang.[64]

Trotsky saw a more insidious role of American beneficence. On the eve of the ARA's departure from Russia, he delivered a speech on the state of the world revolution. According to the summary in *Pravda* on 30 June 1923, he said:

> One factor that has delayed the development of revolution throughout the world is the petty hopes of Europeans based on the "uncle from America" (Wilsonianism, philanthropic feeding, "loans," etc.). The sooner the popular masses come to rely only upon their own strength, the closer they will unite under the banner of the European Union of Workers' and Peasants' Republics—the sooner will revolution break out both here and on the other side of the ocean, since

revolution in Europe will have the same effect upon America as the Russian revolution has had upon Europe.[65]

As the most prominent "uncle from America," Hoover may have been gratified by such expert confirmation of the theory that he had himself advanced during the Armistice period—namely, that American relief would serve to "stem the tide of Bolshevism." More probably, however, Hoover took Trotsky's euphoric pronouncement on the possibilities of revolution in Europe and America as additional proof that the Bolshevik leaders were entirely immune to the influence of America generosity and incapable of reform.

A Letter from Lenin

It was during this period of Soviet antipathy toward the American relief mission that Lenin made his first, and probably his only, attempt to communicate personally with a member of the United States government—the secretary of commerce. On the eve of Haskell's departure for America, he was received by the Bolshevik leader. One of Lenin's secretaries recorded the results of the meeting on 22 November 1922 as follows: "Vladimir Ilyich ordered the distribution of a *very secret* letter about Haskell's proposals to all members of the Politburo and to Chicherin. Send Nazaretyan 8 copies to be distributed for a vote." On the following day, another secretary, Nadezhda Alliluyeva, noted: "If V. I. asks about the letter to Hoover, I am to tell him all that Chicherin has undertaken to do himself. Haskell leaves to-day at 7:20. Letter will be sent through LANDER (since that is what V. I. requested)."[66]

Hoover did not honor the head of the unrecognized government with a written reply. Since the text of Lenin's letter has not yet been revealed, the substance of the unique exchange remains unknown. The outcome of this intriguing, and possibly crucial, episode, however, was disclosed by Haskell in a letter to Quinn from New York: "In regard to the Lenin matter, nothing tangible has developed except that I carry verbal messages to him. I think that they can thank their own stupidity and their failure to cooperate with the A.R.A. for a lack of results in that direction."[67]

If Haskell was correct, the actions taken to cut the ARA down to size and to lower its prestige in Russia may have had the unintended result of removing any possibility that the United States would move from famine relief to economic assistance. As Lenin had realized almost from the start, the American relief mission provided the opportunity for such a momentous development. Hoover had both the standing and the authority to signal the Harding administration that the time had come to resume trade with Russia. In December 1921 Hoover believed that the relief mission was rapidly improving the prospects for such a move. He wrote to Hughes that "the relief measures already initiated are greatly increasing the status and kindliness of relations and their continuation will build a situation which, combined with other factors, will enable the Americans to undertake the leadership in the reconstruction of Russia when the proper moment arrives."[68] By the end of January 1923, however, Hoover was convinced that the Soviet regime had not changed sufficiently to warrant any substantial investment by Americans in the rebuilding of Russia. At the same time, he ordered the ARA to leave the country before the next harvest.

END OF THE MISSION

The withdrawal from Russia was carefully prepared at all levels of the ARA. Upon receiving the news that Hoover had decided to close down the mission, Quinn drew up a central plan for liquidation. On 11 January 1923 he sent his recommendations to New York along with the comment that it would be advisable to withdraw from Russia by early June, before "lukewarm appreciation and support set in."[69] On 29 January the New York office notified Quinn that Hoover had officially approved his plan. The message continued, "We do not wish to make any public announcement either here or in Russia of stoppage as we believe it will solve itself naturally and anticipation of a break in method raises unnecessary alarm."[70]

On 5 February all district supervisors in Russia were informed of the decision to end the mission before the harvest and were cautioned to keep the plan secret.[71] Within a short time, however, rumors about the impending termination of the mission began to circulate in Russia. The Soviet government apparently shared the ARA's desire to avoid "unnecessary alarm." On 27 February *Izvestia* reported that Hoover had denied rumors about the imminent cessation of American relief.[72] On the same day, the ARA New York office requested liquidation reports from all district supervisors and division chiefs.[73]

Preparations for a favorable public reception of the news were made well in advance and in considerable detail. On 15 January Brown asked Lincoln Hutchinson to conduct another survey of Russia's needs and resources. Brown wrote, "Chief has hunch there is enough food in Russia to carry it through."[74] Hutchinson's first report, issued on 3 April, corroborated Soviet estimates of a great increase in sowing during the 1922-23 season.[75] On 19 April the ARA released to the Associated Press an exclusive interview with Ronald Allen, the district supervisor of Samara. Allen was optimistic about conditions in the heart of the famine area: "Samara, the blackest spot of last year's Volga famine, is emerging from the catastrophe with an excellent chance of having a surplus of grain when the summer crop is harvested."[76] Allen foresaw no futher need for relief in this district after the first of June. A week later, Haskell reported that the chiefs of the Moscow offices as well as the district supervisors were "almost unanimous" in agreeing that conditions in Russia had improved to the point where relief was no longer needed to prevent starvation.[77]

Haskell agreed entirely with the decision to withdraw by summer and with the policy of avoiding conflict with the Soviet authorities until the end of operations. "We are prepared," he wrote to Brown on 1 March, "to be as considerate as possible in our dealings with the Soviet government up to the time of closing."[78] He was not willing, however, to submit to Soviet pressure in every instance. On 1 March, for example, he informed Lander that the ARA would not vacate its comfortable quarters in Moscow no matter what the other foreign relief organizations decided to do.[79]

The strategy that he and Quinn followed was to put up a show of resistance at each renewal of earlier Soviet demands and then to space out concessions and compromises that seemed necessary to maintain peace. On 30 March Quinn instructed the district supervisor at Samara to absorb the cost of baking bread rather than attempt to enforce payment by the local government. "It is ridiculous for us to lay down a rule that cannot be enforced," he wrote. "Compromise must necessarily be made."[80] In April, all ARA field offices were ordered to turn over the proceeds from sales of empty grain sacks to local institutions wherever possible and to give the balance to *Posledgol.* In May, the district supervisors were instructed to cooperate with the government's "Mothers' and Children's Week" campaign by donating surplus clothing and food packages.[81]

Released from the obligation to contest each petty violation of the Riga agreement, the ARA staff proceeded to liquidate the mission in relative peace. The only discordant note during this period of general harmony was a dispute about the disposition of surplus ARA supplies. On 26 May Lander instructed his subordinates in the field not to allow the ARA to "squander" its medical supplies by turning them over to hospitals or private individuals. They were also ordered to make sure that all containers and surplus food were turned over to *Posledgol* rather than to institutions directly. His circular concluded, however, with an admonition to all Soviet liaison agents to avoid all friction with foreign relief organizations and to refer all problems to the central office for advice.[82]

The ARA was determined not to be drawn into controversies at this point. When Lander's instructions came to the attention of the Moscow headquarters, a circular was sent out to the field directing the district supervisors to take a complete inventory of all supplies whose "proper distribution" was prevented by *Posledgol* officials and simply to send in a report.[83] The instructions from the leaders of both sides to avoid trouble were generally effective, with one notable exception. Karklin, the bellicose Soviet representative in Samara, ordered his subordinates to prevent any distribution of surplus stocks by the ARA.[84] An overzealous official in Syzran took the order literally. He seized the ARA warehouse, sealed it, and placed it under guard by a Red Army man. The following day, the ARA supervisor had one of his inspectors break the seals and distribute the food to the waiting peasants. The guard prevented the peasants from leaving while the ARA supervisor argued with the Soviet representative. When the ARA supervisor moved to repossess the warehouse, the soldier covered him with his rifle. The American knocked the rifle out of his hand and told the peasants to leave with the food. There was no further interference.[85]

On the following day, the local government issued a formal apology for the incident and expressed its "extreme gratitude to the A.R.A. organization which has accomplished great help to the hungry population of our *uezd*."[86] Thus ended the only recorded episode in which a member of the ARA resisted a Soviet order by force.

After most of the other ARA stations had closed their doors, the one in Samara was still having its difficulties with Karklin. Representatives of institutions complained to the ARA that the supplies that had been turned over to them were being confiscated by Karklin's men.[87] By that time, however, it was too late to appeal to the Americans. The mission was over. On 27 June 1923 the ARA Moscow headquarters informed the New York office that it would close the last station within a week.[88]

Exit—with Applause

On 14 May Hutchinson completed his final report on conditions in Russia; Haskell submitted statements by all division and field supervisors that there was no further need for ARA assistance; and Quinn prepared a draft letter to Kamenev notifying him of the ARA's intentions. After approval by Hoover, Haskell presented the letter to the Soviet leader. It read, in part: "It appears that while small areas may be short, there will be more than enough in the areas of surplus to cover all prospective needs. . . . It has, therefore, been decided to withdraw from Russia. . . ."[89]

Hutchinson's findings were made public on 1 June 1923 in an interview with the Associated Press. If there were no export of grain from Russia, he declared, Soviet resources would be more than sufficient to meet all immediate needs. "The first question, 'Is the famine ended?'" he said, "may therefore be answered in the affirmative."[90] Three days later, Haskell notified the Soviet government officially that relief would end with the coming harvest. In his acknowledgment, Kamenev expressed the deep appreciation of "the working people" of Russia for the help rendered. On the decision to discontinue assistance, he commented:

> I completely join you in the viewpoint expressed by you that this year's harvest promises to be quite satisfactory, and that upon its realization, the government hopes to provide for the basic needs of the former famine region, and to utilize the surplus for the economic reconstruction of the country.[91]

The termination of the mission was formalized on 15 June in a liquidation agreement that was entirely free of ambiguities or residual obligations. As payment for the corn given to the railroad workers during the transport crisis of April 1922, the Soviet government turned over to the ARA the unexpended balance of the security on deposit in London. Each side released the other from all claims connected with the mission. The Soviet government acknowledged that all funds and equipment supplied to the ARA had been properly used and accounted for.[92]

To the copy of the agreement transmitted to the State Department, Herter appended the comment: "I thought it might be of interest for your files, and on the whole, I should consider it an extremely satisfactory agreement. The Soviet authorities have certainly out-shined [*sic*] themselves in trying to be agreeable during the liquidation period."[93]

News of the Americans' imminent departure was conveyed to the Russian people in extravagant testimonials in the Soviet press throughout the country. Newspapers and magazines in Simbirsk, Kharkov, and Moscow carried laudatory descriptions of the ARA's activities, pictures of American supervisors, and effusive messages of praise from Party and government leaders.[94] On 1 July *Pravda* featured an article in which the writer traced the change in his own attitude toward the "American uncles."

> I wrote then [when the ARA arrived in Russia], "It is true that Hoover's messengers carry themselves with a splendid disdain, like a duke visiting the hut of a charcoal-burner. Nevertheless, the A.R.A. carries on loyally. It is not responsive to the overtures of the foreign 'Whites' who have remained here in various guises, but does its work without being swayed by outside influences.
>
> "We accept, without joy, the gifts of bourgeois America. The bread of charity is not sweet. . . ."
>
> Twenty-two months have elapsed. The joint effort of the A.R.A. and the Soviet government is ended, and both sides have studied each other in a practical situation. There is no longer any room for distrust and falsehoods, since we have irrefutable, instructive, and complete facts.

The writer credited the ARA with having fed eleven million people during its stay in Russia and with the rehabilitation of 15,000 hospitals serving eighty million people. On the impact of the experience on the Americans themselves, he wrote:

> And the Americans will carry back to the United States their belief in the possibility of working in a businesslike manner with the Soviet

government, and their impression of the "fanatical" Bolsheviks toward their people.

Colonel Haskell and his staff . . . have decided to work for the recognition of the Soviet government by America.[95]

The 15 July issue of the magazine *Ogonyok* carried a photograph of Haskell together with a factual, appreciative report of the work of the ARA. The article mentioned the conflict with the unions but observed, "To the credit of the A.R.A. men, it must be noted that with them labor discipline was good, strict. Work was carried on sometimes without any limitations of time when the situation at the moment called for it."[96]

Lander's tribute to the ARA, published in *Izvestia* on 18 July, emphasized the concurrence of the Soviet government in the ARA's decision to end relief. The move, he declared, was based solely on "the prospects of a good harvest and the general improvement in our financial situation." The representative plenipotentiary congratulated the district supervisors individually but singled out Colonel Haskell for special praise for his leadership of the mission. The Colonel, wrote Lander, "will work, upon his return to the United States, toward expediting closer relations between the U.S. and the U.S.S.R. and hopes to return soon as a member of some kind of commercial mission."[97]

On the evening of 18 July 1923 the Council of People's Commissars tendered an official banquet in honor of the ARA. At the reception following the banquet, Kamenev, Chicherin, Semashko, and Krasin expressed their gratitude to the ARA and the American people before a gathering of Soviet and foreign press representatives.[98] The final ceremony was the presentation of a handsome plaque on which a valedictory resolution of the Council of People's Commissars had been elegantly inscribed. The text of the resolution more than fulfilled Hoover's request of 23 June for "some documentary communication from the Soviet authorities" acknowledging the value of the ARA's work in Russia.[99]

During the difficult time of enormous natural calamity, the American people, represented by the A.R.A., responded to the needs of the population, already exhausted by intervention and blockade, in the famine-stricken region of Russia and the Union Republics, and unselfishly came to its assistance by organizing on a broad scale the supply and distribution of food products and other articles of prime necessity.

Thanks to the enormous and entirely disinterested efforts of the A.R.A., millions of people of all ages were rescued from death, and whole cities and districts were saved from the horrible catastrophe that threatened them.

At this time, now that the famine is over and the tremendous work of the A.R.A. has come to an end, the Council of People's Commissars, in the name of the millions who have been rescued, and of all the working-people of Soviet Russia and the Union Republics, considers it its duty, before the representatives of the entire world, to express its deepest gratitude to this organization, to its leader, Herbert Hoover, to its representative in Russia, Colonel Haskell, and to all its workers, and to declare that the people of the Union of Soviet Socialist Republics will never forget the help rendered to them through the A.R.A., perceiving in it a guarantee of the future friendship of the two nations.[100]

It was two years—almost to the day—since Gorky had appealed to "all honest people" to come to the assistance of famine-stricken Russia. On 20 July 1923 Haskell and the remaining members of the ARA Moscow staff closed down the headquarters office and left for the United States.

—8—

The Aftermath

The relief mission did not bring about a great change in Soviet-American relations. The fragile connection between the two countries—already attenuated during the last six months of the mission—was severed when relief came to an end. During the following year, both governments took steps to eliminate the side effects of the relief effort on the status quo. The Harding administration acted to remove from the agenda the question of recognition and trade relations with Russia. Lenin's successors renewed the campaign to erase the favorable public image of American philanthropy.

Aftereffects in the United States

Haskell was hardly out of Russia when the administration moved to quell both hopes and fears that the informal ties established by the ARA would be replaced by diplomatic relations with the USSR. On 23 July 1923 the secretary of state declared that he remained firmly opposed to any change in policy toward Russia. The Soviet government, according to Hughes, had failed to provide any compensation for confiscated American property or any guarantees in regard to the future security of American citizens. "What is more serious," he continued, "is . . . conclusive evidence that those in control at Moscow have not given up their original purpose of destroying existing governments wherever they can do so throughout the world."[1]

In the meantime, word had reached Hoover from Europe that

Haskell was planning to issue a public statement in favor of recognition and the resumption of trade relations with Russia. To forestall such a move, Herter cabled the errant former director:

> Press dispatches indicate you considering public statement regarding Russia favorable toward recognition or trade agreement. Personally believe inadvisable in view stand taken by Government you make such statement until conference with Chief here. Certain you understand situation.[2]

Haskell understood. During an interview in Berlin, he said that the Soviet regime had improved, had stabilized its rule, and was eager to be recognized by the United States. When asked about the prospects for recognition, he replied, "It is not my business to talk politics."[3]

Within a week, President Harding reaffirmed the nonrecognition policy. In a statement issued on 31 July, the president declared that it was inadvisable to recognize the Russian government until it corrected the "fundamental error" of its ways.

> International good faith forbids any sort of sanction of the Bolshevist policy. The property of American citizens in Russia, honestly acquired under the laws then existing, has been taken without the color of compensation, without process of law, by the mere emission of countless decrees. . . . If there are no property rights, there is little, if any, foundation for national rights, which we are ever being called upon to safeguard. The whole fabric of international commerce and righteous international relationship will fail if any great nation like ours will abandon the underlying principles relating to sanctity of contract and the honor involved in respected rights.[4]

The language of the statement is strikingly reminiscent of earlier pronouncements by the secretary of commerce, who helped the president prepare the speech and released it during Harding's final illness.[5] Evidently, the experience of his relief mission to Russia had not changed Hoover's attitude toward recognition in the slightest.

Goodrich, the former special representative of the ARA, was apparently unaware of Hoover's role in the decision to maintain the nonrecognition policy. On 9 August 1923 he informed Edgar Rickard that he was still convinced that the United States should establish "some sort of relations with Russia" and that he was disgusted with the State Department's obduracy on the subject. "With respect to

Hoover," he wrote, "it strikes me he is in a position where he will soon have to retire from the Cabinet or put behind him all future political ambitions."[6] Coming from a Hoover aide, this was a remarkable misreading of Hoover's viewpoint and influence in the Harding cabinet. Rickard promptly relayed Goodrich's opinion to Herter, commenting that he had "remonstrated with him" and that "the Chief might be interested in the Governor's letter."[7]

The prorecognition movement gained few recruits among former members of the ARA. Of the veterans of the mission to Russia who were interviewed or polled forty-five years later (an admittedly small sample), none reported having been influenced by his experiences in Russia to change his mind about recognition; only one respondent stated that he had fovored recognition in 1923.[8] An impressive number of former ARA aides obtained executive positions in organizations that favored recognition as little as Hoover did. The list includes the State Department, the Department of Commerce, the U.S. Chamber of Commerce, Standard Oil Company, Wilson and Company, the magazine *Foreign Affairs*, the Hoover War Library, and the vestigial ARA. Christian Herter remained in the Department of Commerce as assistant secretary. A generation later, he was appointed secretary of state by President Eisenhower.[9]

Several former members of the ARA Russian Division joined companies or groups that were directly interested in trade with Russia. They received no encouragement or assistance from Hoover. On 7 November 1923 Hoover refused to ask the secretary of war to extend Haskell's leave of absence from the army so that he might accept a position with the American-Russian Chamber of Commerce.[10] When Walter Brown, the former ARA director for Europe and chief negotiator at the Riga conference, was appointed chief engineer of a group of Russian mines, Hoover asked him to make sure that no misunderstanding arose out of his new association. He wanted all concerned to know that Hoover had no interest or involvement in the project.[11]

To Hoover, one of the most disturbing by-products of the relief mission was the renewal of radical activity in the United States in the form of nationwide relief campaigns. According to the secretary of the Friends of Soviet Russia, practically every major city and factory town in America eventually had a branch of the FSR or a "united front" affiliate. Even children were enlisted in relief-for-Russia work through Famine Scout Clubs. Despite the efforts of the

American Communist party to continue this highly successful activity, however, the FSR gradually withered away after the end of the famine, surviving only as a skeleton group under a succession of different names for about ten years. But the technique of using "front" organizations to attract financial and other support from non-Communists was extremely adaptable. The Communist party continued to create effective "front" groups for several decades after the demise of the FSR.[12]

Did the United States benefit economically from its generosity toward the starving Russians? In 1923, the Department of Commerce claimed that it did. According to a department pamphlet, purchases for the relief program helped to maintain the price of corn during a critical period.[13] According to an ARA official, this added hundreds of millions of dollars to the value of corn sold by American farmers.[14]

At first glance, this estimate seems reasonable. The average price of corn did indeed rise more than 57 percent during the two years of the relief effort. But the price of wheat, which was shipped to Russia in substantial amounts as flour, actually fell by a few percentage points. During the same period, the price of cotton, which was not part of the relief program, went up over 95 percent.[15] It is possible that the purchase of surplus corn had an exhilarating psychological effect on the market generally, but this is difficult to determine. Pending more conclusive proof, the claims by Hoover's colleagues (and the accusations by Soviet critics) that the relief effort substantially improved the American economy remain moot.

Aftermath in Russia

In the spring of 1924, the Soviet government opened a new attack on the reputation of the ARA in Russia. On 2 April a Moscow newspaper reported that a number of Soviet citizens had been arrested in Kiev and charged with accepting ARA food in payment for espionage services. On the same day, the trade union organ in Moscow carried an editorial accusing the ARA of intervening in Soviet internal affairs. From the United States, all that Haskell could do was to deny any involvement of the ARA in improper activities.[16]

More arrests followed. Walter Duranty writes that "a considerable number of men and women who had worked on [ARA] committees or served them in other capacities were arrested by the G.P.U."

Duranty comments that "probably quite a number" of these people had done something that justified action by the GPU, but he offers no evidence to support this charge.[17] On 18 May *Izvestia* reported the trial of two former ARA employees under the headline, "ARA Spies in Role of Philanthropists." According to the article, both defendants confessed to having supplied the ARA with information concerning the number of cultivated fields, cattle, and sheep in Belorussia. One defendant was sentenced to ten years at hard labor; the other, to five.[18]

Hoover was incensed at the arrests. Almost a year later, he declared in a newspaper interview, "While the imprisonment of those assistants continues, it will form an impassable barrier against any discussion of a renewal of official relations."[19] At the time, the threat was relatively unimportant. The new president, Calvin Coolidge, did not favor recognition of the Soviet Union under any circumstance. Less than three years later, Hoover was elected president. The fact that the United States did not recognize Russia during his administration cannot, however, be attributed to the arrests of the Russian employees. Whatever opportunity there may have been to effect even a moderate change in Hoover's views on recognition had been foreclosed while the ARA was still in Russia.

THE CONTINUING REINTERPRETATION

In his final review of the work of the ARA in Russia, Haskell wrote:

> Communism is dead and abandoned and Russia is on the road to recovery. The realization by the Russian people that the strong American system was able and contained the spirit to save these millions of strangers from the death that had engulfed them must have furnished food for thought. . . . To America, this is a passing incident of national duty, undertaken, finished, and to be quickly forgotten. The story of it will be told lovingly in Russian households for generations.[20]

History added an ironic footnote to Haskell's confident verdict that communism was dead. The defeat of the famine not only enabled the Soviet regime to survive but, within four years, to start dismantling the New Economic Policy which Haskell imagined had done away with communism in Russia permanently. In another respect, however, Haskell forecast the course of future events quite accurately. Although the rescue mission excited considerable interest and sympathy in the United States at the time, it has been all but forgotten by American historiography and is almost unknown even to the educated public today. The actual involvement of the American people in the work of the ARA was minimal; in the Soviet Union, by contrast, the impact of the mission was deep and lasting. ARA files contain testimonials from individuals and groups from all sections of Soviet society, including government agencies. Paradoxically, the memory of American philanthropy has been kept alive by the Soviet authorities themselves through the propaganda campaign against the ARA that has continued for fifty years through all changes in Soviet leadership.

The Evolution of the Soviet Image of the ARA

A useful standard for evaluating later Soviet versions of the mission is the strictly factual account that appeared in the original (1926) edition of the *Great Soviet Encyclopedia.* The gist of the entry follows.

> The ARA was a philanthropic organization set up by Hoover to feed the starving children of Europe. When the famine struck in Russia in 1921, the ARA offered its assistance. It distributed almost two billion individual rations in a year and a half, provided drugs and other medical supplies to hospitals, sanitary facilities, and improvements in water supply. When its work was over, it left Russia. At the height of its activity, the ARA distributed supplemental food to approximately 10 million people.[21]

The first hint of substantial revision appeared with the publication of the *Small Soviet Encyclopedia* in 1928. To an abridged version of the earlier article was appended the comment: "Under the guise of charity, the ARA took advantage of this opportunity to relieve the crisis in America arising out of the food prepared in huge amounts for the needs of the imperialist war."[22]

At least one high Soviet official did not share the view that the relief effort was primarily a selfish maneuver. On 10 December 1928 Litvinov told a session of the Central Executive Committee of the

USSR, "We do not forget that, during the difficult years of the famine, the American people gave us vital help through the A.R.A., which was headed by the future president of the United States, H. Hoover."[23] Litvinov's statement was the last unequivocal appreciation of the ARA on record by an official Soviet spokesman. Even in 1937, when the Soviet government was trying to win the United States over to a broad coalition against Nazi Germany, the derogatory interpretation of American motives for the relief mission was repeated in the new edition of the *Small Soviet Encyclopedia.*[24]

Since World War II, Soviet literature has produced a number of criticisms of the ARA that are remarkable for their vehemence and variety. The prototype of the more extreme revisions is an article in a scholarly journal, *Historical Comments,* entitled "Anti-Soviet Acts of the American Relief Administration (ARA) in Soviet Russia in 1921—1922," written by A.N. Kogan and published in 1949. Its central theme is that the relief effort was essentially a continuation of counterrevolutionary intervention by other means. The evidence offered by the author consists of a citation of the social origins of some of the ARA's Russian employees and the fact that the program was financed by the United States government. The Marshall Plan, according to Kogan, was merely another American attempt to implement the plan that failed in 1921—1922.[25]

The 1950 edition of the *Great Soviet Encyclopedia* produced the following variation on the theme.

> The A.R.A. used this opportunity to create an apparatus in Soviet Russia for spying and wrecking activities and for supporting counterrevolutionary elements. The counterrevolutionary activities of the A.R.A. provoked firm protests from the wide masses of toilers in Soviet Russia. "The work" of the ARA in the R.S.F.S.R. was concluded in June, 1923. Soon thereafter, the organization went out of existence.[26]

The entry does not mention actual relief assistance given by the ARA. This total transformation in the official image of the ARA cannot be attributed to Stalin's notorious zenophobia; the attacks continued unabated after his death. In 1958, *Izvestia* responded to an anti-Soviet speech delivered by Hoover with an editorial accusing the ex-President of having directed "the notorious ARA which blasphemously concealed assistance for each and every enemy of

Soviet power as concern for the welfare of the hungry."[27] The edition
of the *Small Soviet Encyclopedia* issued that year repeated the accusations of "spy-wrecking activities" and assistance to "counterrevolutionary elements."[28]

An official history of Soviet foreign relations published in 1961
added a new, international dimension to the earlier versions of the
American relief effort.

> To advance these goals [undermining the USSR], the capitalist
> countries used the "charitable" (actually governmental) organization
> ARA (the American Relief Administration), headed by Herbert
> Hoover. . . . Imperialist England, the U.S., and France hoped, with the
> help of the Kadets, the former ministers of the Provisional Govern-
> ment, Prokopovich and Kishkin, the counterrevolutionist Kuskova,
> and others organized into the Public Famine Relief Committee, to
> create a counterrevolutionary government in Russia. This Committee
> organized anti-Soviet organizations in the country, and established
> connections with foreign interventionists. Kishkin and the rest were
> allied with Antonov's band, which was fighting against the Soviet
> power.
>
> The Soviet government, however, upset the plans of the imperialists.
> The Committee was liquidated and the agents of the foreign interven-
> tionists were arrested.[29]

A considerably amplified treatment of the ARA is included in a
1962 Soviet history textbook. This version is an anthology of earlier
indictments, plus several interesting but undocumented charges not
previously presented. Following is my summary of this version.

> When the famine struck, "the counterrevolutionary forces in
> America rose with new vigor." Hoover decided that the moment had
> come for a revival of his campaign against Bolshevism. Through the
> ARA, the United States expected to gather information, establish con-
> tacts with anti-Soviet elements, and secretly organize an insurrec-
> tionary force. If this plan failed, the American imperialists intended to
> capitalize on Russian gratitude by obtaining profitable concessions. In
> any case, the removal of the food surplus that had accumulated in the
> United States would alleviate the domestic economic crisis.
>
> The Riga agreement made it possible for the Americans to recruit
> counterrevolutionaries and to provide them with special privileges and
> protection. "Former counterrevolutionary activity was the best
> recommendation for anybody who wanted to apply for service in the
> ARA organization."

The ARA "stimulated a definite revival among the White Guard elements in Samara." During 1921-22, the Cheka in Samara arrested many ARA employees for subversive activity, but they were released on the insistence of the American supervisor.

The ARA committees were controlled by kulaks, priests, and others, who refused to give food to the families of Communists and Red Army men and "terrorized the Soviet people." They did not, however, succeed in discrediting Soviet rule. The government invalidated all the agreements whereby the kulaks exacted from the poor their cattle, homes, and seed in exchange for ARA food.

The ARA provided only minimal assistance, amounting to only 25,-000 tons of provisions when even 2 million tons would have been insufficient to meet the needs of the starving.

Workers and farmers in the United States and throughout the world joined the campaign organized by *Mezhrabpom* and thus played a major role in combating the famine. Hoover tried to prevent this campaign by redbaiting. The capitalist press assisted him by publishing slanderous lies about the inability of the Soviet transportation system to handle more relief supplies. "Nothing, however, was able to strangle the mass movement of solidarity with the Soviet people which permeated the United States in 1922." "This time, the plan of American reaction failed. The Soviet government overcame the famine, and the A.R.A. was forced to withdraw from Russia."[30]

To give the author credit, this account is by far the most imaginative version of the relief mission to date. Oddly enough, she offers no explanation why the vigilant Soviet authorities allowed the Americans to engage in subversive activity for almost two years under the cover of insignificant relief assistance.

V. K. Furaev, Soviet analyst of Soviet-American relations, avoids this difficulty by simply omitting mention of the amount of food distributed by the ARA. His major complaint against the ARA is less dramatic than most of the others but no less inventive. "The price of rye, wheat, and corn set by the A.R.A.," he alleges, "was higher than market prices, and Soviet agencies were forced to overpay for seed. The A.R.A. made a fortune on its middleman operations." Later he asserts that the Soviet government spent $12.2 million in gold "to pay for the food provided by the A.R.A."[31]

The Soviet contribution in gold was, of course, not used for the purchase of food but for seed, as stipulated in the agreement of December 1921. How the ARA could have "made a fortune" for itself by overcharging the Soviet government for seed is not explained

According to financial statements rendered to both the United States and Soviet governments, the ARA spent the funds realized from all sources on food and other supplies, which were distributed free of charge. The only ones who could possibly have profited from the ARA's entrepreneurial operations were the starving and the sick—at least, so the Soviet government testified when it acknowledged, in the liquidation agreement, that

> all funds and supplies of whatever nature turned over by [the Soviet government] or its agents to the A.R.A. and disbursed or distributed by the A.R.A. for the Soviet government have been properly expended in accordance with existing agreements and fully and satisfactorily accounted for by the A.R.A.[32]

The failure of the fifty-year effort to produce any evidence that ARA personnel instigated or encouraged counterrevolutionary activity in Russia is not surprising. During the course of the mission, the ubiquitous *Cheka* uncovered no such "distortions" of the relief effort. The vaguer charge that Hoover used the ARA to discredit the Soviet regime is true only in a very broad sense. He certainly intended to demonstrate the superiority of American individualism over Soviet collectivism by carrying out a successful relief operation. But neither he nor his representatives ever belittled the Soviet government's own highly effective relief campaign.

Echoes in the West

In spite of its shortcomings, the Soviet prosecution of the ARA *in absentia* has not been altogether ineffectual. A respectable body of Western scholarly opinion has been influenced by the lurid charges leveled at the ARA and Hoover. The eminent British historian E. H. Carr, for instance, is convinced that the ARA "clearly hoped" to weaken the Soviet government and planned to mesh its activities with the "bourgeois" famine relief committee rather than with the official Soviet agencies.[33] William Appleman Williams finds Hoover guilty of attempting to use the relief program solely for counterrevolutionary purposes but presents no bill of particulars.[34] Peter J. Filene characterizes the relief effort as "more devious than frank counterrevolution."[35]

These critics have quite probably been influenced by Hoover's anti-Bolshevik activities during the Armistice period and by his failure to feed the hungry in the United States during the Depression. Other observers, such as Louis Fischer and George Kennan (neither of whom are Hoover's admirers), have contented themselves with noting the ARA's humanitarian accomplishments in Russia, leaving motivational exploration to future research.[36] A great many other students of Soviet and American politics have made no mention of the relief mission.

The Durable Remembrance

There is no practical way to test the accuracy of the sentiment inscribed in the plaque presented to the ARA by the Council of People's Commissars: "The Soviet people will never forget the help given them by the American people through the A.R.A." The ranks of the famine survivors have been thinned by time and the calamitous events of succeeding years, and the remaining eyewitnesses are, for the most part, in no position to testify. Yet from time to time, faint signs appear that the relief mission has not faded from memory in Russia. In 1962, a Soviet author recalled his childhood impressions of the ARA.

> America—or, as we used to call it, the United States of North America—I know mainly through Mayne-Reid (Ed.—a British author of American and Indian stories) and Cooper, through postage stamps . . . and also through A.R.A. condensed milk which was distributed to us children by Hoover's American relief organization (we also collected the labels from the cans avidly, with their pictures of Indians and bisons). . . . Nor had I yet seen a single live American; at the A.R.A., the milk and snow-white bread, soft as cotton, were handed out by Russians.[37]

Khrushchev objected to the general tone of this book, characterizing it as the work of a man who "has lost the precious qualities of a Communist, the sense of partisanship."[38]

Other evidence that the ARA lingers in Russian memory was provided by the two highest-ranking officials of the Soviet government. During a goodwill visit to the United States in July 1959, the

First Deputy Premier of the USSR, Frol Kozlov, remarked that the United States had demanded and received payment in gold for the food distributed in Russia during the famine. The remark came to the attention of Christian Herter, the secretary of state and former assistant director of the ARA. At an official reception, Herter confronted Kozlov—"I want to straighten you out on one matter"—and informed him that the food sent to the starving in Russia was an outright gift; no payment had been asked or received. "The question is not to be discussed," said Kozlov. "It is not disputed."[39]

Several months later, Khrushchev himself brought up the subject of American relief at a breakfast given in his honor in a Los Angeles movie studio.

> We remember [the help given by the ARA] and we thank you. I consider it necessary to add, however, one "but." And this "but" consists of the fact that our people remember not only that America helped us through the A.R.A., and that, thanks to that, thousands of people were rescued from famine on the Volga; they also remember that, in the difficult time after the October revolution, American soldiers under the leadership of their generals landed on Soviet soil in order to help the White Guards in their struggle against the Soviet system. . . . If you and your Allies had not landed their armies, we would have finished off the White Guards immediately, and we would not have had a civil war, we would not have had destruction, we would not have been starving. And it would not have been necessary, therefore, for you to help the Soviet people through the A.R.A.[40]

This highly inaccurate estimate of the number of people saved by American relief passed without challenge. Surviving members of the ARA, however, may have drawn some comfort from Khrushchev's grudging acknowledgment that the ARA had performed a humanitarian service during the great famine of 1921. It was, after all, the most generous comment from an official Soviet source in many years.

A political theorist who has never been accused of sentimentalism has written, "An act of humanity . . . will at all times have more influence over the minds of men than violence and ferocity."[41] That Russian perceptions of Americans were affected by the relief effort is beyond question. The evidence strongly suggests that the "act of humanity" won the gratitude of the governed and the everlasting resentment of the governors in the Soviet Union. Yet this is by no means certain. The endless campaign of disparagement may only reflect the constant need of the Soviet leadership to adapt aberrant reality to official ideology. An intriguing conjecture on this point is that some of the older Soviet dignitaries who gathered to celebrate the fiftieth anniversary of the Soviet Union may have been rescued from death at an early age by the American relief effort that was inspired and directed by the devout anti-Communist, Herbert Hoover.

—9—

Summary and Conclusions

INSTITUTIONS AND IDEOLOGIES

Despite the disclaimers of Hoover and the State Department, contemporary observers saw the American relief mission as an undertaking of the United States government and therefore as a major political event. There was ample basis for such a view. By appropriating funds for the relief program, Congress tacitly acknowledged its public character and gave its formal approval. The president confirmed the official nature of the project by issuing an executive order delegating exclusive management to the secretary of commerce. The army granted leaves of absence to officers so that they could engage in relief work at the highest level. The navy sent military vessels to the scene of operations in support of the mission. The Treasury Department allowed an exception to its strict rule against the importation of Soviet gold. Finally, the State Department designated the ARA as the clearinghouse in Russia for matters that normally fall under the jurisdiction of a consular office.

Thus, the official position of the United States government that the relief mission was a private matter between a charitable organization and a nonexistent government was only a convenient fiction. The governments of both countries became deeply involved with the ARA's activities in Russia. It was an extraordinary opportunity for each side to observe the interplay of a rival political system with a single series of events.

Decision-making in the Two Systems

The notion that a dictatorship always exhibits greater unity and coherence in framing and carrying out decisions than a more loosely organized political system needs closer examination. In 1921, the leading Bolsheviks disagreed on a variety of issues. These differences broke out of the confines of the Politburo into the larger arena of the Party congress and were articulated in bitter public debates. At times it appeared that the top leadership agreed on very little except the continuance of Bolshevik rule and the need for "iron unity."

The meager evidence available suggests that the ARA was a source of contention within the Politburo. After decisions were arrived at—and a Politburo vote was apparently *de rigueur* even on day-to-day matters—individual members could still use their influence to support or obstruct the mission. Even while Lenin was active in the management of Soviet policy, the Politburo was not merely an instrument of his will. Stalin was able to muster a majority in opposition to the remittance agreement with the ARA, although Lenin clearly favored further ties with the Americans. In this case Lenin was able to overrule the opposition. On the other hand, his suggestion to accept Hoover's offer to act as purchasing agent in Europe for the Soviet government in the procurement of seed was ignored.

In 1922, when Lenin was withdrawing from daily supervision of the Soviet state, official attitudes toward the ARA hovered between reluctant accommodation and restrained hostility. From October 1922 on, the more antagonistic tendency asserted itself and moved to eliminate the ARA's privileged position in the Soviet system. Toward the end of the mission, the more conciliatory Bolshevik leaders made a final gesture of friendship toward the Americans. Symbolic of the sharp division within the Politburo, however, was the absence of such figures as Trotsky, Stalin, Bukharin, Zinoviev, and Tomsky from the farewell ceremonies.

In striking contrast, the American side was represented, for the most part, by a single will. Hoover's international prestige, unique expertise, and strategic position enabled him to achieve close to a monopoly of authority in the initiation and implementation of the mission. His decisions were always subject to approval by Harding and the cabinet, but his practice of informing his colleagues little and late was effective in freeing him from the "frictions, indecisions, and delays" of the consultative routine. The final texts of the Riga and liquidation agreements were transmitted to the secretary of state only after ratification by the ARA and the Soviet government. In his drive for autonomy, Hoover even presumed to trespass on the time-

hallowed domain of the Treasury Department by arranging the con-
tribution of gold by the Soviet government before consulting
Secretary Mellon. Finally, as head of the government-owned U.S.
Grain Corporation, he was able to supervise the placement of sizable
orders for grain and milk without the advice and consent of the
Department of Agriculture.

All in all, it was an extraordinary display of unilateral authority—one not likely to be repeated except under unusual circumstances. A lesser figure than Hoover would undoubtedly have
come to grief for such arrant disregard of the bureaucratic rules of
the game. The fact that Hoover had at his disposal a personal, strictly
disciplined, worldwide organization completes the picture of mono-
lithic control. His decisions were not subject to normal bureaucratic
dilution through neglect or reinterpretation.

For all these reasons, the relief policies that emanated from the
American side were characterized by a coherence and decisiveness
that was noticeably lacking in Soviet policies. Admittedly, the relief
mission was a unique event, but it serves to highlight some of the
latitudes of the American system and some of the limitations of the
Soviet system in regard to the exercise of personal authority during
the period under discussion.

Leaders and Interest Groups

By coincidence, the first effective pro-Soviet interest group in the
United States emerged shortly before the last legal anti-Soviet interest group was dissolved. Thus, for a brief period, Hoover was confronted with the Friends of Soviet Russia while Lenin was contending with the "bourgeois" famine relief committee. Nothing more
than a secret directive from Lenin was needed to dismantle the
"bourgeois" committee and immobilize its recalcitrant members.
The task of discrediting the group was assigned to the controlled
mass media, which carried out Lenin's instructions. No individual or
group outside the top leadership of the Party had the power to oppose these actions.

If Hoover had wanted to proceed against American radical groups
in a similar manner, he would have encountered difficulties. The constitutional bars against proscription of specific organizations were
not breached even at the height of the "Red scare." More important

was the fact that the appetite for wholesale persecution of radicals by the federal government had slackened sharply by 1921. Neither Hoover nor the Harding administration as a whole showed any inclination to revive the anti-Red drive.

Hoover did try to use his official position, both openly and covertly, to discredit and disable the Friends of Soviet Russia and its affiliates. He was not able, however, to curtail the growth of the pro-Soviet relief movement or to prevent the consequent increase in radical agitation throughout the country. To forestall public controversy, Hoover began to modify his own decisions in anticipation of how they would be received and publicized by the groups that he characterized as "pinks and Reds." The decision to remain in Russia after the harvest of 1922 was based in part on his fear of criticism by leftwing groups and of abandoning Russian relief to their control. Thus, in an odd and subtle manner, Hoover came reluctantly to reflect the interests of a small, hostile, but highly cohesive group whose deficiencies in numbers, economic resources, and acceptability would normally have barred it from having any significant influence.

The ARA and Soviet Political Institutions

The question that haunted both sides of the conference table at Riga was whether any way could be found to fit the American relief group into the network of institutions unique to the Soviet system. Litvinov's solution was to turn the distribution of food over to existing Soviet agencies. Under such an arrangement, the ARA would have been restricted to general oversight and accounting. But the Americans refused to countenance Soviet control of ARA food and insisted on independent management of the relief effort. With several modifications, the American plan was adopted in the Riga agreement.

With its own activities effectively shielded from the more repressive Soviet institutions by the Riga agreement, the ARA was able to function with remarkable efficiency in a controlled political system. The constant surveillance by the secret police, the sporadic drives against the Socialist-Revolutionaries and the church, and the restrictions on speech and association were inconveniences but did not hamper relief work appreciably. More disruptive were the refusal of the railroad workers to transport relief supplies until they were given ARA food, the strike of the laborers at Rybinsk, and the resistance of the better-off peasants to the commandeering of their horses. The ARA reacted to these inconvenient assertions of individual rights much as any business firm would to an interruption in production, but with greater determination because of the nature of its work.

From time to time, the ARA found the regime's instruments of control useful in curbing obstructive minor officials. One such useful instrument was the dreaded head of the *Cheka,* Feliks Dzerzhinsky. A hint by Haskell that he might call upon the services of his friend Dzerzhinsky invariably produced results. Government control of the press was also an occasional convenience. When Haskell became particularly annoyed at criticism of the ARA in one of the Soviet newspapers, he did not hesitate to advise the authorities to restrain the offender. On balance, then, it appears that the peculiar institutions of the Soviet system did not seriously hamper the relief mission.

The Role of Ideology

Hoover believed that the Soviet system was irrational and ephemeral. Gorky's appeal for help seemed to confirm this belief and to justify Hoover's early instructions to the ARA to prepare for the possible collapse of the Bolshevik regime. In such an event, the timely arrival of American food would have had a salutory effect on political developments in Russia. But as his earlier experiences in famine relief had demonstrated, a successful relief program could also serve to stabilize the existing Soviet government. Hoover's prompt response to Gorky shows that he spent little time pondering this dilemma. The "foolish economic system" of communism was ultimately doomed anyway. To Hoover, the rescue of a million children was worth the risk of a temporary reprieve of the regime.

Hoover had no difficulty in persuading Secretary of State Hughes that American assistance could be carried out without weakening the official nonrecognition policy. With the two most prominent anti-Communists in the cabinet in agreement, it was impossible for lesser figures in the Harding administration, including the president himself, to raise serious objections. Hoover's record and reputation also promoted more general acceptance of the idea of coming to the aid of Red Russia. In the climate of public opinion created by the "Red scare," such a project would undoubtedly have generated widespread opposition if the sponsor were not equipped with impeccable anti-Bolshevik credentials. The angry protests of liberals and radicals at the terms of Hoover's proposal reinforced the confidence of more influential groups that the relief project was in safe hands.

The first reports from ARA representatives in the field dispelled any illusions that the Bolshevik regime was in imminent danger of being overthrown. But there was still the possibility that an effective demonstration of the superiority of American individualism, conducted in full view of the Bolshevik rulers and the Russian population, would invite comparison with Communist bungling and thus generate pressure for fundamental change in the system. Hoover was thus able to find ample ideological justification, if he needed it, for carrying through and even expanding the relief effort.

To Lenin, Hoover's offer of relief was a sign that the contradictions within capitalism had forced the American bourgeoisie to turn to Soviet Russia to ease the economic crisis in the United States. Since, in Lenin's view, capitalism was doomed anyway, it was no betrayal of the Bolsheviks' revolutionary mission to accept the aid offered by Hoover, even if it meant the temporary recovery of the capitalist system in America. In Lenin's estimation, the prospect of saving the homeland of the proletarian revolution outweighed by far the short-range benefit to the American bourgeoisie. As far as possible counterrevolutionary activity on the part of the relief missionaries was concerned, Lenin was confident that the *Cheka* and Red Army were capable of defending the Soviet power against the one hundred Americans who were expected to enter Russia. Hoover's agreement to an absolute ban on political activity by the ARA and to the conditional right of Soviet authorities to search ARA premises seemed to support Lenin's view that economic opportunity and not subversion was the main objective of the secretary of commerce. Lenin's authority as a revolutionary leader and Marxist theoretician was more than equal to the task of convincing more doctrinaire comrades that the workers' state had to accept the "bitter bread" of the capitalists.

Not entirely by accident, the division of labor between the ARA and the Soviet government was roughly along lines of ideological preference. Lenin's statement during the Riga negotiations that the Soviet government was not providing rations to the rural population placed the major responsibility for feeding the peasants on the ARA. Hoover had always been concerned about the welfare of other non-proletarian groups in Russia. The way things worked out, the Soviet government's relief agency concentrated its efforts on sustaining union members, Communist functionaries, Red Army men, and their families, while the ARA fed the peasants, professional classes, and tradesmen through regular rations or through the remittance program. Although the Soviet government resented what it considered the resuscitation of the bourgeoisie, the tacit assignment of each authority to its natural constituency worked out fairly harmoniously.

It is possible to make a case that the ideological convictions of the leaders on both sides, although antithetical, actually enhanced the prospects for initiating the relief project and did not seriously interfere with its implementation. Apparently, ideology did not impel either side irresistibly toward one or the other alternative—that is, whether to have a relief mission or not. With a little imagination, either course could have been justified by both ideologies. The fact that the decisions of Hoover and Lenin coincided, although their interpretations of reality clashed, arouses a suspicion that these decisions were taken for other compelling reasons and then rationalized to fit each ideology. Thus reinforced, both sides could proceed in good conscience toward the common objective.

GOALS AND OUTCOMES

The Common Objective

Both sides were earnestly committed to the immediate, concrete goal. Hoover's concern for the famine victims stood proof against innumerable difficulties and his own repugnance at collaborating with the Bolsheviks. For the Soviet leaders, halting the march of the devastating famine was the one objective on which all their other goals depended.

The contribution of the ARA cannot be estimated in terms of food shipments alone. The American donation of some 540,000 tons of food over a two-year period was not in itself sufficient to make up the shortage that existed in Russia. No less valuable than Iowa corn and Wisconsin milk, however, were the less tangible resources brought in by the ARA, such as advanced techniques of relief administration, professional dedication, and, not least, a spirit of almost unreasonable optimism. The early successes of the ARA revived fading hopes that the famine could be overcome and inspired Soviet leaders to demand that their own relief workers emulate the Americans. Thus, Hoover's insistence on maintaining the independence of the ARA effort had the collateral effect of stimulating a highly constructive competition between the Soviet and American relief agencies.

The ARA's claim that it sustained over ten million people at the height of its effort is not open to dispute. The Soviet government, through its own agencies, verified this figure and publicly acknowledged its accuracy many times. The Soviet relief effort, which consisted mainly of supplying seed to the famine areas and paying the administrative expenses of the ARA, contributed substantially to the struggle against the famine. In furnishing direct relief to the starving, however, the ARA had no close rival. It is, therefore, no exaggeration to conclude that the major outcome of the American relief mission was the defeat of what the League of Nations called the worst famine in the history of modern Europe.

Collateral American Goals

A basic misapprehension shared by most Soviet leaders was the assumption that saving children from starvation could not possibly have been Hoover's primary interest. Dismissal of this motive inevitably led to an exaggeration of other motives. One group, under Lenin's guidance, saw the relief offer as an effort to achieve predominance in the Russian market. In welcoming such a development, Lenin was joined by his deputy, Kamenev; by Chicherin and Litvinov in the Foreign Commissariat; Krasin in the Trade Commissariat; and Sokolnikov, among others.

As secretary of commerce, Hoover was expected to examine the possibilities for profitable trade with Russia. His extensive probe into all aspects of Soviet economic life satisfied this requirement. In fact, however, Hoover never wavered from his original belief that commercial relations with Russia could serve no useful purpose unless there were a fundamental change in the political and economic institutions of the country. Predictably, he concluded that, even under the NEP, the Soviet government did not provide the guarantees necessary to assure the security of both the funds and personnel of American investors. If one of his goals was to discourage the resumption of trade relations by demonstrating the impracticality of such a move, he achieved his purpose. For the Soviet leaders—including those who were skeptical about reaching a rapprochement with America through Hoover—this was a distinct disappointment.

Another group in the Bolshevik leadership saw Hoover's proposal as a renewal of intervention in the guise of philanthropy. Lenin himself alerted the security forces to the possible danger of counterrevolutionary activity by the relief missionaries. Very early in the mission, however, it became evident to the suspicious hosts that their precautions were unnecessary; the Americans showed no disposition to organize or encourage a revolt against the Bolsheviks. During the rest of the ARA's stay in Russia, Soviet authorities found no occasion to accuse any of the relief workers of any action that could be remotely connected with subversion or counterrevolution. Hoover's initial instruction to all personnel to refrain from political activity in Russia was evidently taken literally.

This is not to suggest that there were no political expectations involved in Hoover's management of the mission to Russia. For a while, he entertained the hope that a demonstration of goodwill would enhance American influence in Russia and somehow induce changes in the Soviet system beyond those instituted by the NEP. As the prospect for such a transformation dimmed, he retreated to the more modest goal of leaving a "lasting impression" in Russia.

Judging by the widespread popularity that the ARA won in Russia, Hoover had reason to congratulate himself on having established an American "presence" in the land of the Soviets. The relief mission did not, however, have any marked effect on Soviet institutions. Here, Hoover's aspirations clearly outran the capabilities of a philanthropic organization. In the absence of a definite understanding with the United States government on trade and recognition, the Soviet leaders were not disposed to institute firm guarantees of person and property out of deference to Hoover's sensibilities.

Collateral Soviet Goals

Undoubtedly the most important goal that the Bolsheviks hoped to attain by overcoming the famine was to stabilize their rule in Russia. At the time, it seemed evident to an American correspondent who was sympathetic toward the Soviet government that the ARA's success "bolstered the strength of the regime." In his dispatch of 7 January 1923, he wrote:

> No government rests securely when its population starves. The A.R.A. has thus very directly aided the present regime through its presence in Russia. It is no disgrace to have done so. It was in fact one of the greatest deeds of charity that history records.[1]

Current Western and Soviet students of the period do not attach such importance to the ARA as a factor in the stabilization of Soviet rule. A notable exception is George F. Kennan, who concludes that "the Soviet government was, thus, importantly aided, not just in its economic undertakings, but in its political prestige and capacity for survival, by A.R.A.'s benevolent intervention. This political aid was desperately needed."[2]

A more typical view is that the easing of the economic and political crises was due almost exclusively to NEP reforms. But the legalization of free trade in farm produce—the most important reform of the NEP—had little meaning in a country paralyzed by famine.[3] As an anonymous Russian eyewitness put it:

> Free trade and certain re-established privileges could not have brought Russia very far at a time when the worst famine ever experienced was raging all over the country, and when all the moral resources of the nation were almost exhausted. The country was in dire need of both moral and physical help from the outside. The A.R.A. broke the mood of desperation. Help from the outside had come. . . .[4]

It was only after the fight against the famine was won that the incentives provided by the NEP began to take effect. The economy recovered. Soviet rule survived. In providing "help from the outside" at a critical point, the American relief mission contributed significantly to the maintenance of the Bolshevik regime in Russia.

As an experiment in international cooperation for the purpose of averting a great human catastrophe, the relief effort was an outstanding success. For a while it seemed as though the mission would be equally successful in ending the estrangement between the United States and Soviet Russia. Leaders on both sides proved that they could submerge their ideological animosities in the interest of a common objective. By establishing the first stable channel of communications between the two countries and by dispelling much of the distrust that had grown up during the war, the intervention, and the four-year alienation, the ARA mission provided an opportunity for reconciliation. When the immediate goal was won, however, the pressure for cooperation was removed. The suppressed hostility of the more dogmatic Soviet leaders was released. At some point during the series of minor conflicts that ensued, the unique opportunity for a significant change in the pattern of Soviet-American relations was lost.

Bibliography

INTERVIEWS

Fisher, Harold H., former Director of the Historical Division of the ARA. Interview, New York, New York, 2 May 1966.

Galpin, Perrin C., former Secretary at New York Headquarters of the ARA. Interview, New York, New York, 14 July 1967.

Quinn, Cyril J. C., former Acting Director of the Russian Unit of the ARA. Interview, New York, New York, 2 May 1966.

Walker, Dr. Herschel C., former District Supervisor with the Russian Unit of the ARA. Interview, New York, New York, 17 May 1966.

Wolfe, Henry C., former member of the Russian Unit of the ARA. Interview, New York, New York, 20 May 1966.

UNPUBLISHED MATERIAL

Ashland, Va. Walter Page Library. "Between Two Worlds" [by J. Rives Childs].

Stanford, Calif. Hoover Institution on War, Revolution and Peace. Documents of the American Relief Administration, 1918-1922.

Stanford, Calif. Hoover Institution on War, Revolution and Peace. Herbert Hoover Archives.

PUBLIC DOCUMENTS

Institut Marksizma-Leninizma Pri TsK KPSS. *Lenin o vneshnei politike sovetskovo gosudarstva.* Moscow: Gos. Izd. Pol. Lit., 1960.

League of Nations. *Report on Economic Conditions in Russia, with Special Reference to the Famine of 1921-22 and the State of Agriculture.* Ser. 2, no. 6. Geneva, 1922.

Ministerstvo Inostrannykh Del SSSR. *Dokumenty vneshnei politiki SSSR.* Vols. 4, 5. Moscow: Gos. Izd. Pol. Lit., 1960, 1961.

Supreme Economic Council—Food Section, Minutes of Meetings. Vol. 7. Paris, 1919.

Tsentralnaya Kommissia Pomoshchi Golodayushchim. *Itogi borby s golodom v 1921-22 gg.: Sbornik statei i otchetov.* Moscow: Izd. TsK Pomgol, 1922.

U.S. Congress. House. *Russian Relief: Hearings before the Committee on Foreign Affairs on H.R. 9459 and H.R. 9548,* 67th Cong., 2d sess., 13 and 14 December 1921.

_____. Senate. *Congressional Record,* 67th Cong., 2d sess., 21 and 22 December 1921, 62, pt. 1.

U.S. Department of Commerce. Bureau of the Census. *Historical Statistics of the United States, Colonial Times to 1957.* Washington, D.C., 1960.

U.S. Department of State. *Papers Relating to the Foreign Relations of the United States: 1919, Russia.* Washington, D.C., 1937.

U.S. National Archives. *Records of the Department of State Relating to the Internal Affairs of Russia and the Soviet Union: 1910-1929.* Microcopy no. 316. Washington, D.C., 1966.

U.S. President. *Executive Orders of a Public Nature.* Washington, D.C., 1919.

COLLECTED DOCUMENTS, WORKS, AND SPEECHES

Baker, Ray S., and Dodd, William E., eds. *The Public Papers of Woodrow Wilson: 1917-1924.* Vol. 1. New York: Harper & Bros., 1925-1927.

Bane, Suda L., and Lutz, Ralph H., eds. *Organization of American Relief in Europe, 1918-1919.* Stanford, Calif.: Stanford University Press, 1943.

Belov, G., ed. *Iz istorii Vserossiiskoi Chrezvychainoi Kommissii, 1917-1921 gg.: Sbornik dokumentov.* Moscow: Gos. Izd. Pol. Lit., 1958.

The Bullitt Mission to Russia: Testimony before the Committee on Foreign Relations, United States Senate, of William C. Bullitt. New York: B. W. Huebsch, 1919.

Eudin, Xenia J., and Fisher, Harold H., eds. *Soviet Russia and the West, 1920-1927.* Stanford, Calif.: Stanford University Press, 1957.

Gay, George I., and Fisher, Harold H., eds. *Public Relations of the Committee for Relief in Belgium: Documents.* Vols. 1 and 2. Stanford, Calif.: Stanford University Press, 1929.

Khrushchev, Nikita S. *Mir bez oruzhia, mir bez voiny.* Vol. 2. Moscow: Gos. Izd. Pol. Lit., 1960.

Lenin, Vladimir Ilyich, *Polnoe sobranie sochineny.* 5th ed. Vols. 43, 44, 45, and 53. Moscow: Gos. Izd. Pol. Lit., 1963, 1964, 1965.

_____. *Selected Works.* Vol. 1. New York: International Publishers, n.d.

Litvinov, Maxim. *Vneshnyaya politika SSSR: Rechi i zayavlenia, 1927-1937,* Moscow: Gos. Sots. Izd., 1937.

Stalin, Joseph V. *Works.* Vol. 5. Moscow: Foreign Languages Publishing Co., 1953.

MEMOIRS AND AUTOBIOGRAPHIES

Daniels, Josephus. *The Wilson Era: Years of War and After, 1917-1923.* Chapel Hill: University of North Carolina Press, 1946.

Duranty, Walter. *Duranty Reports Russia.* New York: Viking Press, 1934.

_____. *I Write as I Please.* New York: Simon & Schuster, 1935.

Golder, Frank A., and Hutchinson, Lincoln. *On the Trail of the Russian Famine.* Stanford, Calif.: Stanford University Press, 1927.

Goldman, Emma. *My Further Disillusionment in Russia.* Garden City, N.Y.: Doubleday, Page & Co., 1924.

Hoover, Herbert. *An American Epic.* Vols. 1 and 3. Chicago: Henry Regnery Co., 1959, 1961.

_____. *The Ordeal of Woodrow Wilson.* New York: McGraw-Hill, 1958.

_____. *Years of Adventure: 1874-1920.* New York: Macmillan Co., 1961.

Nansen, Fridtjof. *La famine en Russie: Conférence faite par le Dr. Nansen au Trocadéro, le 17 février 1922.* Paris, 1922.

_____. *Russia and Peace.* London: Allen & Unwin, 1923.

Steveni, W. Barnes. *Through Famine-Stricken Russia.* London: Sampson Low, 1892.

Strauss, Lewis L. *Men and Decisions.* Garden City, N.Y.: Doubleday & Co., 1962.

Strong, Anna L. *I Change Worlds.* New York: Henry Holt & Co., 1935.

SECONDARY SOURCES

Adams, Samuel H. *The Incredible Era: Life and Times of Warren Gamaliel*

Harding. Boston: Houghton Mifflin Co., 1939.

Ananova, Yelena V. *Noveishaya istoria SShA: 1919-1939 gody*. Moscow: IMO, 1962.

Baker, Ray S. *Woodrow Wilson, Life and Letters: War Leader, April 6, 1917-February 28, 1918*. New York: Doubleday, Doran & Co., 1939.

Baykov, Alexander. *The Development of the Soviet Economic System: An Essay on the Experience of Planning in the USSR*. New York: Macmillan Co., 1947.

Bolshaya Sovetskaya entsiklopedia. Vol. 3. Moscow: Aktsionernoe Obshchestvo Sovetskaya Entsiklopedia, 1926.

Bolshaya Sovetskaya entsiklopedia. Vol. 2. Moscow: Gosudarstvennoe Nauchnoe Izdatelstvo, 1950.

Brandes, Joseph. *Herbert Hoover and Economic Diplomacy*. Pittsburgh: University of Pittsburgh Press, 1962.

Browder, Robert P. *The Origins of Soviet-American Diplomacy*. Princeton: Princeton University Press, 1953.

Brzezinski, Zbigniew. *Ideology and Power in Soviet Politics*. New York: Praeger, 1962.

Brzezinski, Zbigniew, and Huntington, Samuel P. *Political Power: USA/USSR*. New York: Viking Press, 1964.

Carr, E. H. *The Bolshevik Revolution*. Vol. 1. New York: Macmillan Co., 1951.

Commission on Russian Relief. *The Russian Famines: 1921-22, 1922-23*. New York: National Information Bureau, 1923.

Craig, Gordon A., and Gilbert, Felix, eds. *The Diplomats: 1919-1939*. Vol. 1. New York: Atheneum, 1963.

Dallin, Alexander, et al. *The Soviet Union, Arms Control, and Disarmament: A Study of Soviet Attitudes*. New York: Columbia University School of International Affairs, 1964.

Daniels, Robert. *Conscience of the Revolution: Communist Opposition in Soviet Russia*. Cambridge, Mass.: Harvard University Press, 1960.

Dineen, Michael, ed. *Herbert Hoover's Challenge to America: His Life and Work*. New York: Doubleday & Co., 1965.

Dobb, Maurice. *Soviet Economic Development since 1917*. London: Routledge & Paul, 1948.

Dodd, William E. *Woodrow Wilson and His Work*. New York: Doubleday, Page & Co., 1920.

Draper, Theodore. *American Communism and Soviet Russia: The Formative Period*. New York: Viking Press, 1960.

Easton, David. *The Political System: An Inquiry into the State of Political*

Science. New York: Alfred A. Knopf, 1965.

Fainsod, Merle. *How Russia Is Ruled.* Cambridge, Mass.: Harvard University Press, 1963.

Filene, Peter J. *Americans and the Soviet Experiment: 1917-1933.* Cambridge, Mass.: Harvard University Press, 1967.

Fischer, George. *Russian Liberalism: From Gentry to Intelligentsia.* Cambridge, Mass.: Harvard University Press, 1958.

Fischer, Louis. *The Life of Lenin.* New York: Harper & Row, 1964.

———. *The Soviets in World Affairs.* New York: Vintage, 1960.

Fischer, Ruth. *Stalin and German Communism.* Cambridge, Mass.: Harvard University Press, 1948.

Fisher, Harold H. *The Famine in Soviet Russia, 1919-1923: The Operations of the American Relief Administration.* New York: Macmillan Co., 1927.

Furaev, V. K. *Sovetsko-Amerikanskie otnoshenia: 1917-1939.* Moscow: Izd. Sots. Lit., 1964.

Gromyko, Andrei A. et al., eds. *Istoria diplomatii.* 2d ed., rev. Vol. 3. Moscow: Izd. Pol. Lit., 1965.

Gross, Neal; Mason, Ward S.; and McEachern, Alexander W. *Explorations in Role Analysis: Studies of the School Superintendency Role.* New York: John Wiley & Sons, 1958.

Hazard, John N., and Shapiro, Isaac. *The Soviet Legal System: Post-Stalin Documentation and Historical Commentary.* Part 1. Dobbs Ferry, N. Y.: Oceana Publications, 1962.

Hoover, Herbert. *American Individualism.* Garden City, N. Y.: Doubleday, Page & Co., 1923.

Institut Mezhdunarodnykh Otnosheny. *Istoria mezhdunarodnykh otnosheny i vneshnei politiki USSR: 1917-1939 gg.* Vol. 1. Moscow: Izd. IMO, 1961.

Kennan, George F. *The Decision to Intervene.* Princeton: Princeton University Press, 1958.

———. *Russia and the West under Lenin and Stalin.* Boston: Little, Brown & Co., 1961.

———. *Soviet-American Relations, 1917-1920: Russia Leaves the War.* Princeton: Princeton University Press, 1956.

Liggett, Walter W. *The Rise of Herbert Hoover.* New York: H. K. Fly, 1932.

Lipset, Seymour M. *Political Man: The Social Bases of Politics.* Garden City, N.Y.: Anchor Books, 1963.

Lovenstein, Meno. *American Opinion of Soviet Russia.* Washington, D.C.: American Council on Public Affairs, 1941.

Lyons, Eugene. *Herbert Hoover: A Biography.* Garden City, N.Y.: Doubleday, Page & Co., 1964.

Malaya Sovetskaya entsiklopedia. Vol. 1. Moscow: Aktsionernoe Obshchestvo Sovetskaya Entsiklopedia, 1928.

Malaya Sovetskaya entsiklopedia. Vol. 1. Moscow: OGIZ, 1937.

Malaya Sovetskaya entsiklopedia. Vol. 1. Moscow: GNI, 1958.

Marquis, A. N., ed. *Who's Who in America: 1914-1915.* Chicago: A. N. Marquis, 1914.

Mayer, Arno J. *Wilson vs. Lenin: Political Origins of the New Diplomacy.* New York: Meridian, 1964.

Murray, Robert K. *Red Scare: A Study in National Hysteria, 1919-1920.* Minneapolis: University of Minnesota Press, 1955.

Neustadt, Richard E. *Presidential Power: The Politics of Leadership.* New York: John Wiley & Sons, 1962.

Parsons, Talcott. *The Social System.* Glencoe, Ill.: The Free Press, 1951.

Pusey, Merlo J. *Charles Evans Hughes.* Vol. 2. New York: Macmillan Co., 1951.

Robinson, Geroid T. *Rural Russia under the Old Regime.* New York: Macmillan Co., 1949.

Roche, John P. *The Quest for the Dream.* New York: Macmillan Co., 1963.

Rubenstein, N. L. *Vneshnyaya politika Sovetskovo Gosudarstva.* Moscow: Gos. Izd. Pol. Lit., 1953.

Schapiro, Leonard. *The Communist Party of the Soviet Union.* New York: Vintage, 1964.

Schlesinger, Arthur M., Jr. *The Crisis of the Old Order, 1913-1933.* Boston: Houghton Mifflin Co., 1957.

Schriftgiesser, Karl. *This Was Normalcy: An Account of Party Politics during Twelve Republican Years, 1920-1932.* Boston: Little, Brown & Co., 1948.

Schuman, Frederick L. *American Policy toward Russia since 1917.* New York: International Publishers, 1928.

Surface, Frank M. *The Grain Trade during the World War.* New York: Macmillan Co., 1928.

Surface, Frank M., and Bland, Raymond L. *American Food in the World War and Reconstruction Period: Operations of the Organizations under the Direction of Herbert Hoover, 1914-1924.* Stanford, Calif.: Stanford University Press, 1931.

Thompson, John M. *Russia, Bolshevism, and the Versailles Peace.* Princeton: Princeton University Press, 1966.

Tompkins, Stuart R. *The Russian Intelligentsia: Makers of the Revolutionary State.* Norman, Okla.: University of Oklahoma Press, 1957.

Triska, Jan F., and Slusser, Robert M. *The Theory, Law and Policy of Soviet*

Treaties. Stanford, Calif.: Stanford University Press, 1962.

Ulam, Adam. *The Bolsheviks: The Intellectual and Political History of the Triumph of Communism in Russia*. New York: Macmillan Co., 1965.

Veltman, Mikhail L. [Mikhail Pavlovich]. *Sovetskaya Rossia i kapitalisticheskaya Amerika*. Moscow: Gos. Izd., 1922.

Williams, William A. *American-Russian Relations: 1781-1947*. New York: Rinehart & Co., 1952.

Wolfe, Harold. *Herbert Hoover: Public Servant and Leader of the Loyal Opposition*. New York: Exposition Press, 1956.

JOURNALS AND NEWSPAPERS

American Political Science Review. 1965-66.

Current Digest of the Soviet Press. 1963.

Freeman (New York). 1922.

Istoricheskie zapiski (Moscow). 1949.

Izvestia (Moscow). 1921-24, 1958.

Nation (New York). 1921-23.

New Republic (New York). 1921-22.

New York Call. 1922-23.

New York Evening Post. 1923.

New York Globe. 1922.

New York Times. 1921-24, 1967.

New York Tribune. 1921-22.

Novy mir (Moscow). 1962.

Novy zhurnal (New York). 1954.

Pravda (Moscow). 1921-23.

Slavic Review. 1966.

Sputnik kommunista (Moscow). 1921.

Survey (London). 1965.

Times (London). 1921-22.

Vestnik Narodnovo Kommissariata Inostrannykh Del (Moscow). 1921.

Washington Post. 1924.

World's Work (New York). 1921.

Notes

INTRODUCTION

[1]Harold H. Fisher, *The Famine in Soviet Russia, 1919-1923.*

[2]George F. Kennan, "Our Aid to Russia: A Forgotten Chapter," *New York Times Magazine,* 19 July 1959.

[3]Herbert Hoover Archives, Hoover Institution on War, Revolution and Peace, Stanford Calif., Box no. 17, Folder no. 6 (hereafter cited as HHA 17-6).

[4]See Zbigniew Brzezinski, *Ideology and Power in Soviet Politics,* p. 4; Joseph LaPalombara, "Decline of Ideology: A Dissent and an Interpretation," *American Political Science Review* 60, no. 1 (March 1966): 7; and James B. Christoph, "Consensus and Cleavage in British Political Ideology," *American Political Science Review* 59, no. 3 (September 1965): 629. Christoph comments on his own definition, "Perhaps the best-known paradigms are classical Christianity and classical Marxism."

[5]See Zbigniew Brzezinski and Samuel P. Huntington, *Political Power,* p. 23, for a comparison of "Soviet ideology" and "American political beliefs."

[6]Richard E. Neustadt, *Presidential Power,* pp. 1-8, uses the term "clerk" to describe the president's relationship to the many constituencies that he is expected to serve.

[7]David Easton, *The Political System,* p. 185.

1: THE POLITICS OF FAMINE RELIEF

[1]Geroid T. Robinson, *Rural Russia under the Old Regime,* pp. 94-96, 116-18.

[2]Stuart R. Tompkins, *The Russian Intelligentsia,* p. 145; W. Barnes Steveni, *Through Famine-Stricken Russia,* pp. ix, 19.

[3]George Fischer, *Russian Liberalism,* p. 72.

[4]Tompkins, *The Russian Intelligentsia,* p. 162.

[5]Ibid., p. 145.

[6]Adam Ulam, *The Bolsheviks,* pp. 106-7; V. Sorin, "Vladimir Ilyich Lenin (1870-1924): A Short Biography," in Vladimir Ilyich Lenin, *Selected Works,* 1:21.

[7]Vladimir Ilyich Lenin, "Doklad o zamene razvyorstki naturalnym nalogom," 15 March 1921, *Polnoe sobranie sochineny,* 43:71 (hereafter cited as *Pss*).

[8]Lenin, "O prodovolstvennom naloge," 21 April 1921, *Pss,* 43:219.

[9]G. Aronson, "E. D. Kuskova," *Novy zhurnal* (New York), no. 37 (1954), p. 246.

[10]*Pravda* (Moscow), 30 June 1921.

[11]A. Morozanov, "Famine in the Volga Region," *Ekonomicheskaya zhizn,* 30 June 1921, from a translation in HHA 5-2.

[12]Admiral Mark Bristol to Secretary of State, 21 July 1921, in U.S., National Archives, *Records of the Department of State Relating to the Internal Affairs of Russia and the Soviet Union: 1910-1929,* File no. 861.48/1562 (hereafter cited as *NA* 861.48/1562).

[13]Bristol to Secretary of State, 26 July 1921, *NA* 861.48/1562.

[14]Ministerstvo Inostrannykh Del SSSR, *Dokumenty vneshnei politiki SSSR,* 4:251 (hereafter cited as *Dokumenty vneshnei politiki)*; English translation in *NA* 861.48/1494.

[15]Gibson, Warsaw, to Secretary of State, 10 August 1921, *NA* 861.48/1527; *Izvestia* (Moscow), 12 August 1921.

[16]*Times* (London), 13 September 1921.

[17]*Times* (London), 13 August 1921.

[18]Wheeler, London, to Secretary of State, 14 August 1921, *NA* 861.48/1529.

[19]Tsentralnaya Kommissia Pomoshchi Golodayushchim, *Itogi borby s golodom v 1921-22 gg.,* pp. 427-28 (hereafter cited as *Itogi borby s golodom).*

[20]Ibid., pp. 230, 232.

[21]Ibid., p. 256.

[22]Ibid., p. 258.

[23]Report to Hoover by James Goodrich, 21 November 1921, HHA 81-1.

[24]Frank A. Golder and Lincoln Hutchinson, *On the Trail of the Russian Famine.* p. 13.

[25]Fridtjof Nansen, *La famine en Russie,* p. 9.

[26]League of Nations, *Report on Economic Conditions in Russia, with*

Special Reference to the Famine of 1921-22 and the State of Agriculture.

[27]Maurice Dobb, *Soviet Economic Development since 1917*, p. 103; Alexander Baykov, *The Development of the Soviet Economic System*, p. 22.

[28]*Izvestia* (Moscow), 15 July 1921.

[29]*Itogi borby s golodom*, pp. 207-8.

[30]*London Daily Telegraph*, 20 May 1922, cited in HHA 10-4.

[31]W. H. Coleman to Liaison Division, ARA, Moscow, 6 February 1922, HHA 10-3.

[32]A vivid account of the course of the famine in a Russian village is contained in an unpublished manuscript, "Famine in Ekaterinoslav, 1921-22," by Professor Guskov, HHA 6-2.

[33]Lenin, *Pss*, 45:285.

[34]Ibid., p. 283

[35]Ibid., 53:109.

[36]Louis Fischer, *The Soviets in World Affairs*, p. 342.

[37]Ibid., p. 321.

[38]See, for instance, Lenin's instructions to Litvinov on the Riga negotiations, 11 August 1921, in *Dokumenty vneshnei politiki*, 4:781.

[39]Ulam, *The Bolsheviks*, p. 233.

[40]Lenin, *Pss*, 44:77.

[41]Golder and Hutchinson, *Russian Famine*, p. 126.

[42]P. Krasnev, "The Starving Ukraine," *Kommunist*, 28 December 1921, cited in HHA 10-4.

[43]J. Schleimann, "The Life and Work of Willi Münzenberg," *Survey*, no. 55 (April 1965), p. 71.

[44]Nansen to Gorky, 14 July 1921, *NA* 861.48/1501.

[45]Lenin to Chicherin, 15 July 1921, in Lenin, *Pss*, 53:34-35.

[46]Chicherin to Lenin, 18 July 1921, in Lenin, ibid, p. 384.

[47]*Dokumenty vneshnei politiki*, 4:250.

[48]Louis Fischer, *The Life of Lenin*, p. 557.

[49]V. I. Lenin, "Concluding Remarks on Business Concessions at Meeting of the Russian Communist Party Faction of Eighth Congress of Soviets," 21 December 1920, cited in *Current Digest of the Soviet Press* 15, no. 16 (May 1963): 11.

[50]Lenin, *Pss*, 43:129.

[51]Magruder, American Legation at Helsingfors, to Secretary of State, 13 March 1921, *NA* 861.48/1400.

[52]M. Gorky, *The Russian Peasant* (1922), quoted in Ulam, *The Bolsheviks*, p. 450.

[53]E. Kuskova, "Tragedia Maksima Gorkovo," *Novy zhurnal* (New York), no. 38 (1954), p. 235.

[54]Aronson, "E. D. Kuskova," p. 246.

[55]Lenin, *Pss,* 53:4.

[56]Aronson, "E. D. Kuskova," p. 246.

[57]Lenin, *Pss,* 53:24.

[58]*Pravda* (Moscow), 21 July 1921.

[59]*Pravda* (Moscow), 23 July 1921.

[60]*Izvestia* (Moscow), 22 July 1921, quoted in *NA* 861.48/1637.

[61]Spargo to Secretary of State, 25 July 1921, *NA* 861.48/1993.

[62]N. Avksentiev to American Ambassador, Paris, 27 July 1921, *NA* 861.48/1542.

2: THE ROLES OF HERBERT HOOVER

[1]*Freeman* (New York), 28 June 1922.

[2]See, for instance, William A. Williams, *American-Russian Relations,* p. 193.

[3]George F. Kennan, *Russia and the West under Lenin and Stalin,* p. 180.

[4]Peter J. Filene, *Americans and the Soviet Experiment,* p. 78.

[5]*Sputnik kommunista* (Moscow), no. 3 (4 September 1921), p. 15.

[6]Harold H. Fisher, *The Famine in Soviet Russia, 1919-1923,* fn. 13, p. 57.

[7]Herbert Hoover, *Years of Adventure,* chap. 7.

[8]Ibid., chap. 8; Eugene Lyons, *Herbert Hoover,* pp. 67-71.

[9]Sen. Joseph I. France to Hoover, 8 February 1923, HHA 245-4.

[10]Hoover to France, 10 February 1923, HHA 245-5.

[11]Hoover, *Years of Adventure,* pp. 102-3 and 107-8; A. N. Marquis, ed., *Who's Who in America,* p. 1153.

[12]Urquhart, London, to Hoover, 8 August 1921, *NA* 861.48/1880.

[13]Hoover to Urquhart, 10 August 1921, *NA* 861.48/1880.

[14]Herbert Hoover, "American Relations to Russia," address before the International Chamber of Commerce, 15 May 1922, in *ARA Bulletin* 2, no. 25 (June 1922): 2-6.

[15]Herbert Hoover, press release, 10 February 1923, HHA 271-17.

[16]See, for instance, Walter W. Liggett, *The Rise of Herbert Hoover,* pp. 282-93, 382.

[17]George I. Gay and Harold H. Fisher, eds., *Public Relations of the Committee for Relief of Belgium,* 1:3; Herbert Hoover, *An American Epic,* 1:21-22. For a brief summary of the Belgian relief mission, see Frank M. Surface and Raymond L. Bland, *American Food in the World War and Reconstruction Period,* pp. 12-14.

[18]Ambassador Page to Secretary of State, 16 October 1914, in Gay and Fisher, *Public Relations,* 1:6-7.

[19]Baron von der Goltz to Comité Central, 16 October 1914, in ibid., 1:10-11; Acting Secretary of State to American Ambassador, London, 20 October 1914, in ibid., 1:13.

[20]Hoover, *Years of Adventure,* pp. 157-58.

[21]According to Hoover *(An American Epic,* 1:21-22), Kitchener and Churchill were opposed to any program for feeding the Belgians. In *Years of Adventure,* p. 162, Hoover states that Churchill formally accused him of acting as a spy for the Germans.

[22]Hoover to David Lloyd George, 17 February 1915, in Gay and Fisher, *Public Relations,* 1:265-66.

[23]Hoover, memorandum of a conversation with von Jagow, 7 February 1915, in ibid., 1:252.

[24]Brand Whitlock, American Minister to Belgium, to Ambassador Page, 19 July 1915, ibid., 1:62-65; Baron von der Lancken to Whitlock, 29 July 1915, ibid.

[25]Ibid., 1:167; Hoover, *Years of Adventure,* p. 225.

[26]Gay and Fisher, *Public Relations,* 1:v and 2:473.

[27]Hoover, *Years of Adventure,* pp. 199-201.

[28]Edgar Rickard, "American Relief in Russia," talk before a group of mining engineers, 4 May 1922, HHA 83-1.

[29]Josephus Daniels, *The Wilson Era,* p. 316.

[30]Herbert Hoover, "We'll Have to Feed the World Again," original manuscript of article published in *Collier's* 28 November and 5 December 1942, cited in Suda L. Bane and Ralph H. Lutz, eds., *Organization of American Relief in Europe, 1918-1919,* p. 11.

[31]This description of a Hoover relief organization is derived from Hoover's accounts in *An American Epic* and *Years of Adventure, passim:* Gay and Fisher, *Public Relations,* vols. 1 and 2; the writer's interviews with former ARA officials; and intraorganizational communications in HHA.

[32]Hoover, *Years of Adventure,* pp. 228-29; Gay and Fisher, *Public Relations,* 1:39-42 and 2:473.

[33]Hoover, *Years of Adventure,* pp. 241-42.

[34]Ibid., p. 244; Ray S. Baker and William E. Dodd, eds., *The Public*

Papers of Woodrow Wilson, 1:43-44.

[35]William E. Dodd, *Woodrow Wilson and His Work,* p. 226; Hoover, *Years of Adventure,* p. 253; *Official U.S. Bulletin,* 11 November 1918, p. 7, cited in Bane and Lutz, *American Relief,* p. 36.

[36]Hoover to Wilson, 24 October 1918, in Bane and Lutz, *American Relief,* pp. 26-27.

[37]Hoover to Cotton, 7 November 1918, in ibid., p. 33.

[38]Hoover, interoffice memorandum for American officials, 14 November 1918, in ibid., p. 50.

[39]Lord Reading to Hoover, 12 December 1918, in ibid., p. 89; Hoover to Rickard, 16 December 1918, in ibid., pp. 115-16.

[40]Stephen Pichon to House, 23 December 1918, in ibid.; Announcement of the American Commission to Negotiate Peace, 3 January 1919, in ibid., p. 142; Statement by Herbert Hoover, 3 January 1919, in ibid., p. 143.

[41]Surface and Bland, *American Food,* p. 36.

[42]Bane and Lutz, *American Relief,* pp. 714-19.

[43]Hoover to Wilson, 9 November 1918, in ibid., p. 36; Wilson to Secretary of the Treasury, 1 January 1919, in ibid., pp. 139-40.

[44]Hoover to Wilson, 25 January 1919, in ibid., pp. 211-13; Executive Order no. 3035B, 24 February 1919, in U.S., President, *Executive Orders of a Public Nature.*

[45]Hoover, *An American Epic,* 3:xix.

[46]Herbert Hoover, "Analysis and Comparison of the Plans of President Wilson and the Plans of the Allied Representatives," 16 December 1918, in Bane and Lutz, *American Relief,* p. 93.

[47]Herbert Hoover, "Memorandum on Reconstruction," 22 November 1918, in ibid., pp. 52-53.

[48]Wilson to Hon. Swager Sherley, 13 January 1919, in Baker and Dodd, *Wilson Papers,* 1:389.

[49]*The Bullitt Mission to Russia,* pp. 31-48, 65-66.

[50]For a similar view of the susceptibility of the lower classes to anti-democratic ideas, see Seymour M. Lipset, *Political Man,* p. 51.

[51]Hoover to Wilson, 28 March 1919, HHA 17-6.

[52]*Bullitt Mission,* pp. 39-43, 74-75; Hoover, *Years of Adventure,* p. 414.

[53]Fridtjof Nansen, *Russia and Peace,* pp. 23-32.

[54]*Bullitt Mission,* pp. 75-79.

[55]Ibid., pp. 83-89.

[56]Lewis L. Strauss, *Men and Decisions,* p. 32. In *Russia and the West,* pp. 136-41, George F. Kennan states that Hoover wrote the Nansen letter and the reply by the Council of Four. For a well-documented argument that

Auchincloss and David Miller were the actual authors of the reply to Nansen, see John M. Thompson, *Russia, Bolshevism, and the Versailles Peace,* pp. 249-55.

[57]Hoover, *Years of Adventure,* pp. 416-17.

[58]Fisher, *Famine in Russia,* pp. 18-19.

[59]Nansen, *Russia and Peace,* p. 27.

[60]Chicherin to Nansen, ibid., pp. 28-33.

[61]Ibid., pp. 33-34; Nansen to Hoover, 14 May 1919, HHA 17-6, and Robert Cecil to Sir Maurice Hankey, 16 May 1919, HHA 17-6.

[62]Hoover, *Years of Adventure,* p. 418.

[63]Hoover, *An American Epic,* 3:120-21.

[64]Herbert Hoover, *The Ordeal of Woodrow Wilson,* p. 138; Hoover, *Years of Adventure,* pp. 399-400. For a claim by a former ARA official, T. T. C. Gregory, that he and Hoover actually planned the ouster of the Kun regime, see Gregory's "Overthrowing a Red Regime," *World's Work* (New York), June 1921.

[65]Fisher, *Famine in Russia,* p. 27, describes a meeting between Hoover and Pichon during which Hoover attacked foreign support of the counter-revolutionary forces as invasions in behalf of the Russian landlord class and thus doomed to failure.

[66]Woodrow Wilson, "Preliminary Report of Receipts and Expenditures under the Act of Congress Approved 24 February 1919," 30 June 1919, in Documents of the American Relief Administration, 1918-1922 (unpublished compilation, 24 vols., Hoover Institution on War Revolution and Peace, Stanford, Calif.), 2:231 (hereafter cited as ARA Documents).

[67]Announcement of the American Relief Administration European Children's Relief, 14 July 1919, in ARA Documents, 2:319.

[68]Hoover to ARA, New York, 7 July 1919, ibid., 2:310; Hoover to Wilson, 6 June 1919, in Bane and Lutz, *American Relief,* pp. 540-42.

[69]Hoover, *An American Epic,* 3:166-67.

[70]"Special Agreement between the American Relief Administration and the Provisional Government of Russia," 16 July 1919, in U.S., Department of State, *Papers Relating to the Foreign Relations of the United States,* pp. 693-96.

[71]Hoover to Secretary of State, 30 August 1919, ibid., p. 707.

[72]Hoover, *An American Epic,* 3:166.

[73]George Stewart, *The White Armies of Russia* (New York: Macmillan Co., 1933), p. 226.

[74]Commander, Northwest Russian Army, to Hoover, 26 July 1919, HHA Special Testimonials File.

[75]Hoover, *Years of Adventure,* p. 410; Rickard to State Department, 3

November 1919, *NA* 861.48/1409.

[76]ARA, London, to ARA, New York, 22 July 1920, HHA 17-6.

[77]ARA, New York, to ARA, London, 23 July 1920, HHA 17-6.

[78]Ibid.; ARA, New York, to ARA, London, 4 August 1920, HHA 17-6.

[79]Brown to Chicherin, 24 July 1920, HHA 17-6.

[80]Chicherin to Lansbury, 4 August 1920, contained in Brown to ARA, New York, 4 August 1920, HHA 17-6.

[81]Brown to Chicherin, 5 August 1920, HHA 17-6.

[82]Pate to Brown, 15 August 1920, HHA 17-6.

[83]Interview with Dr. Herschel C. Walker, 17 May 1966; Walker-Pate Report, 22 August 1920, HHA 17-6.

[84]Chicherin to ARA, London, 28 August 1920, HHA 17-6.

[85]Pate to S. Nuorteva, Anglo-American Department, People's Commissariat of Foreign Affairs, 9 September 1920, HHA 17-6.

[86]ARA, London, to ARA, New York, 24 September 1920, HHA 17-6.

[87]Pate to People's Commissar for Foreign Affairs, 29 August 1920; Nuorteva to Pate, n.d. (probably 30 August 1920), HHA 17-6; Brown to Hoover, 10 September 1920, HHA 17-6.

[88]Hoover to Friends Service Committee, 26 January 1921, HHA 271-21.

[89]Wilbur Thomas to Hoover, 31 January 1921, HHA 271-21; Hoover to Thomas, 24 February 1921, HHA 271-21.

[90]Friends Service Committee, Moscow, to Hoover, 10 March 1921, HHA 271-21; Anna J. Haines, Moscow, to W. K. Thomas, 14 March 1921, *NA* 861.48/1442.

[91]Anna Haines to Friends Service Committee, 24 June 1921, HHA 271-21; Edgar Rickard, ARA, to ARA, London, 31 May 1921, *NA* 861.48/1536.

[92]Hoover to Hughes, 13 August 1921, *NA* 861.48/1536.

[93]Samuel H. Adams, *The Incredible Era,* pp. 205-6.

[94]Arthur M. Schlesinger, Jr., *The Crisis of the Old Order, 1919-1933,* p. 82.

[95]Merlo J. Pusey, *Charles Evans Hughes,* 2:427.

[96]*New York Times,* 22 March 1921, p. 1.

[97]Ibid.

[98]*New York Times,* 25 March 1921, p. 2.

[99]*New York Times,* 26 March 1921, p. 1.

[100]Robert K. Murray, *Red Scare,* p. 273.

[101]U.S. Department of Commerce, Bureau of the Census, *Historical Statistics of the United States, Colonial Times to 1957,* p. 283.

[102]Address to American Institute of Banking, "New York Newsletter of the ARA," 4 March 1922, HHA 295-2.

[103]U.S., Department of Commerce, Bureau of the Census, *Historical Statistics*, p. 67.

[104]Rickard, ARA, New York, to Brown, ARA, London, 3 June 1921, HHA 18-2.

3: CONFRONTATION AT RIGA

[1]Gorky to Nansen, 13 July 1921, cited in American Legation at Christiania to Secretary of State, 15 July 1921, *NA* 861.48/1501.

[2]Hoover to Secretary of State, 22 July 1921, HHA 282-6.

[3]Herter to De Witt C. Poole, Department of State, 23 July 1921, HHA 282-16.

[4]Poole to Herter, 25 July 1921, HHA 282-16.

[5]Hoover to Maxim Gorky, Petrograd, 23 July 1921, HHA 254-16.

[6]Gorky to Hoover, 26 July 1921, via Brown to Rickard, 27 July 1921, *NA* 861.48/1540½.

[7]Gorky to Hoover, 28 July 1921, *Dokumenty vneshnei politiki,* 4:246.

[8]Hoover to Brown, 1 August 1921, HHA 15-6.

[9]Lenin to Kamenev, 5 August 1921, *Pss,* 53:97.

[10]*New York Times,* 26 July 1921, p. 17.

[11]Editorial, *Nation* (New York), 10 August 1921.

[12]Herter, memorandum, 8 August 1921, HHA 18-2.

[13]Hughes to Hoover, 12 August 1921, enclosing Mark Bristol to Secretary of State, 9 August 1921, HHA 288-3.

[14]George Harvey, Paris, to Secretary of State, 10 August 1921, HHA 288-3.

[15]*Izvestia* (Moscow), 4 August 1921.

[16]Hoover to Brown, 6 August 1921, HHA 17-6.

[17]Hoover to Brown, 9 August 1921, HHA 17-6.

[18]Harold H. Fisher, *The Famine in Soviet Russia, 1919-1923,* pp. 59-60.

[19]Louis Fisher, *The Soviets in World Affairs,* pp. 176-77.

[20]Lenin to Chicherin, 11 August 1921, *Dokumenty vneshnei politiki,* 4:781.

[21]Rickard to Brown, 1 August 1921, HHA 17-6.

[22]Hoover to Brown, 3 August 1921, HHA 17-6.

[23]Hoover to Brown, 5 August 1921, HHA 17-6.

[24]Michael P. Dineen, ed., *Herbert Hoover's Challenge to America,* p. 28.

[25]Brown to Hoover, 8 August 1921, HHA 17-6.

[26]Hoover to Brown, 9 August 1921, HHA 17-6.

[27]Hoover to Brown, no. 12, 9 August 1921, HHA 17-6.

[28]Arthur C. Ringland to Brown, 30 July 1921, HHA 71-1.

[29]Brown to Hoover, 10 August 1921, HHA 17-6.

[30]Hoover to Brown, 10 August 1921, HHA 17-6.

[31]Brown to Hoover, 13 August 1921, HHA 17-7; and Fisher, *Famine in Russia,* p. 60.

[32]Chicherin to Litvinov, 11 August 1921,. *Dokumenty vneshnei politiki,* 4:262. See also ibid., fn. 45, p. 781, for comment that Lenin was referring to the Allied Council session in Paris.

[33]Lenin to Molotov, 11 August 1921, *Pss,* 53:110.

[34]*Novy put* (Riga), 12 August 1921, cited in HHA 82-4.

[35]Hoover to President Harding, 11 August 1921, HHA 271-1.

[36]Harding to Hoover, 12 August 1921, HHA 271-1.

[37]Secretary of State to Hoover, 4 August 1921, HHA 271-17.

[38]Hoover to Secretary of State, 11 August 1921, HHA 250-1.

[39]Hoover to Brown, 13 August 1921, HHA 271-17.

[40]Brown to Hoover, 15 August 1921, HHA 271-17.

[41]Fisher, *Famine in Russia,* pp. 62-67.

[42]Hoover, press release, 11 August 1921, HHA 271-17.

[43]Fisher, *Famine in Russia,* pp. 64-65.

[44]Hughes to Hoover, 12 August 1921, *NA* 861.48/1515.

[45]*Pravda* (Petrograd), 31 August 1921, cited in HHA 253-2.

[46]Cited in *NA* 861.48/1625.

[47]Brown to Hoover, 13 August 1921, HHA 17-7.

[48]Hoover to Brown, 15 August 1921, HHA 17-7.

[49]Lenin to *Narkomindel* [People's Commissariat of Foreign Affairs] and *Pomgol,* 13 August 1921, *Dokumenty vneshnei politiki,* 4:263.

[50]Brown to Hoover, 13 August 1921, HHA 17-7.

[51]Brown to Hoover, 15 August 1921, no. 20, HHA 17-7.

[52]Brown to Hoover, 15 August 1921, no. 21, HHA 17-7.

[53]Hoover to Brown, 15 August 1921, HHA 17-7.

[54]Brown to Hoover, 17 August 1921, HHA 17-7.

[55]*New York Times,* 17 August 1921, p. 1.

[56]*New York Times,* 16 August 1921, p. 1.

[57]Hoover to Brown, 16 August 1921, HHA 17-7.

[58]Hoover to Brown, 17 August 1921, HHA 17-7.

[59]*Krasnaya gazeta,* 18 August 1921, cited in Quarton to Secretary of State, 18 August 1921, HHA 288-3.

[60]Brown to Hoover, 17 August 1921, HHA 17-7.

[61]Brown to Hoover, 18 August 1921, HHA 17-7.

[62]*New York Times,* 18 August 1921, p. 1.

[63]Chicherin to Litvinov, 19 August 1921, *Dokumenty vneshnei politiki,* 4:275-80.

[64]Hoover to Brown, 18 August 1921, HHA 17-7.

[65]Brown to Hoover, 20 August 1921, HHA 17-7.

[66]*New York Tribune,* 21 August 1921.

[67]*Sevodnia* (Riga), 21 August 1921, cited in HHA 17-7.

[68]*New York Times,* 21 August 1921, p. 1.

[69]Brown to Hoover, 27 August 1921, HHA 243-7.

[70]*New York Tribune,* 17 August 1921.

[71]*Manchester Guardian,* 19 August 1921, cited in HHA 17-7.

[72]Brown to Hoover, 27 August 1921, HHA 243-7.

[73]Informal notes on Riga negotiations by Cyril J. C. Quinn, Warsaw, 29 August 1921, HHA 17-7.

[74]Interview with Cyril J. C. Quinn, 2 May 1966.

[75]*Times* (London), 22 August 1921.

[76]"Agreement between the American Relief Administration and the Russian Socialist Federative Soviet Republic," Riga, Latvia, 20 August 1921, in *Dokumenty vneshnei politiki,* 4:281, and HHA 243-4.

[77]Brown to Litvinov, 20 August 1921, HHA 17-1.

[78]Jan F. Triska and Robert M. Slusser, *The Theory, Law, and Policy of Soviet Treaties,* p. 192.

[79]*Sputnik kommunista* (Moscow), no. 4 (16 September 1921), p. 13.

[80]*Sputnik kommunista* (Moscow), no. 3 (4 September 1921), p. 13.

[81]Karl Radek, "Golod v Rossii i kapitalistichesky mir," *Vestnik Narodnovo Kommissariata Inostrannykh Del* (Moscow), no. 7-8 (1 October 1921), p. 9.

[82]*New York Times,* 23 August 1921, p. 4.

[83]Lenin to Zinoviev, 22 August 1921; *Pss,* 53:134.

[84]*Novy put,* 23 August 1921, cited in HHA 86-5.

[85]*Pravda* (Moscow), 23 August 1921.

[86]Herbert Hoover, *An American Epic,* 3:428.

[87]*New York Times,* 21 August 1921, p. 3.

[88]Bristol to Secretary of State, 25 August 1921, HHA 288-3.

[89]*New York Times,* 19 August 1921, p. 1.

[90]Hoover to Brown, 9 August 1921, HHA 17-6; Hoover to Brown, 22 August 1921, HHA 5-1.

[91]Hoover to ARA, London, 18 August 1921, HHA Document no. A 50-05163.

[92]Minutes of meeting at Department of Commerce, 24 August 1921, HHA 243-4.

[93]*New York Tribune,* 15 August 1921.

[94]Fisher, *Famine in Russia,* fn. 13, p. 57; T. T. C. Gregory, "Overthrowing a Red Regime," *World's Work* (New York), June 1921, p. 161; *Nation* (New York), 24 August 1921, p. 187. According to an undated telegram from the American consul at Viborg, Finland, to Secretary of State, 1921 (HHA 228—State Dept.), Bela Kun, then in Soviet Russia, was opposed to accepting foreign assistance in fighting the famine.

[95]*Nation* (New York), 31 August 1921, p. 215.

[96]*New Republic* (New York), 24 August 1921, p. 341.

[97]John P. Roche, *The Quest for the Dream,* pp. 120-21.

[98]Hoover to Henry Ford, 9 September 1921, HHA 266-1.

[99]*Fremont (Ohio) Independent,* 17 August 1921, cited in HHA 261-1.

[100]Acting Secretary, United Cloth and Cap Makers Union, to President Harding, 31 August 1921, *NA* 861.48/1608.

[101]*New York Times,* 27 August 1921, p. 2.

[102]*Times* (London), 25 August 1921.

[103]*Manchester Guardian,* 19 August 1921, cited in HHA 17-7.

[104]*New York Times,* 28 August 1921, p. 2.

4: THE UNIQUE ENCOUNTER

[1]*New York Times,* 22 August 1921, p. 2.

[2]Ibid., p. 1.

[3]*New York Times,* 24 August 1921, p. 3.

[4]Lenin to Stalin and all members of the Politburo, 26 August 1921, *Pss,* 43:140.

[5]G. Aronson, "E. D. Kuskova," *Novy zhurnal* (New York), no. 37 (1954), p. 246.

[6]Agreement between Nansen and Chicherin, 27 August 1921, HHA 1-4.

[7]Lenin to Stalin, 26 August 1921, *Pss,* 43:140.

[8]U.S. Commissioner, Riga, to Secretary of State, 10 September 1921, *NA* 861.48/1673.

[9]*Izvestia* (Moscow), 30 August 1921, and *Pravda* (Moscow), 30 August 1921.

[10]E. H. Carr, *The Bolshevik Revolution,* 1:178.

[11]E. Kuskova, "Tragedia Maksima Gorkovo," *Novy zhurnal* (New York), no. 38 (1954), p. 237.

[12]*Pravda* (Moscow), 30 August 1921.

[13]G. Belov, ed., *Iz istorii Vserossiiskoi Chrezvychainoi Kommissii, 1917-1921 gg.,* pp. 464-66. Antonov's group had mounted a massive but futile revolt in the Tambov area.

[14]Hughes to Hoover, 1 September 1921, HHA 282-6.

[15]Interview with Cyril J. C. Quinn, 2 May 1966.

[16]Harold H. Fisher, *The Famine in Soviet Russia, 1919-1923,* p. 79.

[17]Ibid., pp. 73-74.

[18]Ibid., pp. 80-81.

[19]Lenin to Chicherin, 5 September 1921, *Pss,* 43:177.

[20]Mandate of All-Russian Central Executive Committee to A. I. Palmer, 24 September 1921, HHA 230-1.

[21]*Izvestia* (Moscow), 7 October 1921.

[22]Fisher, *Famine in Russia,* p. 74.

[23]Archibald C. Coolidge, "Liaison Work with the American Relief Administration in Russia, September, 1921, to February, 1922," in ARA Documents, 4:143-51.

[24]*Izvestia* (Moscow), 30 November 1921.

[25]Eiduk to Lonergan, 16 October 1921; Eiduk to Carroll, 5 October 1921, and Eiduk to Carroll, 6 October 1921, HHA 230-1.

[26]Order no. 17 of Representative Plenipotentiary with ARA, HHA 15-10.

[27]Interview with Dr. Herschel C. Walker, 17 May 1966.

[28]Preston Kumlor, Acting District Supervisor, Tsaritsyn, to ARA, Moscow, 3 November 1921, HHA 83-5.

[29]Interview with Henry C. Wolfe, 20 May 1966.

[30]Interviews with Quinn and Walker; Walter Duranty, *I Write as I Please,* p. 133.

[31]Alexei Yakovlev, "The ARA Men and their Work in a Russian Province: 1921-1922" (unpublished manuscript), 21 November 1922, HHA 6-2.

[32]Rickard to Brown, 1 August 1921, HHA 254-16.

[33]Kellogg to Hoover, 8 September 1921, HHA 259-5.

[34]Brown to Rickard, 15 October 1921, HHA 270-1.

[35]List of ARA personnel in Moscow, HHA 62-5.

[36]Interviews with Quinn and Walker.

[37]Interview with Wolfe.

[38]H. H. Fisher to Herter, 11 September 1923, and Rickard to *Atlantic Monthly,* 17 September 1923, HHA 284-1.

[39]ARA, New York, to ARA, London, 7 December 1921, HHA 283-19.

[40]Personnel of the ARA, HHA 266-2, 3, 4; J. Rives Childs, "Between Two Worlds" (unpublished manuscript, copy at Walter Page Library, Ashland, Va.), pp. 131-32.

[41]Haskell to Goodrich, 14 November 1921; Hoover to Haskell, 5 December 1921, HHA 269-4.

[42]John N. Hazard and Isaac Shapiro, eds., *The Soviet Legal System,* 1:3.

[43]Ibid., p. 59.

[44]Riga Agreement, HHA 243-4; *Dokumenty vneshnei politiki,* 4:281.

[45]President, Council of Commissars, Tatar Socialist Soviet Federative Republic, to the American Relief Administration, 14 November 1921, HHA 18-2; I. W. Wahren to ARA, Moscow, 15 November 1921, HHA 18-2; and Eiduk to Haskell, 20 November 1921, HHA 18-2.

[46]Eiduk to Haskell, 20 November 1921, HHA 18-2.

[47]Lonergan to Eiduk, 21 November 1921, HHA 18-2.

[48]Eiduk to Lonergan, 29 November 1921, HHA 15-10.

[49]Haskell to Eiduk, 6 December 1921, HHA 237-2.

[50]Fisher, *Famine in Russia,* p. 127.

[51]Eiduk to Lonergan, 3 November 1921, and Eiduk to Lonergan, 31 October 1921, HHA 230-1.

[52]Hughes to Brown, 2 September 1921, HHA 248-16.

[53]Brown to Herter, 16 November 1921, HHA 267-6.

[54]Haskell to Hoover, 20 October 1921, in ARA Documents, 1:127.

[55]Haskell to Hoover, 5 November 1921, HHA 81-2.

[56]Dickinson to Podashevksy, 14 November 1921, HHA 15-10.

[57]*New York Tribune,* 4 April 1921.

[58]Memorandum by George Barr Baker, 10 April 1922, HHA 19-1.

[59]Memorandum by Lieutenant Dunn, U.S.S. *Gilmer,* Novororossisk, for Admiral Bristol, 23 September 1921, *NA* 861.48/1723.

[60]Hoover to Hughes, 24 October 1922, HHA 282-3.

[61]Haskell to Lander, 23 November 1922, HHA 240-1.

[62]Hughes to Hoover, 30 September 1921, HHA 282-6.

[63]Weinstein to Haskell, 8 October 1921, HHA 236-2.

[64]Haskell to Weinstein, 11 October 1921, HHA 15-10.

[65]Haskell to Weinstein, 21 October 1921, HHA 15-10.

[66]Hoover to Hughes, 9 November 1921, HHA 282-6.

[67]Riga Agreement, HHA 243-4.

[68]Hoover to Brown, 6 September 1921, HHA 271-17; Brown to Hoover, 6 September 1921, HHA 271-17.

[69]Haskell to Weinstein, 12 October 1921, HHA 15-10.

[70]Weinstein to Lonergan, 15 October 1921, HHA 236-2.

[71]Kuskova, "Tragedia Maksima Gorkovo," p. 237.

[72]D. C. Poole, Division of Russian Affairs, U.S. State Department, to Secretary of State, 22 September 1921, *NA* 861.48/1609.

[73]Hoover to Brown, 23 September 1921, *NA* 861.48/1662A.

[74]Haskell to Kamenev, 29 September 1921, HHA 15-6.

[75]Brown to Hoover, 3 October 1921, HHA 286-3.

[76]Kuskova, "Tragedia Maksima Gorkovo," p. 237.

[77]Richard Pipes, *The Formation of the Soviet Union,* rev. ed. (New York: Atheneum, 1968), pp. 253-54.

[78]Eiduk to Lonergan, 16 November 1921, HHA 15-10.

[79]Lonergan to Eiduk, 18 November 1921, HHA 15-10.

[80]Eiduk to Lonergan, 21 November 1921, HHA 15-10.

[81]Report by F. Golder and L. Hutchinson to Colonel Haskell, 4 December 1921, HHA 81-4.

[82]Frank A. Golder and Lincoln Hutchinson, *On the Trail of the Russian Famine,* pp. 119-23.

[83]P. Krasnev, "The Starving Ukraine," *Kommunist,* 28 December 1921, cited in HHA 10-4.

[84]Lincoln Hutchinson, report on the Ukraine, 19 January 1922, HHA 10-4.

[85]Fisher, *Famine in Russia,* pp. 252-53; Golder and Hutchinson, *Trail of the Famine,* pp. 126, 130.

[86]Eiduk to Haskell, 25 January 1922, HHA 231-2.

[87]Fisher, *Famine in Russia,* p. 528.

[88]*Itogi borby s golodom,* pp. 189 ff., pp. 257-58.

[89]Fisher, *Famine in Russia,* pp. 71, 80, 82, 84, 111.

5: EXPANSION OF THE MISSION

[1]ARA, London, to ARA, New York, 7 October 1921, HHA 259-5.

[2]Haskell to Brown, 1 December 1921, HHA 81-2.

[3]Haskell to ARA, London, 8 December 1921, HHA 81-2.

[4]Harold H. Fisher, *The Famine in Soviet Russia, 1919-1923,* p. 146.

[5]Brown to Rickard, 6 January 1922, HHA 19-1.

[6]U.S., Congress, House, *Russian Relief: Hearings before the Committee on Foreign Affairs on H.R. 9459 and H.R. 9548,* 67th Cong., 2d sess., 13 and 14 December 1921, p. 12 (hereafter cited as *Russian Relief: Hearings).*

[7]Ibid., p. 49.

[8]Ibid., p. 39.

[9]Goodrich to Hoover, 6 December 1921, HHA 269-4.

[10]*Russian Relief: Hearings,* p. 13.

[11]Ibid., p. 41.

[12]Ibid.

[13]Fisher, *Famine in Russia,* p. 149.

[14]U.S., Congress, Senate, *Congressional Record,* 67th Cong., 2d sess., 21 December 1921, 62, pt. 1:704-5.

[15]Ibid., p. 704; ibid., 22 December 1921, pp. 814-15.

[16]Ibid., 21 December 1921, pp. 661, 663, 666.

[17]Fisher, *Famine in Russia,* p. 149.

[18]Ibid., pp. 153-54.

[19]Hoover to Harding, 20 December 1921, HHA 271-1; Executive Order Appointing the Purchasing Commission for Russian Relief, 24 December 1921, HHA 271-1.

[20]Frank M. Surface, *The Grain Trade during the World War,* pp. 419-20.

[21]A. W. Mellon, Secretary of the Treasury, to Edwin P. Shattuck, 19 December 1921, HHA 283-1; Shattuck to Mellon, 20 December 1921, HHA 283-1; Mellon to Shattuck, 27 December 1921, HHA 283-1.

[22]Mellon to Hoover, 13 January 1922, HHA 283-1.

[23]Fisher, *Famine in Russia,* p. 552.

[24]Hoover to Brown, 26 August 1921, HHA 281-8.

[25]Herter to D. C. Poole, State Department, 23 September 1921, HHA 251-8; Hughes to Hoover, 23 September 1921, HHA 251-8.

[26]Hoover to Secretary of the Treasury, 26 October 1921, HHA 283-1.

[27]Hoover to Brown, 16 December 1921, HHA 251-8.

[28]Brown to Hoover, 29 December 1921, HHA 251-8; Agreement between Walter Lyman Brown, ARA Director for Europe, and Leonid Krasin, on Behalf of RSFSR, 30 December 1921, HHA 243-7.

[29]Hoover to S. P. Gilbert, Jr., Undersecretary of the Treasury, 31 December 1921, HHA 282-6.

[30]Mellon to Hoover, 7 January 1922, HHA 251-8.

[31]Herter to Perrin C. Galpin, ARA, 27 January 1922, HHA 243-4.

[32]Lenin, Report to the Ninth All-Russian Congress of Soviets, 23 December 1921, *Pss,* 44:312.

[33]William C. Redfield to Hoover, 22 November 1921, HHA 243-12.

[34]Redfield to Rep. Frank W. Mondell, 22 November 1921, HHA 243-12.

[35]*Russian Relief: Hearings,* p. 49.

[36]Hoover to Rep. Edward E. Browne, 11 January 1922, HHA 256-10.

[37]Hoover to Rep. G. N. Haugen, 30 January 1922, HHA 256-11.

[38]Hoover to Haugen, 18 February 1922, HHA 256-11.

[39]United Committee of Russian Organizations, Paris, to Russian Ambassador, Washington, D. C., 13 December 1921, *NA* 861.48/1823.

[40]*New Republic* (New York), 4 January 1922.

[41]*Nation* (New York), 21 September 1921 and 14 December 1921.

[42]Rep. O. J. Larson to Hoover, 26 January 1922, HHA 256-11; Herter to Larson, 30 January 1922, HHA 256-11.

[43]Theodore Draper, *American Communism and Soviet Russia,* p. 176.

[44]*New York Call,* 30 July 1922.

[45]Instruction Bulletin no. 1 of the Friends of the Soviet Union, n.d., HHA 79-1.

[46]Herter to Brown, 28 October 1921, HHA 79-1.

[47]Brown to Herter, 3 January 1922, HHA 267-6.

[48]Hoover to Hon. D. W. Davis, Governor of Idaho, 11 January 1922, HHA 281-7.

[49]Draper, *American Communism,* p. 176.

[50]Letterhead, American Federated Russian Relief Committee, HHA 79-1.

[51]*New York Call,* 30 July 1921.

[52]Frank Page, ARA, London, to Baker, ARA, New York, 4 February 1922, HHA 14-5; Hoover to Sen. Porter McCumber, 17 January 1922, HHA 278-18.

[53]Hoover to McCumber, 17 January 1922, HHA 278-18.

[54]Hoover to Davis, 11 January 1922, HHA 281-7.

[55]Hoover to Attorney General Daugherty, 25 November 1921, HHA 255-4.

[56]W. J. Burns, Director, Department of Justice, to Lawrence Richey, Department of Commerce, 12 January 1922, HHA 255-9.

[57]*New York Globe,* 9 February 1922.

[58]Hoover to President, Nowaco Package Confectionery Company, 31 October 1921, HHA 260-MC.

[59]Hoover to Rufus Jones, American Friends Service Committee, 6 January 1922, HHA 18-4.

[60]Hoover to Jones, 13 February 1922, ARA Document A50-05812.

[61]Ibid.

[62]Richard W. Child to Secretary of State, 16 November 1921, *NA* 861.48/1784.

[63]De Witt C. Poole to Secretary of State, 13 October 1921, *NA* 861.48/1784.

[64]Hutchinson to Brown, 9 November 1921, HHA 81-5.

[65]Goodrich to Hoover, 3 April 1922, HHA 81-1.

[66]J. P. Goodrich, "Impressions of the Bolshevik Regime," *Century,* May 1922, in HHA 81-1.

[67]Hoover to Dwight Morrow, 24 November 1921, HHA 260.

[68]Hoover to Hughes, 6 December 1921, cited in William A. Williams, ed., *The Shaping of American Diplomacy* (Chicago: Rand McNally, 1956), pp. 718-19.

[69]Fisher, *Famine in Russia,* p. 524.

[70]Report on Kiev by "A Friend of America," 1923, HHA 6-2. Another anonymous observer wrote that questions about American food shipments "absorbed the life of Kiev. The interest in A.R.A. was the interest in life itself" ("The Moment Is the Mother of the Ages," HHA 6-2).

[71]Quinn to ARA, London, weekly letter, 3 April 1922, HHA 19-1.

[72]Will Shafroth, District Supervisor of Samara, to ARA, Moscow, 9 January 1922, HHA 89-1.

[73]Shafroth to Lonergan, 13 March 1922, HHA 89-1.

[74]Shafroth to Karklin, 30 April 1922, HHA 89-1.

[75]Quinn to ARA, London, 10 April 1922, HHA 15-10.

[76]Eiduk to Haskell, 3 March 1922, HHA 232-1.

[77]Haskell to Eiduk, 20 April 1922, HHA 238-2.

[78]Haskell to Kamenev, 27 April 1922, HHA 238-2.

[79]Quinn to Eiduk, 23 May 1922, HHA 89-1.

[80]Samara *Gubispolkom* to Karklin, 13 June 1922, HHA 89-1.

[81]Eiduk to Haskell, 3 June 1922, HHA 232-3; Interview with Cyril J. C. Quinn, 2 May 1966.

[82]Fisher, *Famine in Russia,* pp. 188-200.

[83]Haskell to Eiduk, 4 March 1922, HHA 238-1.

[84]Quinn to ARA, London, weekly letter, 3 April 1922, HHA 19-1.

[85]Fisher, *Famine in Russia,* p. 199.

[86]Adam Ulam, *The Bolsheviks,* p. 488.

[87]Brown to Rickard, 13 April 1922, HHA 19-1; ARA, New York, to ARA, London, 14 April 1922, HHA 19-1.

[88]Fisher, *Famine in Russia,* pp. 200-201.

[89]Minutes of Conference between Haskell and Kamenev, 11 April 1922, HHA 19-1.

[90]Haskell to Hoover, 12 April 1922, HHA 15-10; Haskell to Brown, 13 April 1922, HHA 19-1.

[91]Ibid.; Fisher, *Famine in Russia,* pp. 206-7.

[92]Haskell to Hoover, 27 April 1922, HHA 15-10.

[93]Cited in ARA, London, to ARA, New York, 19 April 1922, HHA 259-3.

[94]Haskell to Eiduk, 9 May 1922, HHA 238-2.

[95]Board of Health, Kosmodemiansk Canton, Mari Autonomous Territory, to ARA Medical Division, n.d., HHA 236-2.

[96]Dr. M. Jukelson, Jewish Hospital, Kiev, to ARA, Kiev, 9 May 1922, HHA 6-2.

[97]Bolshoi Ballet Company to ARA, 24 January 1922, HHA 236-2.

[98]Kalmyk Representation to ARA, 25 October 1921, HHA 236-2.

[99]Mari Representation to Children's Section of Central Relief Commission, 26 October 1921, HHA 236-2.

[100]Kirghiz Republic Representation to Eiduk, 9 January 1922, HHA 236-2.

[101]*Itogi borby s golodom,* p. 239.

[102]Interview with Professor P——, Putney, Vt., 9 August 1963.

[103]*Itogi borby s golodom,* p. 266.

[104]Ibid.

[105]Fisher, *Famine in Russia,* p. 292.

[106]Haskell to Eiduk, 18 February 1922, HHA 238-1; Eiduk to Haskell, 27 February 1922, HHA 232-1.

[107]Shafroth to ARA, Moscow, 18 April 1922, HHA 89-1.

[108]J. C. R. Hall, ARA Representative, Rybinsk, to Director, ARA, Moscow, 11 May and 21 May 1922, HHA 83-2; Eiduk to Quinn, 12 June 1922, HHA 83-2.

[109]Haskell to Lander, 30 June 1922, HHA 239-1.

[110]Edward Fox, District Supervisor, Simbirsk, to Director, ARA, Moscow, 5 September 1922, HHA 86-5.

[111]Eiduk to Lonergan, 15 November 1921, HHA 230-2.

[112]Eiduk to Lonergan, 26 December 1921, HHA 15-10.

[113]Leonard Schapiro, *The Communist Party of the Soviet Union,* pp. 334-36.

[114]Lander to Quinn, 27 July 1922, HHA 233-2; Quinn to Lander, 2 August 1922, HHA 239-2.

[115]Lander to Quinn, 21 September 1922, HHA 232-2; Interview with Quinn.

[116]Memorandum on inspection trip to Tsaritsyn, 17 July - 12 August 1922, by Arthur Ruhl, HHA 83-2.

[117]Bimonthly reports from District Supervisor, Orenburg, 15 May and 3 June 1922, HHA 59-3.

[118]Clipping from *Rabochaya diktatura* (n.d.), sent by ARA, Odessa, to ARA, Moscow, 4 August 1922, HHA 86-5.

[119]E. G. Burland, Chief, Remittance Division, ARA, to Eiduk, 24 April 1922, HHA 238-2.

[120]Eiduk to Burland, 22 March 1922, HHA 232-1; Burland to Eiduk, 22 April 1922, HHA 238-2.

[121]Lander to Burland, 24 June and 15 July 1922, HHA 233-1.

[122]Weekly Newsletter, ARA, Moscow, 14 May 1922, HHA 15-10.

[123]*Itogi borby s golodom,* p. 341.

[124]Memorandum of conference between ARA and Joint Distribution Committee, 3 June 1922, HHA 258-12.

[125]Lenin, *Pss,* 44:246-47.

[126]Fisher, *Famine in Russia,* pp. 514-16.

[127]Lenin, *Pss,* 44:555.

[128]Ibid., p. 179.

[129]Ibid., p. 555.

[130]Lenin to Chicherin, 16 October 1921, in Institut Marksizma-Leninizma Pri TsK KPSS, *Lenin o vneshnei politike sovetskovo gosudarstva,* p. 457.

[131]Lenin, *Pss,* 53:299.

[132]Lenin, *Pss,* 44:312-13.

[133]Ibid., p. 333.

[134]*Izvestia* (Moscow), 30 August 1922.

[135]*New York Times,* 22 March 1921, p. 2.

[136]Goodrich to Hoover, 3 April 1922, HHA 81-1.

[137]M. M. Mitchell to Brown, 27 February 1922, HHA 19-1.

[138]Memorandum of interview between Professor A. C. Coolidge and Kamenev, 15 February 1922, HHA 82-2.

[139]Joseph V. Stalin, *Works,* 5: 121.

[140]Interviews with Quinn; Dr. Herschel C. Walker, 17 May 1966; and Henry C. Wolfe, 20 May 1966; writer's poll of former ARA personnel, April –September 1966.

[141]Goodrich to Hoover, 3 April 1922, HHA 81-1.

[142]Brown-Rickard Report, in Barnes to Hoover, 7 July 1922, HHA 82-7.

[143]Interview with Walker.

[144]Interview with Quinn.

[145]*Pravda* (Moscow), 11 May 1922.

[146]*Izvestia* (Moscow), 13 May 1922.

[147]*Pravda* (Moscow), 8 June 1922.

[148]*Pravda* (Moscow), 15 August 1922, cited in HHA 86-5.

[149]*Pravda* (Moscow), 25 October 1921.

[150]Interview with Quinn.

[151]Golder to Fisher, 4 December 1922, HHA 254-12.

[152]Golder to Herter, 2 December 1922, HHA 254-12.

[153]*Izvestia* (Moscow), 28 January 1922.

[154]M. M. Mitchell to ARA, New York, 13 June 1922, HHA 284-10.

[155]Goodrich to Hoover, 20 June 1922, in Hughes to Hoover, 28 June 1922, HHA 282-4.

[156]*New York Times,* 26 March 1921, p. 1.

[157]Fisher, *Famine in Russia,* p. 556. These figures, compiled by the ARA, match those cited in a Soviet report in *Izvestia* (Moscow), 8 September 1922, and in the summary of foreign aid in *Itogi borby s golodom,* p. 335.

[158]Report for publication, London, 14 July 1922, by Rickard and Brown, HHA 82-7.

[159]*Izvestia* (Moscow), 16 September 1922.

[160]H. C. Walker to Director, ARA, Moscow, 19 July 1922, in HHA Testimonials Folder.

[161]Cablegram, in Hughes to Hoover, 6 June 1922, HHA 282-4.

6: THE POLITICS OF RETREAT

[1]Poole to Secretary of State, 10 April 1922, *NA* 861.48/1925.

[2]Memorandum by H. H. Fisher to George Barr Baker, 22 April 1922, HHA 80-6.

[3]Brown to Rickard, 13 April 1922, HHA 19-1.

[4]Edgar Rickard, "American Relief in Russia," talk before a group of mining engineers, 4 May 1922, HHA 83-1.

[5]ARA Documents, 1:559-90.

[6]Haskell to Hoover, 24 June 1922, HHA 269-6 and *NA* 861.48/1991.

[7]Hoover to Hughes, 28 June 1922, *NA* 861.48/2011.

[8]Hoover to Rickard and Brown, 12 July 1922, HHA 288-15.

[9]Harold H. Fisher, *The Famine in Soviet Russia, 1919-1923,* pp. 303-6.

[10]Circular Letter to District Supervisors, 12 September 1922, HHA 32-1.

[11]Circular Letter to District Supervisors, 18 September 1922, ARA Documents, 2:189; Circular Letter to District Supervisors, 30 September 1922, ARA Documents, 2:195-99.

[12]Rickard, "American Relief in Russia," HHA 83-1.

[13]Hoover to Hughes, 15 June 1922, HHA 282-4.

[14]Hughes to Hoover, 23 June 1922, HHA 282-4.

[15]Letter enclosed in Hughes to Hoover, 28 June 1922, HHA 282-4.

[16]Haskell to Hoover, 8 September 1922, HHA 269-6.

[17]*Izvestia* (Moscow), 19 September 1922.

[18]Golder to Herter, 20 September 1922, HHA 254-12.

[19]Golder to Herter, 2 October 1922, HHA 254-12.

[20]Leighton W. Rogers, London, weekly report, 28 November to 5 December 1921, HHA 251-8.

[21]Goodrich to Hoover, 2 June 1922, HHA 254-16.

[22]Mowatt M. Mitchell to ARA, New York, 13 June 1922, HHA 284-10.

[23]Herter to Poole, 30 August 1922, HHA 282-3.

[24]Haskell to Hoover, 30 September 1922, HHA 269-6.

[25]*Pravda* (Moscow), 7 October 1922.

[26]Golder to Herter, 9 October 1922, HHA 276-24.

[27]Hoover to Sen. Joseph I. France, 10 February 1923, HHA 251-8.

[28]Louis Fischer, *The Soviets in World Affairs,* pp. v, 321.

[29]*Pravda* (Moscow), 2 August 1922, and *Izvestia* (Moscow), 2 August 1922.

[30]Fisher, *Famine in Russia,* p. 311.

[31]Hoover to Haskell, 26 September 1922, HHA 269-6; Haskell to Kamenev, 9 October 1922, HHA 259-3.

[32]Hoover to Haskell, 25 October 1922, HHA 269-6.

[33]Lander to Haskell, 24 October 1922, HHA 269-6.

[34]Kamenev to Haskell, 13 October 1922, HHA 269-6.

[35]Kamenev to Haskell, 6 November 1922, HHA 259-3.

[36]Haskell to Hoover, 9 November 1922, HHA 7-6.

[37]Hoover to Haskell, 18 November 1922, HHA 269-6.

[38]Fisher, *Famine in Russia,* p. 327.

[39]*Izvestia* (Moscow), 23 May 1923.

[40]F. D. Stephen, District Supervisor, Tsaritsyn, to Director ARA, Moscow, 14 September 1922, HHA 83-5.

[41]John Ellingston to Haskell, 4 October 1922, HHA 83-5.

[42]Arthur Ruhl, ARA Inspector, to Quinn, 6 September 1922, HHA 89-1; Ronald H. Allen to ARA, Moscow, 7 September 1922, HHA 89-1; and Charles M. Willoughby, ARA, Pugachov, to District Supervisor, ARA, Samara, 29 August 1922, HHA 89-1.

[43]*Izvestia* (Moscow), 5 October 1922.

[44]Quinn to Lander, 13 December 1922, HHA 240-2.

[45]Ronald H. Allen to ARA, Moscow, 16 January 1923, HHA 89-1; Harold M. Fleming, ARA Inspector, to ARA, Moscow, 18 February 1923, HHA 89-1.

[46]Fleming to Fisher, New York, 29 March 1923, HHA 80-7.

[47]*Nation* (New York), 21 September 1921.

[48]Fisher, *Famine in Russia,* pp. 234-35, HHA 266-1; George Barr Baker correspondence, HHA 266-1.

[49]Ralph M. Easely to Hoover, 18 December 1922, HHA 264-9; Hoover to Easely, 20 December 1922, HHA 264-9.

[50]Arthur J. Burns, Department of Justice, to Lawrence Richey, ARA, 24 July 1922, HHA 258-16.

[51]*Nation* (New York), 8 November 1922.

[52]*New York Times,* 16 October 1922, p. 1.

[53]Fisher, *Famine in Russia,* pp. 314-15.

[54]*Call* (New York), 8 January 1923.

[55]Allen Wardwell, Graham R. Taylor, and Allen T. Burns, "Draft Report on the Russian Famine, 1921-22, 1922-23," HHA 264-10.

[56]Frank C. Page, ARA, New York, memorandum on report of National Information Bureau, 3 February 1923, HHA 264-10.

[57]Hoover to Goodrich, 7 February 1923, HHA 264-10.

[58]Herter to Rickard, 3 February 1923, HHA 264-10.

[59]Commission on Russian Relief, *The Russian Famines.*

[60]Haskell to Hoover, 20 October 1921, HHA 81-5.

[61]Rickard to Hoover from Brown, 15 February 1922, HHA 79a-7.

[62]*Izvestia* (Moscow), 8 August 1922.

[63]*Izvestia* (Moscow), 29 September 1922.

[64]Haskell to Herter, 12 February 1923, HHA 81-2.

[65]C. E. Herring, American Commercial Attaché in Berlin, to Herter, 9 January 1923, HHA 259-9; Herter to Herring, 3 February 1923, HHA 259-9.

[66]Haskell to Brown, 20 February 1923, HHA 81-2; Haskell to Hoover, 6 March 1923, HHA 81-2.

[67]Hoover, press release, 8 March 1923, HHA 81-2.

[68]*Nation* (New York), 10 March 1923.

[69]*Izvestia* (Moscow), 11 and 16 March 1923.

[70]Hoover to C. V. Hibbard, 23 March 1923, HHA 251-8.

[71]Fisher to Herter, 14 November 1922, HHA 243-15; Herter to Fisher, 16 November 1922, HHA 243-15.

[72]John R. Ellingston to Fisher, 16 May 1923, HHA 80-4.

[73]Ellingston to Fisher, 30 May 1923, HHA 80-6.

7: DISENGAGEMENT IN RUSSIA

[1]Haskell to Hoover, 8 September 1922, HHA 269-6.

[2]*Izvestia* (Moscow), 16 August 1922.

[3]Charles M. Willoughby, ARA Representative, Pugachov, to District Supervisor, Samara, 29 August 1922, HHA 89-1.

[4]Eiduk to Quinn, 31 August 1922, HHA 89-1.

[5]Harold H. Fisher, *The Famine in Soviet Russia, 1919-1923,* p. 309.

[6]*Izvestia* (Moscow), 14 September 1922.

[7]Lander to Haskell, 1 October 1922, ARA Documents, 3:8-16.

[8]Haskell to Lander, 2 October 1922, ARA Documents, 3:16-18.

[9]Lander to Haskell, 2 and 4 October 1922, ARA Documents, 3:19-21.

[10]Haskell to Brown, 4 October 1922, ARA Documents, 3:24-27.

[11]Circular to All *Posledgol* Committees from Kameneva, 31 October 1922, ARA Documents, 3:28.

[12]Haskell to Lander, 4 November 1922, ARA Documents, 3:29; Lander to Haskell, 15 November 1922, ARA Documents, 3:31.

[13]Quinn to ARA, New York, 28 December 1922, ARA Documents, 3:34-37.

[14]Lander to Quinn, nos. 2721 and 2755, 27 November 1922, HHA 234-2; Lander to ARA, Moscow, 30 November 1922, HHA 32-1.

[15]Lander to Quinn, 22 December 1922, HHA 234-2.

[16]Quinn to Lander, 27 December 1922, HHA 240-2.

[17]Quinn to Lander, 22 December 1922, HHA 240-2.

[18]Quinn to ARA, New York, 28 December 1922, ARA Documents, 3:34-37.

[19]Quinn to Lander, 5 December 1922, HHA 32-1; Lander to Quinn, 8 December 1922, HHA 32-1.

[20]Circular Letter to ARA District Supervisors, 14 December 1922, HHA 32-1.

[21]Quinn to Lander, 22 December 1922, HHA 240-2.

[22]Quinn to ARA, New York, 28 December 1922, ARA Documents, 3:34-37.

[23]Quinn to Haskell, 28 December 1922, ARA Documents, 3:34-37.

[24]Memorandum by Arthur T. Dailey, Assistant Secretary, ARA, New York, 6 January 1923, HHA 18-4.

[25]Fisher, *Famine in Russia,* p. 557.

[26]*Izvestia* (Moscow), 14 October 1922.

[27]Quinn to J. S. Bashkovich, 1 December 1922, HHA 240-2.

[28]Lander to Quinn, 4 January 1923, HHA 234-2; Lander to Quinn, 6 January 1923, HHA 235-1; and Lander to Quinn, 13 February 1923, HHA 235-1.

[29]Haskell to Lander, 24 February 1923, HHA 241-2.

[30]Quinn to Lander, 4 December 1922, HHA 83-5; Lander to Quinn, 8 December 1922, HHA 83-5.

[31]*Izvestia* (Moscow), 31 January 1923.

[32]Allen to Director, ARA, Moscow, 3 February 1923, HHA 89-1.

[33]Quinn to Lander, 23 February 1923, HHA 89-1.

[34]Lander to Quinn, 1 March 1923, HHA 235-1.

[35]Richard W. Bonnevalle to District Supervisor, Samara, 9 March 1923, HHA 89-1.

[36]Fisher, *Famine in Russia,* fn. 19, p. 395.

[37]M. Shapiro to George A. Daum, ARA Remittance Division, 23 December 1922, and a series of letters of a similar nature, HHA 234-2.

[38]Elmer G. Burland, Chief, ARA Remittance Division, to Eiduk, 15 June 1922, HHA 239-1.

[39]M. Shapiro to James F. Hodgson, Acting Chief, ARA Remittance Division, 9 December 1922, HHA 234-2.

[40]Lander to Quinn, 13 February 1923, HHA 235-1.

[41]Haskell to Lander, 24 February 1923, HHA 241-2.

[42]Quinn to Lander, 8 March 1923, HHA 241-2.

[43]Walter Duranty, *Duranty Reports Russia,* p. 18.

[44]M. Farmer Murphy, Chief, Permanent Records Division, Moscow, to George Barr Baker, New York, 16 April 1922, HHA 19-1.

[45]*Pravda* (Moscow), 24 September 1922.

[46]See Adam Ulam, *The Bolsheviks,* pp. 516-18, for a description of Lenin as a virtual prisoner of the Politburo during this period.

[47]Haskell to Hoover, 7 February 1923, HHA 270-2.

[48]Ellingston to Fisher, 28 February 1923, HHA 80-4.

[49]Circular Letter no. 128, 25 October 1922, HHA 32-1.

[50]Interview with Cyril J. C. Quinn, 2 May 1966; Fisher, *Famine in Russia,* pp. 369-70.

[51]*Izvestia* (Moscow), 16 December 1922.

[52]Anna L. Strong, *I Change Worlds,* p. 180.

[53]Quinn to ARA, New York, 21 December 1922, HHA 81-2.

[54]Haskell to Quinn, 18 December 1922, HHA 81-2.

[55]*Izvestia* (Moscow), 22 December 1922.

[56]*Itogi borby s golodom,* p. 335. Ruth Fischer, *Stalin and German Communism,* p. 611, states that *Mezhrabpom* collected, in all, some $2 million worth of supplies, some of it secondhand, but that the "value of these collections [as propaganda] was inestimable; everyone who donated his little bit felt tied to the new workers' fatherland."

[57]*Pravda* (Moscow), 16 September 1921.

[58]*Pravda* (Moscow), 23 November 1922.

[59]*Izvestia* (Moscow), 11 August 1922.

[60]*Izvestia* (Moscow), 23 September 1922.

[61]*Izvestia* (Moscow), 31 October 1922.

[62]*Izvestia* (Moscow), 10 March 1923.

[63]*Izvestia* (Moscow), 11 March 1923.

[64]*Pravda* (Moscow), 28 March 1923.

[65]*Pravda* (Moscow), 30 June 1923.

[66]Lenin, *Pss,* 45:458.

[67]Haskell to Quinn, 23 January 1923, HHA 81-2.

[68]Hoover to Hughes, 6 December 1921, cited in William A. Williams, ed., *The Shaping of American Diplomacy* (Chicago: Rand McNally, 1956), pp. 718-19.

[69]Quinn to ARA, London and New York, 11 January 1923, HHA 27-3.

[70]Brown to Quinn, 29 January 1923, HHA 27-3.

[71]Confidential Circular to District Supervisors from Quinn, 5 February 1923, HHA 27-3.

[72]*Izvestia* (Moscow), 27 February 1923.

[73]Brown to Haskell, 27 February 1923, HHA 27-3.

[74]Brown to Hutchinson, 15 January 1923, HHA 81-5.

[75]Hutchinson to Brown, 3 April 1923, HHA 81-5.

[76]ARA News Release, 19 April 1923, HHA 89-1.

[77]Haskell to Brown, 26 April 1923, HHA 27-3.

[78]Haskell to Brown, 1 March 1923, HHA 27-3.

[79]Haskell to Lander, 1 March 1923, HHA 241-2.

[80]Quinn to District Supervisor, Samara, 30 March 1923, HHA 89-1.

[81]ARA Circular Letter, 5 May 1923, HHA 32-1.

[82]Circular Letter from Lander to Soviet Representatives with ARA, 26 May 1923, HHA 27-3.

[83]ARA Circular Letter, 4 June 1923, HHA 27-3.

[84]Allen to ARA, Moscow, 5 June 1923, HHA 89-1.

[85]Bonnevalle, Report to ARA, Moscow, 6 June 1923, HHA 27-3.

[86]Fokeev, Acting Chairman, *Ispolkom,* Syzran, to ARA, 6 June 1923, HHA 27-3.

[87]Allen to Director, ARA, Moscow, 13 July 1923, HHA 27-3.

[88]ARA, Moscow, to ARA, New York, 27 June 1923, HHA 27-3.

[89]Lincoln Hutchinson, "Report on Food Conditions in Russia, 14 May 1923," HHA 81-5; Haskell to Hoover, 14 May 1923, HHA 27-2; Quinn to Herter, 14 May 1923, HHA 259-3; and Haskell to Kamenev, 17 May 1923, HHA 269-5.

[90]Lincoln Hutchinson, interview with Associated Press, London, 1 June 1923, HHA 81-5.

[91]Haskell to Kamenev, 4 June 1923, HHA 27-3; Kamenev to Haskell, 8 June 1923, HHA 27-3.

[92]"Liquidation Agreement, 15 June 1923, between L. Kamenev for RSFSR and William N. Haskell for ARA," HHA 27-2.

[93]Herter to A. W. Klieforth, Russian Division, Department of State, Washington, D. C., 11 July 1923, HHA 282-2.

[94]*Proletarsky Kharkov,* 24 June 1923, translated in HHA 27-3; *Proletarsky Put* (Simbirsk), 21 June 1923, HHA 86-6.

[95]*Pravda* (Moscow), 1 July 1923.

[96]*Ogonyok,* no. 16 (15 July 1923).

[97]*Izvestia* (Moscow), 18 July 1923.

[98]*Izvestia* (Moscow), 20 July 1923.

[99]Hoover to Herter, 28 June 1923, HHA 282-2.

[100]"Resolution of the Council of People's Commissars, 10 July 1923," HHA Special Testimonials File.

8: THE AFTERMATH

[1]*New York Times,* 23 July 1923, p. 1.

[2]Herter to Haskell, 24 July 1923, HHA 245-26.

[3]*New York Times,* 26 July 1923, p. 26.

[4]New York Times, 1 August 1923, p. 1.

[5]Harold Wolfe, *Herbert Hoover,* p. 93.

[6]Goodrich to Rickard, 9 August 1923, HHA 251-11.

[7]Rickard to Herter, 11 August 1923, HHA 251-11.

[8]Writer's poll of former ARA personnel, April-September 1966.

[9]ARA Association Bulletin, December 1923, HHA 266-8.

[10]Hoover to S. R. Bertram, 7 November 1923, HHA 269-5.

[11]Hoover to Brown, 20 October 1923, HHA 267-7.

[12]Theodore Draper, *American Communism and Soviet Russia,* pp. 176-85.

[13]Cited in Joseph Brandes, *Herbert Hoover and Economic Diplomacy,* p. 11.

[14]Frank M. Surface and Raymond L. Bland, *American Food in the World War and Reconstruction Period,* p. 114.

[15]U.S., Department of Commerce, Bureau of the Census, *Historical Statistics of the United States, Colonial Times to 1957,* pp. 297, 301.

[16]*Washington Post,* 4 April 1924.

[17]Walter Duranty, *I Write as I Please,* pp. 133-34.

[18]*Izvestia* (Moscow), 18 May 1924.

[19]*Washington Evening Star,* 21 April 1925, cited in HHA 271-22.

[20]Haskell to Hoover, 27 August 1923, HHA 81-2.

[21]*Bolshaya Sovetskaya entsiklopedia* (1926), 3:190.

[22]*Malaya Sovetskaya entsiklopedia* (1928), 1:385.

[23]Maxim Litvinov, *Vneshnyaya politika SSSR,* p. 23.

[24]*Malaya Sovetskaya entsiklopedia* (1937), 1:451.

[25]A. N. Kogan, "Anti-sovetskie deistvia Amerikanskoi Administratsii Pomoshchi (ARA) v Sovetskoi Rossii," *Istoricheskie zapiski* 29 (1949): 5-7.

[26]*Bolshaya Sovetskaya entsiklopedia* (1950), 2:582.

[27]*Izvestia* (Moscow), 30 June 1958.

[28]*Malaya Sovetskaya entsiklopedia* (1958), 1:474.

[29]Institut Mezhdunarodnykh Otnosheny, *Istoria mezhdunarodnykh otnosheny i vneshnei politiki SSSR,* 1:222.

[30]Yelena V. Ananova, *Noveishaya istoria SShA,* pp. 87-93.

[31]V. K. Furaev, *Sovetsko-Amerikanskie otnoshenia,* pp. 81, 83.

[32]Harold H. Fisher, *The Famine in Soviet Russia, 1919-1923,* p. 552.

[33]E. H. Carr, *The Bolshevik Revolution,* 1:178.

[34]William A. Williams, *American-Russian Relations,* p. 193.

[35]Peter J. Filene, *Americans and the Soviet Experiment,* p. 78. Filene, incidentally, in his only mention of the number of people fed, uses the figure 568,000, citing Fisher, *Famine in Russia,* p. 111, as his source. This, indeed, was the number fed in December 1921. The maximum figure, however, is 10 million—the number of relief recipients fed during the height of the mission in August 1922. This statistic is also available in Fisher, *Famine in Russia,* p. 557.

[36]Louis Fischer, *The Soviets in World Affairs,* p. 228; and George F. Kennan, *Russia and the West under Lenin and Stalin,* p. 180.

[37]Viktor Nekrasov, "Po obe storony okeana," *Novy mir* (Moscow) 38, no. 12 (December 1962): 110.

[38]N. S. Khrushchev, "Marxism-Leninism Is Our Banner, Our Fighting Weapon," *Pravda* (Moscow) and *Izvestia* (Moscow), 22 June 1963, cited in *Current Digest of the Soviet Press* 15, no. 24 (July 1963): 4.

[39]*New York Times,* 2 July 1959, pp. 1-2.

[40]Speech at Twentieth Century-Fox Studio, Los Angeles, Calif., 19 September 1959, in Nikita S. Khrushchev, *Mir bez oruzhia, mir bez voiny,* 2:193-94.

[41]Niccolo Machiavelli, *The Prince and the Discourses* (New York: Modern Library, 1950), p. 472.

9: SUMMARY AND CONCLUSIONS

[1]Louis Fischer, *New York Evening Post,* 7 January 1923.

[2]George F. Kennan, *Russia and the West under Lenin and Stalin,* p. 180.

[3]For similar evaluations that the NEP was effective only when the famine ended, see E. H. Carr, *The Bolshevik Revolution: 1917-1923,* 3 vols. (Baltimore: Penguin, 1966), 2:286; and Seth Singleton, "The Tambov Revolt: 1920-1921," *Slavic Review* 25, no. 3 (September 1966): 510.

[4]"Effect of Relief Work by the ARA from Various Angles," HHA 6-2.

Index